FERTILE MATTERS

Chicana Matters Series
Deena J. González and Antonia Castañeda, editors

Chicana Matters Series focuses on one of the largest population groups
in the United States today, documenting the lives, values, philosophies,
and artistry of contemporary Chicanas. Books in this series may be
richly diverse, reflecting the experiences of Chicanas themselves,
and incorporating a broad spectrum of topics and fields of inquiry.
Cumulatively, the books represent the leading knowledge and scholarship
in a significant and growing field of research and, along with the literary
works, art, and activism of Chicanas, underscore their significance
in the history and culture of the United States.

FERTILE MATTERS

The Politics of Mexican-Origin Women's Reproduction

ELENA R. GUTIÉRREZ

UNIVERSITY OF TEXAS PRESS

AUSTIN

Requests for permission to reproduce material
from this work should be sent to:
Permissions
University of Texas Press
P.O. Box 7819
Austin, TX 78713-7819
www.utexas.edu/utpress/about/bpermission.html

♾ The paper used in this book meets the minimum requirements of
ANSI/NISO Z39.48-1992 (R1997) (Permanence of Paper).

Library of Congress Cataloging-in-Publication Data

Gutiérrez, Elena R., 1970–
Fertile matters : the politics of Mexican-origin women's reproduction /
Elena R. Gutiérrez. — 1st ed.
p. cm. — (Chicana matters series)
Includes bibliographical references and index.
ISBN 978-0-292-71681-0 (cloth : alk. paper) —
ISBN 978-0-292-71682-7 (pbk. : alk. paper)
1. Fertility, Human—United States. 2. Mexican Americans—
Population. 3. Mexican American women. 4. Involuntary
sterilization—United States—History. I. Title. II. Title: Politics
of Mexican-origin women's reproduction.
HB915.G88 2007
305.48'868073—dc22
2007023269

For my parents, Félix Frank Jr. and Maria Elena Gutiérrez

CONTENTS

A NOTE ON TERMINOLOGY

Throughout this book, I use the terms *women of Mexican origin* and *Mexican-origin women* to designate both women who have migrated from Mexico and those of Mexican descent who were born in the United States. I also refer to those who have migrated from Mexico during their lifetime as *Mexican immigrant women.* The same terms are used for their male counterparts.

Fertile Matters is an exploration of the ways we have come to think about the reproduction of women of Mexican origin in the United States. In particular, I look closely at one of the most popular and longstanding public stereotypes that portray Mexican American and Mexican women as "hyper-fertile baby machines" who "breed like rabbits." Although these labels have become colloquially acceptable, I use them to also signify the related beliefs that Mexican families are unduly large and that Mexican-origin women do not use birth control. By examining the historical and sociopolitical evolution of these racial stereotypes, I reveal a complex network of character, ideology, time, and place that has yielded the collectively accepted image of women of Mexican origin as prolific "breeders."

Chicana feminist scholars have previously documented the existence of this stereotype. However, during the course of writing this book, I was struck by the resilience of these images within public perceptions. For example, almost without fail, when I mentioned that I was researching the reproductive politics of Mexican American women, I received the response, "That is *such* an important topic. They have so many children!" Latino and non-Latino individuals alike often pointed out the "huge problem" of teenage pregnancy in Latino communities or commented that Latinas do not use birth control. Many asked me to explain *why* Mexican women have so many children. This widespread perception that Mexican women have too many children, and the belief that this reproductive behavior is a social problem that requires fixing, compelled me to continue trying to understand the sources and consequences of these ideas.

Although the stereotype of Mexican-origin women as perpetually pregnant is longstanding, our reproduction has been targeted for the past fifteen years as a major U.S. social problem. Newspapers carry headlines about the changing composition of the nation's racial and ethnic makeup, the so-called Latinization of America. Due to a higher than average birth rate among Mexican Americans and a steady stream of immigrants from Mexico, Mexican-origin people are the fastest growing minority group in the United States. As a consequence, the reproduction of Mexican immigrant women has been a central theme in contemporary U.S. politics since the 1990s.

There is no clearer marker of this phenomenon—that is, the construct of Mexican women's fertility as a social problem—than the passage of Proposition 187, proposed in 1994. The initiative, passed by California voters, was intended to take strong and deliberate measures to "Save Our State" from Mexican immigration. The campaign denied prenatal care and other social services to undocumented immigrants, specifically those of Mexican origin, and particularly women and children. Many of the proposition's backers identified pregnant immigrants as the problem, claiming that they come to the country illegally to have their babies on U.S. soil in order to achieve citizenship for their children and benefits—namely, access to welfare and other public services.

Although Prop. 187 was eventually overturned in 1996, its original passage demonstrated the growing public concern over the so-called problem of Mexican reproduction and the increased public support for proposals to stop it. While some scholars suggest that this recent focus on women signals a new twist in nativist and anti-immigrant sentiment, I demonstrate that public concern about the reproductive behaviors of women of Mexican origin has a much longer presence in the United States, beginning as far back as the turn of the twentieth century.

Throughout *Fertile Matters* I demonstrate the gradual crystallization of widespread interest in the reproduction and "hyper-fertility" of women of Mexican origin during the 1970s. My purpose is in large part to systematically document the development of discourse about women of Mexican origin as "breeders" over the second half of the twentieth century.

Another goal of the book is to demonstrate the impact that such discourses have on the reproductive experiences of the women themselves. Specifically, I examine the coercive sterilization of women of Mexican origin at the University of Southern California–Los Angeles County Medical Center (LACMC) during the early 1970s. My research reveals that the perception of women of Mexican origin as "breeding like rabbits" was manifested in the coercive actions of doctors and other health providers at LACMC who believed they had the right to sterilize women who, in their opinion, had too many children. The case of *Madrigal v. Quilligan* provides strong evidence that racializing images and beliefs were crucial factors in the abusive handling of these women, both during their deliveries at LACMC and in the Los Angeles County courtroom where their case was tried.

Since I began this project ten years ago, a growing body of literature has documented that reproductive politics are central to racial politics and vice versa. U.S. racial politics and *all* women's childbearing capacities have been intimately linked and manipulated throughout history. My research has shown that for women of color, racist stereotypes exist to justify the control of their fertility, and that activists in all communities have resisted accepting these images in their struggles for reproductive justice. However, we still know little about how these stereotypes *work*.

Fertile Matters intends to deepen public understanding of how the racial politics of reproduction have developed for women of Mexican origin in the United States. It shows that how we talk and think about reproduction is part of a system of racial domination that shapes social policy and impacts individual women's lives. And finally, it aims to convince readers that reproductive politics are indeed fertile matters for discourse and disclosure, not only for women of Mexican origin, but for all communities.

CHAPTER OVERVIEW

Chapter One provides an overview of the theoretical perspectives and issues that frame my analysis, primarily social constructionist approaches to the study of social problems, racial formation theory, and feminist studies of the racial politics of reproduction. I also sketch a general picture of the ways in which Mexican-origin women's reproduction has been racialized historically, particularly as they have been cast as "breeders."

Chapter Two presents the historical background necessary to understand the development of the social construction of Mexican-origin women during the second half of the twentieth century. Focusing on social concerns about overpopulation and immigration that developed after World War II, this account highlights the primary actors and institutions considered in the remainder of the book.

Chapter Three is an empirical case study of the coercive sterilization of Mexican-origin women at Los Angeles County Medical Center, and the trial of *Madrigal v. Quilligan* that followed. I focus on how the idea that women of Mexican origin have too many children led to the abuses that occurred in both the hospital and the courtroom.

Chapter Four examines the construction of the category of "Mexican-origin women's fertility" through a review of the development of social scientific interest in the topic. I critically assess the empirical findings of this research trajectory and suggest that this mode of inquiry plays a fundamental role in the social construction of Mexican-origin women's hyper-fertility.

Chapter Five is a case study based on primary analysis of the platforms of Zero Population Growth (ZPG) Inc., and its offshoot, the Federation of American Immigration Reform (FAIR). I highlight the interests of John Tanton, a former president of ZPG and the founder of FAIR, who was concerned about the "indirect effect" of immigration: the reproduction of Mexican women.

Through consideration of the published writings and public discussions of Chicana activists, in Chapter Six I show how they contest predominant characterizations of Mexican-origin women as breeders and develop a reproductive justice agenda that reflects their position as a racially oppressed group in the United States.

The final chapter discusses the centrality of the reproduction of Mexican immigrant women to more contemporary politics (the 1990s–present), focusing on the controversies over granting birthright citizenship to children born in the United States, changes in California over welfare reform, and the denial of prenatal care to Mexican immigrant women. These legislative and public battles not only represent the most recent incarnations in the lengthy historical trajectory of attempts to control Mexican-origin women's reproduction, but also indicate that the social construction of these women's fertility as a social problem has become institutionalized.

ACKNOWLEDGMENTS

This book is truly a product of my entire academic trajectory and political journey, and was born from the support, inspiration, and intelligence of many. I began writing about reproductive politics fifteen years ago when I researched my first paper on Chicanas and abortion during my undergraduate years at Pomona College. Joanne Badagliacco, Raymond Buriel, and Gilbert Cadena all provided generous mentorship as I first explored the terrain of race relations, Chicano studies, and reproductive politics. Margaret Anderson, whom I met through the American Sociological Association's Minority Opportunity Summer Training Program, was an initial and continuing source of encouragement as I dedicated myself to a professional career in sociology, and I am grateful for her tender insistence that there was a place for me in the academy.

My doctoral work in the Department of Sociology at the University of Michigan convinced me of the interconnection between reproductive and racial politics. I am grateful to Tomás Almaguer, Eduardo Bonilla-Silva, Donald Deskins, and Silvia Pedraza for their exceptional training in this field and their encouragement to develop my thinking in this area. My dissertation committee was an outstanding group of scholars with whom I was honored to work. George Sánchez provided the initial encouragement to begin researching and writing about the case of *Madrigal v. Quilligan*, and Karin Martin and Renee Anspach provided acute theoretical insights and consistently reminded me of how this project worked. To Sonya Rose and Tomás Almaguer I owe my utmost gratitude; their patient faith that I could see this project through made their generous guidance even more humbling.

As is often the case, my graduate student colleagues provided my most crucial support system throughout my years at Michigan, and it is to those with whom I shared both academic and "real life" lessons that I am most indebted. I'd particularly like to thank Moon-kie Jung, Christine Garza, Amanda Lewis, Hyun-Joo Oh, Teri Rosales, Tyrone Forman, Nicole Pagán,

Susan Chimonas, and Gloria Martínez for helping me to walk toward the Ph.D.

During a year as a Dissertation Fellow at the Chicana/Latina Research Center at the University of California at Davis I found a generous home in the Department of Chicano Studies. *Muchísimas gracias a* Beatriz Pesquera, Yvette Flores Ortiz, and Lorena Oropeza for opening their arms and bringing me into a vibrant community. Carole Joffe and Jim Cramer, in the Department of Sociology, also encouraged my knowledge of reproductive politics and demography, and generously read parts of the manuscript. Finally, Adeljíza Sosa-Riddell, for all of your knowledge, vision, *apoyo y ánimo*, I cannot thank you enough. Your fearless commitments to Latina reproductive politics and student-centered education is an inspiration. To you, and the other early scholars of Latina reproductive politics (Adelaida Del Castillo, Irís Lopez, Helen Rodriguez-Trías, Carlos Vélez-Ibáñez), I am greatly indebted.

I was able to complete additional research for this book and bring it to completion through the aid of two post-doctoral research fellowships that provided uninterrupted time to dedicate to the manuscript. While a Chancellor's Post-doctoral Fellow in the Department of Sociology at UC Berkeley, under the sponsorship of Kristen Luker, I also received engaged feedback on my research from Troy Duster, Patricia Macias, Raka Ray, Michael Burawoy, Evelyn Nakano Glenn, and Davíd Hernández. *Un abrazo a* Laura Enríquez, who took particular interest in me when she didn't have to and helped me negotiate the job market as well as make decisions about the publication of this book.

Meeting and working with Aída Hurtado has been a true blessing in my life. As I completed this book during my early years as an assistant professor, her consistent mentorship and exhortations to "Write!" was truly sustaining. I am grateful to Aída and the University of California at Santa Cruz for providing an institutional home while I completed my manuscript. I would also like to thank Patricia Zavella, who encouraged me to research Chicana reproductive politics early in my graduate training and has read several parts of the manuscript since then.

Maylei Blackwell, Adele Clark, Moon-Kie Jung, Janet Shim, Keta Miranda, Laurie Schaffner, Gayatri Reddy, Amanda Lewis, Nilda Flores-González, Gabriela Sandoval, and Lorena García have all read chapters of the manuscript and provided generous feedback. To John D'Emilio, Margaret Anderson, Aída Hurtado, and Rickie Solinger, who each meticulously read the entire manuscript at different points, I am humbly honored for your help in making this manuscript better.

I also extend sincere gratitude to my colleagues at the University of Illinois, Chicago, who have provided the academic home I once thought did not exist. In particular, Phil Bowman and the Institute for Research on Race and Public Policy, Aída Giachello, María de los Angeles Torres, Beth Richie, Jennifer Brier, Peg Strobel, Tyrone Forman, Amalia Pallares, Javier Villa-Flores, Nilda Flores-González, Gayatri Reddy, and Laurie Schaffner, each in their own way, have helped me become the kind of academic that I want to be, and I am grateful for their constant encouragement.

Beyond my academic affiliations I have deep appreciation to the many others who have helped me bring strength and self-knowledge, as well as political efficacy, into my life. I would first like to thank those many activists in the reproductive and sexual justice movements who have taught me more about the realities of reproductive politics than I could learn from any book. While the words and articulations contained herein are mine, the history and much of the analysis come from the many communities with whom I have engaged. It is particularly through working with the National Latina Health Organization, the National Latina Institute of Reproductive Health, Sistersong, and the ACCESS/Women's Health Rights Coalition that I have gained the strength and clarity to voice the ideas in this book. I thank them for providing community and spirited support as I wrangled with these words over the years, and for teaching me how to live the politics of reproduction in my own life. This includes a special note of gratitude to my *Undivided Rights* co-authors Jael Silliman, Loretta Ross, and Marlene Fried, all of whom read parts of this manuscript and served as magnificent models of how to be fearless academic activists.

My *amiga-colegas* have consistently provided the crucial support during the everyday ups and down of writing: RoseAnn Rentería, Amalia Cabezas, Christine Garza, Laurie Schaffner, Dolores Inés Casillas, Maythee Rojas, and Gabriela Sandoval have been steadfast *hermanas* throughout my professional experience and always offer the best *consejos*. Only they know what this book truly took.

I have been able to conduct this research, which began by examining the sterilization abuse at LACMC, only because of the willingness of others to share their recollections, their time, and often, their own personal documents. Carlos Vélez-Ibáñez provided an initial entrée into the case of *Madrigal v. Quilligan,* and he generously provided me with many of his own materials and contacts. I was also blessed to collaborate at times with historian Virginia Espino. Over the years we have collaborated in the archive, shared documents, conducted interviews together, and worked through the extensive collection of Bernard Rosenfeld. Having someone to "compare notes" with was critically important as I began to make meaning of the sterilization abuse of Mexican-origin women in L.A. Knowing that she is capably telling more stories about this case has freed to me to write my own.

To the many people who have shared the events of their daily lives, often painful memories, thank you for allowing me to write your recollections here. It is my hope that this work honors your visions. Over the years various people have sent news clippings, articles, and other relevant data. They are too many to name, but I would particularly like to thank the late Frank Del Olmo and Virginia Pérez, who both provided primary sources and contacts for interviews early on in my research. Many family friends hosted me while I conducted research in Los Angeles, and I'd particularly like to thank the Wallerstein and Delgadillo families and Mona Jhawar for having me.

This project has additionally been aided by funding from a small grant from the Center for Research on Social Organization at the University of Michigan, a Department of Sociology Dissertation Thesis Grant, and a fellowship at the Institute for the Research of Women and Gender at the University of Michigan. I also received support from the University of California at Davis Chicana/Latina Research Center, the Ford Foundation, and Rackham Graduate School at the University of Michigan.

Several "lifesavers" provided research assistance at crucial stages of the data collection and completion process: Nicole Romero, Angela Duursma, Juliana and Dolóres Inés Casillas, Marisol Salgado, and Araceli Martínez. Kim Lorettucci and Amanda Krupman both lent a careful eye to the final editing of the manuscript; I am grateful for their insight and Kim's encouragement, which helped me see the light at the end of the tunnel.

Luna Calderón and Gail London were "lifesavers" of another kind, without whom I could not have completed this book. To those tried and true friends who have offered me faith and love over the long haul—Julie Weng-Gutiérrez, Alex Gradilla and Beatriz Tapia, Maythee Rojas, Amalia Cabezas, Mona Jhawar, David Maynard, and Nathaniel Silva: thank you for keeping me laughing and dancing. For bringing me to Chicago and loving me while I grew into it, I am very grateful to Isabella Garza-Narváez, Christine Garza, Rosa Narváez, and the entire Garza *familia*.

Finally, I must thank my own family for their enduring inspiration, love, and support. Several times over the past ten years my parents took me into their home and provided me with the physical and mental space to think, write, and complete this project. They were the first to teach me how to think critically about race, class, gender, and sexual politics. They have both read the manuscript in its entirety several times and have patiently helped me let it go. My two sisters, Anita and Alicia, have always encouraged me to continue writing, and at crucial times they listened to my frustrations, helped me gather and organize materials, and encouraged me to think through partial thoughts. In recent years Rosa Amalia has been the light of my life. I love you all.

FERTILE MATTERS

ONE

THE FERTILITY OF WOMEN
OF MEXICAN ORIGIN

A Social Constructionist Approach

" I think what we are trying to show is that throughout the entire period that the doctors were not using medical reasons to perform these sterilizations, but were using social reasons. That is very pertinent to this case."[1]

Attorney Antonia Hernández spoke these words as she implored federal district court judge Jesse Curtis to hear the testimony of her next witness. Along with co-counsel Charles Nabarette, Hernández represented ten women of Mexican origin filing a class-action civil suit against physicians at the University of Southern California–Los Angeles County Medical Center (LACMC). The plaintiffs in the case of *Madrigal v. Quilligan,* which was tried in 1978, accused the doctors of coercively sterilizing each of them between June 1971 and March 1974. Many alleged that hospital personnel forced them into signing consent forms while under the duress of labor pains, or that they were never approached and informed about the procedure at all. All of the women had various levels of English comprehension, and most testified that they did not understand that tubal ligation would irreversibly terminate their childbearing. The plaintiffs filed suit against state and federal officials, and the administrators and doctors at LACMC for violation of their constitutionally guaranteed right to procreate.[2] In addition to financial compensation, the plaintiffs requested that the U.S. Department of Health, Education and Welfare require federally funded hospitals to provide thorough sterilization counseling and consent forms in Spanish.[3] On this, the sixth day of the trial, tension in the courtroom was high.

The contested witness was Karen Benker, a medical student at the University of Southern California Medical School, and an employee of the Women's Hospital of LACMC during the period when the alleged forced sterilizations of countless Mexican-origin women occurred. As the only witness who had observed the alleged coercive practices of the doctors firsthand and was willing to testify in court, Benker's observations confirmed Hernández's argument that the sterilization of her clients at this hospital was "socially motivated."[4]

What Dr. Benker would share with the court could prove that the coercive sterilization of these ten plaintiffs was not incidental, accidental, or medically necessary, but was part of a concerted attempt by the doctors at the Women's Hospital of LACMC to reduce the birth rate of Mexican-origin women. Based on this testimony, Hernández would maintain that many of the physicians deceptively pushed women into sterilization in accordance with an attitude widespread in the hospital community that the high childbearing rates of Mexican-origin women contributed to many social problems and could be effectively remedied through sterilization.

I begin this book with an empirical case study of the forced sterilization at LACMC because it illustrates the convergent discourses around Mexican-origin women's fertility and the material ramifications of ideological notions of Mexican-origin women as "hyper-fertile" that surfaced during this period. The case of *Madrigal v. Quilligan* lucidly illustrates the central argument of this book: namely, that during the 1970s a confluence of ideas crystallized to construct the fertility of Mexican-origin women as a social problem to be remedied. These issues are part of a larger public policy discourse that has continued into the twenty-first century.

THE DEMOGRAPHY AND POLITICS OF THE POPULATION GROWTH OF PEOPLE OF MEXICAN ORIGIN

The 2000 U.S. census statistically confirmed that Latinos have become the largest racial-ethnic group living in the United States, totaling over forty million people. Between 1990 and 2000, the U.S. Latino population increased by 58 percent.[5]

In what has been called a demographic revolution, Latinos were 12.5 percent of the nation's population in 2000, and are expected to comprise 25 percent of the U.S. population by 2050.[6] An ever-increasing volume of academic study, public policy investigation, and social commentary addresses this demographic change. Due to both higher birthrates than the national average and continued immigration from Mexico, persons of Mexican origin represent the largest portion of the Latino population growth in the last thirty plus years. In March 2002, Mexicans comprised 66.9 percent of the Latino population.[7]

Demographic and government interest in the birthrates of the Mexican-origin community have also grown steadily over the past three decades. In

1998, the U.S. government conducted a first-ever, multiyear analysis of Hispanic birthrates, which established that, even within the rising rates for Hispanic women as a group, women of Mexican origin display markedly higher rates of childbirth than other Latinas.[8] Media coverage of the 1998 report by the National Center for Health Statistics publicized the "dramatic rise" in Hispanic births between 1989 and 1995, attributing much of this growth to the "soaring" rates of teenage pregnancy.[9] Commentators expressed an almost singular preoccupation with the ascending birthrates of Latina teens (which notably overtook those of African Americans for the first time in history) and pondered the social and political ramifications of such a demographic pattern. One commentator from the conservative journal *National Review* warned,

> For those who cluck cheerfully about the 'strong family ties' of Hispanic immigrants, the new figures are ominous: two-thirds of young Latina mothers have no husbands. . . . Because the Latino share of the population is expanding, any burgeoning Latino culture of poverty will make its impact widely felt. Thirty-three years ago Sen. Daniel Patrick Moynihan (D-NY) gave a prescient warning about the breakdown of the African American family, for which he had no easy remedy. Now, thanks to feckless immigration policies, the United States is sowing difficulties which could prove of at least comparable scope.[10]

Alluding to Senator Moynihan's much-critiqued analysis of black family life, which faulted the matriarchal family structure of African Americans as the core cause of their poverty, the above statements suggest a similar case for national action concerning the reproductive behavior of Latinas.[11]

Social and political interest in controlling the fertility of Latinas is of course nothing new. Control of the reproduction of Mexican, Mexican American, and Puerto Rican women's reproduction served as a crucial tool of colonization and social repression of entire communities. Puerto Rico's population has long served as a social laboratory for the U.S. birth control industry, and ideologies of population control and economic development justified the massive sterilization abuse of Puerto Rican women.[12] With 33 percent of Puerto Rico's women sterilized, and similar rates for Puerto Rican women living on the U.S. mainland, anthropologist Irís Lopez argues that the procedure has now become an institutionalized, or "medicalized," practice of women faced with limited options.[13] She writes, "Once Puerto Rican women's reproductive decision-making is medicalized, they lose the ability to control their own fertility. . . . The medicalization of women's reproductive behavior infused and gave medical and state authority more control."[14]

Other commentators similarly portray immigrant families as opportunists who are sapping social services and other scarce public resources. Public discourse surrounding California's Proposition 187 (passed in November 1994), a paradigmatic embodiment of contemporary nativism in the United States, provides a classic case in point.[15] The fertility of women of Mexican origin assumed center stage in the debates surrounding this controversial proposition, which was a measure designed to deny undocumented immigrants access to education and health care services. Proponents of the "Save Our State" initiative persistently alluded to the high fertility of Mexican women as one of the primary problems with recent immigration from Mexico (births to Hispanic mothers outnumber all other groups in the state). The very substance of the policy prescriptions of Proposition 187 (which I explore in greater detail in Chapter Seven) assumes that the allure of social benefits (i.e., health care, education, welfare) is the driving motivation for Mexican women to cross the border to bear their children on U.S. soil.

Supporters of the anti-immigration proposition encouraged strict sanctions to deter migrants from coming to the United States and "stealing" health and social service benefits that were not rightfully theirs.[16] Although the proposition's expressed goal was to halt all immigration, especially from Mexico, women were particularly targeted.[17] Proposition 187 singled out "poor, pregnant immigrant women who, with their children, come to the United States to give birth in publicly-financed county hospitals, allowing the newborns to become U.S. citizens, and all their children to receive public assistance, medical care, and public school education."[18]

Fear of the "Latinization" of California and the possible ascent of people of Mexican origin to political power has led to vociferous anti-immigrant and anti-Mexican mobilization in the state and in the larger Southwest, sentiments that are increasingly echoed across the nation.[19]

Consider the message in *Mexifornia*, a book written by classics professor Victor Davis Hanson of California State University, Fresno. Published in 2003, the title reflects "the strange society that is emerging as the result of a demographic and cultural revolution like no other in our times."[20] Hanson attributes a transformation of U.S. culture to a lack of assimilation by recent immigrants. At the heart of the complaint, though, is the ultimate culprit. Hanson bemoans that "every year the state must continue to deal with a succession of first-generation immigrant families with three to six children at or below the poverty line. Moreover, no advocate in the university promotes family planning as a means of economic self-sufficiency; there is no campaign in Chicano studies departments encouraging immigrant families to have only one or two children so as to ensure financial solvency."[21] According to Hanson, the continuing immigration of large, poor families has led to an unassimilated class of Mexicans that is changing the very nature of the state of California.

Again in 2003, Samuel Huntington, a distinguished Harvard professor, received national recognition for his treatise on "The Hispanic Challenge." In *Who Are We? The Challenge to America's National Identity*, Huntington wrote that "the single most serious challenge to America's traditional identity comes from the immense and continuing immigration from Latin America, especially Mexico, and the fertility rates of these immigrants compared to black and white American 'natives.'" Huntington clearly identifies the growth of the Mexican-origin population as a very real problem for the United States. He further warns that if these "floods" of immigrants are not stopped, the country's cultural and political integrity will be endangered.[22]

Some scholars suggest that the recent focus on women signals a "new twist" in nativist and anti-immigrant sentiment.[23] However, criticisms of immigrant motherhood have prevailed in the United States since at least 1890. According to Katrina Irving, between 1890 and 1925 "all writers, no matter what their ideological position—nativism ('scientific racism'), Americanization, or cultural pluralism—drew upon discourses that articulated feminine gender in order to construct an immigrant woman who would, in turn, embody their particular version of the immigrant 'problem.'"[24] In particular, nativists questioned the eugenic quality of children of very fertile immigrant mothers, predating contemporary concerns about the fertility of Mexican immigrant women. Later in this chapter, I will show that over the course of the twentieth century not only nativists, but some social scientists, members of the medical community, and population control proponents have expressed a similar racial anxiety over the reproduction of women of Mexican origin in the United States. First, I clarify my argument and review the major theoretical threads upon which my analysis is built.

THE TOOLS OF SOCIAL CONSTRUCTIONISM: SITUATING THE FERTILITY OF WOMEN OF MEXICAN ORIGIN

To explore the politics of Mexican women's reproduction, I draw upon the analytical perspective represented by sociological research on the social construction of social problems. Such an approach (well articulated by Malcolm Spector and John Kitsuse, and Joseph Gusfield, and perceptively deployed by Constance Nathanson) posits that it is not the putative social conditions that should be the focus of study, but the processes central to the definition of any social occurrence as a "social problem."[25]

The construction of a social problem is a collective process within which individuals or groups define some set of putative circumstances as unduly problematic.[26] While objectivists believe that social problems are literal conditions that pose a concretely real and objective threat to the good of society, social constructionists approach social problems from an alternative standpoint. Contextual constructionists argue that social problems do not objectively exist, but are fundamentally conceived by certain interests within a particular context; they are "constructed in the human mind, constituted by the definitional process."[27] Proponents of contextual constructionism argue that it is impossible for any given set of conditions to be considered a social problem outside of its sociopolitical context, and thus historical analysis is necessary to any project engaging the construction of such a problem.

The epistemological approach offered by social constructionism relies on an empirical focus on the actors, historical moments, and interests that contribute to the construction of the fertility of Mexican women as a matter of public interest and concern. Moreover, in his thoughtful analysis of drinking and driving, Joseph Gusfield notes that "analyzing public problems as structures means finding the conceptual and institutional orderliness in which they emerge in the public arena. The public arena is not a field on which all can play on equal terms; some have greater access than others and greater power and ability to shape the definition of public issues."[28] My research thus focuses centrally on those institutions that claim ownership of the problem of the fertility of Mexican women—that is, demographers, medical professionals, population policymakers, and Chicana feminists.

Accordingly, my intention is to "turn the camera around" to investigate those institutions, groups, and policies that have observed the reproduction of women of Mexican origin. Such a maneuver helps us shift the focus from attempting to unravel the "truth" of what is happening with the fertility and reproduction of women of Mexican origin toward an exploration of perspectives, interests, and policies that have played a role in creating "truths" about this topic.

A social constructionist perspective provides a completely different vantage point from which to engage the topic of the fertility of women of Mexican origin. In this vein, Sally Andrade, one of the first scholars to trace the biased nature of social science research about women of Mexican origin, wrote in 1982,

If one's primary interest were research on the family size of Chicanas, the primary question remaining to be clarified would be whether the cultural background or the educational status of Mexican American women is the more important factor in terms of understanding their fertility regulation attitudes and behaviors. If one wants to examine the implications of social sciences' inability to confront issues of racism, sexism, and social class bias with reference to research on Mexican women, however, different questions emerge.[29]

Thus, principles of social constructionism provide a useful corrective to most of the extant social scientific research on the reproduction of women of Mexican origin, which primarily attempts to document and understand their "unusually high rates" and focuses on the attitudinal and behavioral aspects of their family planning practices. Typically based on secondary analysis of quantitative data, such projects conceptualize the reproduction of Mexican-origin women as a culturally dictated behavior to be understood.[30] These projects largely reinscribe the reproduction of women of Mexican origin as the primary locus of inquiry, and the women themselves as the principal unit of analysis, often ignoring the sociopolitical context within which the reproductive activities of Mexican-origin women occur. A social constructionist approach considers academic scholarship as complicit in the creation of ideas about the fertility of women of Mexican origin. As such, demographic research about Mexican-origin women's fertility is treated as a focal object of study in my analysis rather than as literature upon which my analysis is built.

Diverging from the previous social scientific research, in this project I argue that the important question is *not* how many children are born to women of Mexican origin or whether abortion intervention or birth control is practiced. Rather, I explore why the fertility of women of Mexican origin is in itself such a significant issue in so many sociopolitical discourses. This is not a study of the fertility of Mexican women per se, but an investigation of the sociohistorical context within which such a topic, and the structures that shape it, become significant.

Because such emphasis has been placed on enumerating and tracking the actual rates of fertility for Mexican-origin women (the number of children they bear), this project is particularly interested in exploring the concept of "fertility." Popular discussions of such a category are inevitably tied up with a host of other related issues such as reproductive behavior, birth control practices, and attitudes toward the family. This project will thus envelop any and all topics related to reproduction with respect to Mexican-origin women, and the terms *fertility* and *reproduction* will be used as synonyms throughout to encompass this variety.

When anthropologists Faye Ginsburg and Rayna Rapp theorize the politics of reproduction—which bridges the micro-level of reproductive behavior and practices, and the macro-level of the politics involved in that process—they stress that reproductive issues are largely discursive terrain and that discourse analysis "can be used to analyze 'reproduction' as an aspect of other contests over hegemonic control."[31] Since I am primarily concerned with the ideological construction of the fertility of women of Mexican origin as a social problem, this project pays considerable attention to discursive realms. Such a focus on discourse fundamentally assumes its political nature.

Moreover, my focus on the "ideological effects" of these discursive constructions implies that "these practices are *always more* than semiotic because they inscribe signs within social practices as a condition of existence of the meanings and subjectivities produced."[32] Thus, discourse is also located in public policy, social institutions, and practices.

Racialized reproductive images about women of Mexican origin circulating in public discourse are central to this project. I am equally interested in how these ideological constructs are tied to structural and institutional modes of reproduction and racial control. Drawing from racialization theory, most extensively articulated by Omi and Winant,[33] I argue that the social construction of women of Mexican origin as hyper-fertile is a racial project and that the discourse surrounding and constructing their reproductive behavior as problematic must be viewed as racially based. Omi and Winant define racial formation as "the historical process by which racial categories are created, inhabited, transformed, and destroyed," and as "a process of historically situated projects in which human bodies and social structures are represented and organized."[34] Imperative to my perspective is the vigilant consideration of racial projects in both their ideological and structural nature.[35] I argue that ideological representations of women of Mexican origin as hyper-fertile must not only be analyzed in their form and content, but additionally in their relation to the structural associations within which they historically emerge.

I further draw upon a growing body of critical analyses that argue that race and reproductive politics are fundamentally intertwined.[36] Research since the 1980s has traced the systemic intrusions on the reproductive liberty of African American and other women of color and the historical control of fertility as a mechanism of racial domination and economic exploitation.[37] Legal scholar Dorothy Roberts's treatise *Killing the Black Body: Race, Reproduction, and the Meaning of Liberty* deftly demonstrates that racial domination and reproductive control have been intricately tied throughout history. Central to her examination is how images about African American women render significant implications for their reproductive freedom. According to Roberts, "Regulating Black women's fertility seems so imperative because of the existence of powerful stereotypes that propel these policies; myths are meaningful as expressions of what we believe to be true; [and] have justified the restrictions on Black women's childbearing."[38]

Other authors have documented how the development of racializing images and ideologies is central to the reproductive control of women of color. Sociologist Patricia Hill Collins has identified that "controlling images" such as the mammy, welfare queen, and Jezebel are historically deployed to devalue African American women.[39] Collins's groundbreaking work theorizes how controlling images of African American women serve as "powerful ideological justifications" for class, race, gender, and sexuality domination. Stressing the ubiquity of these ideas in her now-classic treatise *Black Feminist Thought*, Collins writes that "schools, the news media, and government agencies constitute important sites for reproducing these controlling images. Scholarship has helped produce and disseminate controlling images."[40] It is in these spaces where the discourse of reproductive politics is created and communicated.

Through the denial of black motherhood and the characterization of African American women as "bad mothers," the material deprivation of their reproductive rights to bear children has been symbolically justified.[41] This dichotomization of good/bad, black/white motherhood is indeed a significant aspect of the racial politics of reproduction in the United States. However, in contrast to the depiction of African American women as neglectful mothers, historically and contemporarily, women of Mexican origin are more typically cast as overly identified mothers and reproducers.

THE POLITICS OF THE FERTILITY OF WOMEN
OF MEXICAN ORIGIN: HISTORICAL ANTECEDENTS

Women's procreation has been a subject of political interest from the time of the Spanish colonization of Mexico. Spanish colonizers claimed a state imperative to control the childbearing of native women. Because a growing California needed a Hispanicized Indian population, missionaries took affirmative steps to encourage reproduction. Historian Antonia Castañeda has documented that in addition to encouraging marriages of converted Amer-Indian women and mestizo soldiers by offering bounties, colonial officials also brought *niños* and *niñas de cuna* (foundlings) from Spain to populate California.

Castañeda's research further demonstrates how women of Mexican origin first came to be depicted as hyper-fertile. In particular, impressions collected in the narratives of Euro-American pioneers (many of which were commissioned by Hubert Howe Bancroft during the 1870s and 1880s) provide some of the first documented characterizations of the Mexican family, which dominated subsequent histories of early California. According to Castañeda, descriptions of the patriarchal Spanish-Mexican family, their reproductive patterns, and family size abound in the recordings of Euro-Americans and elite Californios: "the texts described California women as 'remarkably fecund' and frequently commented that families were exceptionally large, with women bearing twelve, fifteen, and twenty children."[42] These stereotypical narratives provided a foundation on which most of the history of Mexican California is written. However, the research of Castañeda and others has dispelled these common mischaracterizations, suggesting that there was significant regional variation in the size of Spanish-Mexican California families, many of which had much smaller numbers of children than noted in founding texts.

Accounts of the reproduction of women of Mexican origin in the United States continued into the twentieth century. For example, in 1929 Samuel J. Holmes, a University of California professor, posed a foreboding question in an article entitled "Perils of the Mexican Invasion," published in the *North American Review*: "At a recent state fair in Sacramento, California, when prizes were offered for the largest families, the first prize went to a Mexican family with sixteen children. . . . This excessive fecundity is of course exceptional, but it is indicative of the breeding habits of this class of our population. Is it not evident, then, that the Mexican invasion is bound to have far-reaching effects upon our national life?"[43] Concerns about a possible "Mexican invasion" of the United States are clearly expressed here, with particular speculation about the resulting cultural effects on the nation.

From the beginning of the century into the early 1940s, growing nativist sentiment blamed Mexican immigrants for societies' ills and commonly bemoaned their fertility. In a 1929 issue of the *Saturday Evening Post*, the editor offered his opinion under the heading "The Mexican Conquest": "The very high Mexican birth rate tends to depress still further the low white birth rate. Thus a race problem of the greatest magnitude is being allowed to develop for future generations to regret and in spite of the fact that the Mexican Indian is considered a most undesirable ethnic stock for the melting pot."[44]

This concern about the fertility of Mexican women was wholeheartedly adopted by those associated with eugenic efforts. Sociologist David Montejano wrote:

> The outcry about social decay reached near-hysterical levels. Eugenicists pointed out with alarm that Mexicans were not only intellectually inferior—they were also quite "fecund." Imaginative calculations were formulated to drive home the point. C. M. Goethe, president of the Immigrant Study Commission, speaking of a Los Angeles Mexican with thirty-three children, figured that "it would take 14,641 American fathers . . . at a three-child rate, to equal the descendants of this one Mexican father four generations hence."[45]

Goethe, a Sacramento realtor, wrote in 1935, "It is this high birthrate that makes Mexican peon immigration such a menace. Peons multiply like rabbits."[46] The social panic that eugenicists instigated often incited public outcries to deport Mexicans (immigrant or not); at times their messages were informed by germ theories and hereditarianism.[47]

Alternatively, proponents of the Americanist agenda (1915–1929) believed that efforts should be made to assimilate the Mexican population in the United States. A growing body of literature has shown that these efforts primarily focused on the assimilation of Mexican immigrant women and their children into American culture.[48] Historian George Sánchez has noted that for Americanists, motherhood represented "the juncture at which the Mexican immigrant women's potential role in Americanization was most highly valued."[49] Ideas about fertility, reproduction, and motherhood all gained significant racial meaning within the process of Americanization, as female Mexican immigrants were believed to be the bearers and sharers of culture.[50]

In her study of the Houchen Settlement, a "Christian Americanization" program run in El Paso, Texas, from 1920 to 1960, historian Vicki Ruiz argues that this and other groups like it paid particular attention to expectant mothers. Millie Rockford, who worked at the settlement, shared the logic behind this approach with Ruiz: "If we can teach her [the mother to be] the modern methods of cooking and preparing foods and simple hygiene habits for herself and her family, we have gained a stride."[51]

In some cases Americanization policies bore important implications for the birth control practices of Mexican immigrant women. Americanists attempted to inculcate Anglo ideals of family planning and family size into the women's values in hopes of ultimately changing behavior as well. Efforts to transform the reproductive ideas and behavior of recent immigrants were fueled by nativist and Americanist fears of race suicide. According to Sánchez, "the nativists wanted to control Mexican population growth for fear of a 'greaser invasion,' while Americanists viewed unrestricted population growth as a vestige of Old World ways that would have to be abandoned in a modern industrial world."[52] Regardless of their motivations, both nativists and Americanists centered their efforts on the reproduction of Mexican immigrant women.

More recently, social science literature on Mexican American women provides an acute example of these racializing images. Prevalent among depictions of Mexican-origin women in this body of research are assumptions that they are solely defined by their capacity to bear children. In a 1982 review of such representations in the extant social scientific literature, Sally Andrade wrote, "An exaggerated 'super-mother' figure emerges from a summary of the above impressions about Mexican American women: the unceasingly self-sacrificing, dedicated, ever-fertile woman totally without aspiration for self or initiative to do other than reproduce."[53]

While dissimilar to the ideological constructs that shape the reproductive context for African American women, images of Mexican women as overly identified mothers are also embedded in a framework of racial domination. One important component of the circumvention of Mexican women's motherhood is the social construction of their hyper-fertility. Chicana feminist scholars have challenged these prevailing notions, showing that not only are these women complex in their identification as mothers, but that they are sexual beings who have diverse opinions regarding reproductive matters.[54] Such efforts to deconstruct existing racist discourse and contribute to more accurate representations and analyses of the reproduction of women of Mexican origin are deliberately part of a Chicana feminist project. As Aida Hurtado explains, "Chicana feminisms proclaim that creating and controlling their own discourse are essential to decolonization. Passive silence has been the enemy that allowed others to construct who Chicanas are, what they can and cannot do, and what they are capable of becoming."[55]

While scholars demonstrate the complex construction of racializing images and ideologies central to the reproductive control of African American women and women of Mexican origin, less obvious are the ways that these images impact women's lives. I argue that beyond serving as key components of a "generalized ideology of domination," by which the oppression of women of color is justified, these notions are often manifested in social institutions and actors that construct individual experience.[56] In this volume, I advance such an examination by considering both the discursive dimensions of fertility and reproduction as they pertain to women of Mexican origin and their circulation in policy and public attitudes—or rather, how these social constructions work.

Throughout the following chapters I explore ideas about Mexican-origin women's fertility in public discourse, assess the reasons for their deployment, and grapple with the relationship between "ideas" about fertility and the actual abuses enacted on the bodies of Mexican-origin women, including forced sterilization. I examine multiple forms of data (including written texts, oral statements, and other documents gathered through archival research) that construct social knowledge about Mexican-origin women's fertility. I empirically ground notions of Mexican-origin women as "breeders" in historical context, and explore the implications of these ideas in the discursive practices of various social actors.

CHAPTER TWO

THE TWIN PROBLEMS
OF OVERPOPULATION
AND IMMIGRATION IN
1970S CALIFORNIA

W hen the physicians at LACMC identified Mexican-origin women as excessively fertile and as prime candidates for sterilization, they were defining a key "social problem" of the 1970s and its solution. Indeed, during the 1960s and 1970s a host of interests converged that collectively created a watershed period in the social construction of Mexican-origin women's fertility as problematic. In addition, several national discourses and political controversies flourished during this pivotal period, all of which defined new social problems.

Although these problems are sometimes understood as separate social issues, each attracting different constituencies with often contradictory claims, the interrelationships between them were particularly evident during the 1970s in the state of California, the geographical focus for this study. The intersection there of the immigration and overpopulation issues and the ensuing discourses were sharp and consequential. In my discussion of the various approaches to population and immigration control, I introduce a number of primary actors involved in policy debates and controversies, each of whom contributed to the evolving depiction of women of Mexican origin as particularly problematic child bearers.

THE POPULATION BOMB

Prior to 1945, the dominant population-related anxiety in the United States was about *under*population (or race suicide, in its eugenical formulation), and governmental leaders did not view other countries' population problems as relevant to demanding U.S. interests. Over time demographers introduced evidence of "overpopulation" in the United States to the public, often stressing the motifs of eugenic stability and the underscored distinctions between the moderate, restrained "us" and the teeming, profligate "them."[1]

The U.S. government paid increasing attention to the growth of the world's population after World War II.[2] Experts initially considered overpopulation as a problem primarily attributable to underdeveloped nations, with growth in Asia, Latin America, and Africa drawing particular attention. By the mid-1960s world population growth became a "measurable, publicly documented, economically defined problem of the third world" and an increasing concern of foreign policy experts.[3]

While population research was primarily initiated and supported by private foundations and organizations, by the late 1960s government monies were directly funneled to studies that addressed these issues.[4] According to Wilmoth and Ball (1995), foundations "contributed to the development of a cadre of scientific professionals who could offer expert advice on questions of population, economic development, and family planning."[5] Betsey Hartmann elaborates:

> Beginning in the 1950s large amounts of money began to flow into U.S. universities from the Ford Foundation, the Population Council, and the Rockefellers to finance population studies, facilitating the development of what some observers have called a "powerful cult of population control" in U.S. academia. Government funding followed soon thereafter, until, with few exceptions, demography and related social sciences came to serve the population establishment's goal of promoting the machine model of family planning as the solution to this population "crisis."[6]

Although a 1958 annual report of the Population Council, founded in 1952, argued that "even in the United States, present rates of growth may well handicap education and cultural advances and make more difficult the adjustments to the rapid rate of urbanization," governmental authorities were not sharply focused on such concerns at this point.[7] It was not until the late 1960s and early 1970s that the American public turned its attention to the issue of population growth within the United States, a development primarily triggered by a growing concern about the environmental and social ramifications of "overpopulation." A decade later policymakers, government officials, and population control advocates directed considerable effort toward implementing a national population policy, justified by the new internationalist initiative and an increased understanding of the population issue.[8] The population movement was comprised of a variety of invested groups—citizen-activists, ecologists, scientists, and governmental officials among them.[9] In particular many population control activists stressed t increased population growth would have disastrous consequences on both the nation's natural resources and the operation of the federal government, ultimately decreasing the quality of life for American citizens.

THE COMMISSION ON POPULATION GROWTH
AND THE AMERICAN FUTURE

Issues of family planning and population growth entered formal political discourse while Richard Nixon was the nation's president. Earlier administrations had viewed population issues under the rubric of reproduction and family planning, thus placing them outside the realm of governmental interference.[10] In 1969, newly inaugurated President Nixon delivered the first-ever presidential message on population, in which he stated his belief that many current "social problems" were related to recent rates of population increase. Nixon committed the government to providing family planning services "to all those who want them but cannot afford them" during the next five years.[11] Nixon's promise was realized eight months later with the passage of the 1970 Family Planning Services and Research Act.[12] This legislation provided federal funding for family planning services and research, and supported the formation of the Office of Population Affairs within the Department of Health, Education and Welfare.[13] Enacted by the 91st Congress, this was the first piece of federal legislation exclusively concerned with family planning and thus demonstrated a new government investment in population concerns.

Simultaneously, Congress passed the act establishing the Commission on Population Growth and the American Future (CPGAF).[14] This commission—which was mandated to complete a two-year assessment of the relationship between changing demographics in the U.S. and quality of life—was also charged with formulating U.S. policy on the issue. Specifically, members were to "examine the probable extent of population growth and internal migration in the United States between now and the end of the century, to assess the impact that population change will have upon government services, our economy, and our resources and environment, and to make recommendations on how the nation can best cope with that impact."[15]

Headed by John D. Rockefeller III, founder of the Population Council and longtime benefactor of population control efforts, the commission was made up of twenty-four prominent businessmen, academics, medical professionals, congressmen, and citizens.[16] As was true of virtually every government-sponsored examination of population from the beginning of the century, "one of the first steps was to enlist the cooperation of U.S. academics."[17] Although most members of the commission were not population experts, academic demographers conducted all of the research work for the commission's review. The list of those involved in the research efforts for the CPGAF has been described as "quite literally a 'Who's Who' in demography."[18] Directed by Charles Westhoff and Robert Park Jr., both preeminent population specialists, more than ninety experts from all areas of demography were contracted to produce research papers for consideration and inclusion in the report.[19]

The commission's final report, published in 1972, strongly advocated the development of a national policy of population control. Focusing on the maintenance of a good standard of living for American citizens, the report offered a series of recommendations addressing social policies geared to enhance personal freedom—with respect to family planning, but also with respect to the economy, the environment, education, health, family life, immigration, sexuality, religion, and leisure. In addition to its recommendation that effective contraceptives be made available to all citizens, the report encouraged nationwide liberalization of abortion laws and government funding of voluntary abortion.[20] President Nixon ultimately rejected these recommendations based on his belief that abortion was "an unacceptable means of population control" and that supplying contraception to minors was wrong.[21] Although Nixon's presidency was cut short by his resignation, the president's Commission on Population Growth and the American Future has been called "the closest the nation has come to considering the formulation of a national population policy."[22] Congressional support for creating the commission clearly reflects mounting concerns about population and reproduction. The implementation of government initiatives was also in large part a response to the efforts of population control advocates.[23]

THE PUBLIC DISCOURSE AND CITIZEN ACTIVISM

A number of publications and other developments reflected and contributed to widespread concerns about the repercussions of uncontrolled reproduction during this era. Paul Ehrlich's classic treatise, *The Population Bomb*, published in 1968, emphasized the effects of declining natural resources and a less prosperous future. This influential volume heightened public awareness of birthrates and the need for birth control in developing countries, and stimulated the creation of an influential population control lobby.[24] Ehrlich, a biology professor at Stanford University, brought public attention to how overpopulation could affect the earth's resources and quality of life. His most direct influence on the public was to make the perils of overpopulation a recognizable issue. Ehrlich aggressively pressed for reforms in tax laws that would discourage reproduction, for mandatory birth control education in public schools, for a sharply increased budget for the study of population problems, and, if necessary, compulsory birth control. Basically Ehrlich was a staunch advocate of immediate population reduction. A self-proclaimed "doom-sayer," Ehrlich warned that if population control was not implemented, the repercussions for the nation and the world would be apocalyptic. In his view, only drastic measures might forestall the imminent situation: "The pain will be intense, but the disease is so far advanced that only with radical surgery does the patient have any chance of survival."[25]

The similarly alarming Campaign to Check the Population Explosion, funded by Hugh Moore, president of the Dixie Cup Company, also fueled public fears of overpopulation. Anxiety-ridden propaganda, often expressing thinly veiled racial panic, appeared in the nation's newspapers, endorsed by influential national policymakers and industry leaders.[26] For example, a full-page advertisement in the *New York Times* with the headline "How Many People Do *You* Want in Your Country?" declared, "Our city slums are packed with youngsters—thousands of them idle, victims of discontent and drug addiction. And millions will pour into the streets in the next few years at the present rate of procreation. You go out after dark at your peril. Last year one out of every four hundred Americans was murdered, raped or robbed. Birth control is an answer."[27] However, some in population control circles thought Moore's efforts misguided, and opted for less "hysterical" strategies to implement change.[28]

Fueled by paranoia about personal safety, the deterioration of the environment, and world chaos, citizen-action groups like Moore's pressed for government action to deter further population increases. Many of these associations became the primary proponents of population control after government interest waned. The largest and most influential of these groups, Zero Population Growth, Inc. (ZPG), was founded by Paul Ehrlich, Charles Remington (of Yale University), and Richard Bowers (a Connecticut attorney). The only grassroots political action organization focusing on U.S. population growth, ZPG proposed to "conduct and support programs of education and information . . . stressing the need for achieving zero population growth in the United States and elsewhere as soon as possible."[29] Adopting the simple slogan "Stop at Two" and electing Ehrlich as its honorary president, ZPG quickly attracted a large membership, reaching 34,250 members belonging to three hundred chapters in fifty states by spring of 1971.[30] Along with other groups, ZPG organized various programs to encourage wide-spread change in societal views about family size. In 1973, the group's board of directors realized that replacement-level fertility would not adequately reduce the size of the nation's population and began to advocate for a below-replacement fertility rate of 1.2 to 1.5 children per family.[31]

This drive for smaller families was similarly proposed by CPGAF, whose 1971 interim report began with an extended example of how "small differences in family size" significantly alter future population predictions and "make big differences in the demands placed on our society."[32] Advocacy for smaller families was a primary mode of instituting the normative change necessary to achieve zero population growth, which argued that the difference between a two- and three-child family "bears vitally upon . . . the nation's future."[33]

Government officials and population activists together criticized the pronatalist ideology pervasive in American culture.[34] In 1971 members of Congress and organizations including Zero Population Growth, Planned Parenthood, the Sierra Club, and the Audubon Society formed the Coalition for a National Population Policy. With Senator Joseph Tydings and Dr. Milton S. Eisenhower as its co-chairs, the coalition declared a nation-wide campaign to persuade American couples to have no more than two children in an effort to reduce the nation's population growth rate to zero.[35]

THE MEDICAL PROFESSIONALS

From federal policy to daily reading material, ideas about population growth and the need to control its escalation were widely circulated during the late 1960s and 1970s.[36] President Nixon's science advisor Dr. Lee A. DuBridge declared, "Every human institution, school, university, church, family, government and institutional agency should set this [zero population growth] as its prime task."[37]

Many professional individuals and organizations took this charge seriously. For example, in 1972 the California Department of Social Welfare mandated increasing the effort to offer family planning services to "all current recipients of childbearing age."[38] California's director of social welfare, Robert B. Carleson, notified all county welfare directors in the state that he would "expect statistical data to reflect closer correlation between the total AFDC caseload during a given quarter and the number of persons offered family planning services as well as an increase in the number of persons referred."[39]

Members of the medical community also expressed a heightened commitment to rectify the "population problem." Some physicians believed their professional status and resources granted them the authority and responsibility to protect the public welfare by taking deliberate actions to reduce high rates of population growth. The comments of Dr. Curtis Wood, president of the Association for Voluntary Sterilization, provides one example of similar sentiments printed in the pages of medical journals during this time: "People pollute, and too many people crowded too close together cause many of our social and economic problems. These, in turn, are aggravated by involuntary and irresponsible parenthood. As physicians we have obligations to our individual patients, but we also have obligations to the society in which we are a part. The welfare mess, as it has been called, cries out for solutions, one of which is fertility control."[40]

In 1966 the American Medical Association (AMA) adopted an official policy regarding population growth. Although the AMA had previously relegated matters of reproduction to the individual practitioner, the new stance was that "the medical profession should accept a major responsibility in matters related to human reproduction as they affect the total population and the individual family" and that each doctor should be prepared to counsel patients on matters of family planning, no matter his or her specialty.[41]

Many physicians believed that it was indeed their duty to help resolve the problem of "overpopulation" because the medical community had defined issues of human reproduction and birth control as essentially medical in nature.[42] One doctor wrote in the *Journal of the American Medical Association*, "historically, physicians have been leaders in medicine and in the furtherance of human welfare, and only if the medical profession recognizes its opportunity and responsibility can it meet its clear obligation to help solve what is now widely regarded as the world's number one problem."[43] The AMA's newly adopted position was an affirmative step in this direction, and certain members advocated that the medical community assume leadership in solving this problem.

C. Lee Buxton, a doctor from New Haven, Connecticut, wrote at the time, "We must also realize that medical responsibility demands more action than just passing resolutions and making recommendations. We must do our part in lay education, research, teaching, and the dissemination of appropriate contraceptive advice."[44] Buxton clearly portrayed the population "explosion" as a disease that the medical profession had, up to that point, failed to take responsibility for curing. In his words, "It's as though there were an ever-growing, raging, small-pox epidemic being fought with a vaccine so attenuated that no protective effort could be observed."[45] Because the medical community had been successful in controlling the death rate but not in managing the birthrate, Buxton held the medical profession accountable for the problem of overpopulation. He asked his colleagues, "Are we going to capitulate to an even more incredible pestilence—the destruction of our own civilization by our own progeny? We can, and must, be leaders in attempts to solve, as we have in the past, problems in future human welfare and happiness. Now is the time for action."[46]

Many doctors shared Buxton's opinions in medical journals and during professional meetings, educating their peers about the perils of overpopulation and urging medical intervention to solve the problem in both the undeveloped and developed world. Most called for "an immediate commitment of medical and social resources in order to curtail the continuing population flood" and considered the various ameliorative efforts medicine might take to achieve this goal.[47] Toward the end of the 1960s these cries mirrored the apocalyptic urgency expressed by other advocates of population control such as Paul Ehrlich.

Of course, practitioners in the specialty of obstetrics and gynecology felt particular pressure. In his address to the Central Association of Obstetricians and Gynecologists in 1971, president George L. Wulff, M.D., clearly delineated the problem facing obstetrics practitioners and asked them to become involved in family planning. His question to his fellow colleagues asked, "Will we be part of the solution, or part of the problem?"[48]

In sum, during the late 1960s and early 1970s, a committed and proactive medical community joined an already strong population control lobby of citizen activists, government officials, and demographers who were concerned with curbing the birthrate as a means to avoid overpopulation. The reduction of fertility rates became the primary means through which advocates hoped to control the impending "population bomb," placing women's fertility (and thus, their bodies) at the center of national interest. This diverse group of lobbyists played a large role in advocating for and inciting government action on issues of population. As I show in the following discussion, a similar process of public outcry and advocacy emerged at this time around the issue of immigration control.

"ALIEN INVASION": THE CRISIS OF ILLEGAL IMMIGRATION

Reducing the nation's fertility rates was not the only focus of those concerned with population control during the 1970s. Policymakers and others paid increasing attention to illegal immigration at this time; by mid-decade attention was especially keen. At the federal level, immigration emerged in tandem with population control as a pressing issue. In fact, the CPGAF report included an extensive analysis that attributed about 20 percent of U.S. population growth to immigration.[49] The commission's attention to immigration increased public awareness of the issue (as did a national recession, which left many Americans without jobs in 1970 and 1971). The report also stimulated debate regarding its negative impact. Particular attention was paid to the changing composition of post-1965 immigration.[50] The commission itself noted that the Immigration Act of 1965 led to "a dramatic shift in the geographic origins of our immigrants."

> From 1945 to 1965, 43 percent of immigrants came from Europe. But, from 1966 to 1970, only one-third of the immigrants were European, while one-third were Canadian and Latin American, and the remaining third were West Indian, Asian, and African. This geographic change has also affected the racial composition of immigrants, increasing the number of nonwhites. Because of earlier changes in composition, women now outnumber male immigrants, and there are more families with dependents.[51]

Although the report primarily focused on population growth by reproductive means, the commission identified illegal immigration as "a major and growing problem." Most of its analysis regarding immigrants dealt with "illegal aliens," noting that 80 percent of them migrate from Mexico.[52] It is important to point out that after 1964 "illegal" immigration rates rose in part due to the cessation of the Bracero program, which had allowed the importation of Mexican contract labor for work in U.S. farming communities.[53] Assuming a large number of Mexicans were "illegal aliens," the commission report recommends a concerted effort to eliminate immigration across the U.S.-Mexico border through enforcement of sanctions against employers who hire undocumented workers. Compared with their other recommendations, the suggestions relating to immigration were fairly well received by the general public and were considered to be "the one area in which practical results are possible."[54]

PUBLIC DISCOURSE AND MEDIA HANDLING

The public's warm reception of these recommendations on immigration control may in part be seen as a willingness to accept the perspective that illegal immigration from Mexico was a growing social problem. Media coverage of undocumented immigration intensified during the 1970s, signifying that it had indeed become a prominent topic of public interest and concern. In their quantitative content analysis of national and regional newspapers (including all articles published in the *Los Angeles Times, New York Times,* and *Washington Post* from 1972 through 1978), Celestino Fernández and Lawrence Pedroza concluded that "the public was bombarded with 'information,' albeit not necessarily accurate information, on undocumented Mexican immigration. On a regular basis, one could pick up a newspaper or magazine, listen to the radio, or watch television and encounter an item on illegal immigration. . . . the phenomenon captured the attention of the mass media and, in turn, of the American public."[55]

Moreover, Fernández and Pedroza argue, the news media indirectly convinced the American public "that the 'problem' of illegal immigration was out of control because of the influx of Mexicans."[56] A 1976 Gallup poll confirmed the impact of the media, finding that over half of the nationally representative population sampled had recently read or heard something negative about illegal aliens. Of those citizens residing in states bordering Mexico, over two-thirds polled reported that they had read or heard about this "problem."[57]

Much of the public discourse around the "illegal alien crisis" used sensational rhetoric comparable to the invective deployed by extremists against population growth.[58] The media broadcast an image of undocumented immigrants "stealing" American jobs, and immigration as a "human flood," invoking both criminality and destruction.[59] In 1973 journalist Clarence La Roche warned readers of the *San Antonio Express* that "there's a new invasion going on. Thousands and thousands of Mexican nationals are crossing the U.S.-Mexico border, heading north for jobs and higher pay."[60]

Many journalists stressed that this group of undocumented workers were a "new breed of wetbacks." Some reported that the immigrants were no longer satisfied with crossing the border to perform stoop labor and were now more aggressively searching for white-collar jobs in urban areas.[61] Presumably taking advantage of welfare, food stamps, and/or unemployment benefits during off-seasons, the new "modernized" alien was often feared because he would bring his family with him later. Since this new mode of illicit entry into the nation was "invisible" to most, it earned the moniker of "silent invasion," a phrase that associated Mexican immigration with disease, war, and communist threat.[62]

Documenting the rapidly increasing numbers of immigrants entering the country each year, in 1977 Leonard Chapman, director of the Immigration and Naturalization Service (INS), described the problem of illegal immigration from Mexico as a "critical problem . . . completely out of control." In another comment, Chapman declared, "It's a national dilemma that threatens to worsen rapidly. We're facing a vast army that's carrying out a silent invasion of the United States."[63] Chapman, a retired Marine officer who was INS commissioner from 1973 to 1977, launched a nationwide campaign to publicize this "silent invasion." While delivering speeches to local Rotary and Kiwanis Clubs, congressional committees, and national business organizations—and during many interviews with the news media—Chapman decried the "epidemic proportions" of illegal immigration. Garnering support for federal efforts to defeat this formidable "army" of Mexican illegals, Chapman lobbied for increased funding of the INS and tighter immigration laws.[64]

The issue of Mexican immigration was often raised within the context of contemporaneous discussions about world "overpopulation." Drawing on a metaphoric trope of the atomic age, commentators often described illegal immigration from Mexico to the United States as the result of the "sizzling time bomb" of overpopulation that was ominously ticking away in Mexico.[65] New York Times columnist James Reston put it bluntly: "Mexico has been producing more people than jobs."[66] Thus Mexico's high birthrate, which resulted in an annual growth rate of 4 percent, and its large population of young people were often blamed for generating "alien hordes" crossing the border to take advantage of the nation's generous social benefits and higher wages, and contributing to overpopulation.[67] Commentators of every stripe named population control as a solution. For example, Donald Mann, the president of Negative Population Growth, Inc., stated that "because of present overpopulation and continued population growth, its [Mexico's] employment and economic problems are, beyond any question, insoluble without population control."[68] Advocates of stricter immigration laws argued that the United States could no longer serve as the "safety valve" for the "explosive" populations of developing countries such as Mexico.

Many journalists highlighted the social implications of continued high rates of immigration. A U.S. News & World Report article commented, "Great waves of Latin-American immigrants appear well along the way to accomplishing what their Spanish ancestors couldn't: the 'conquest' of North America."[69] The claim that this second "Spanish invasion" would not just have a "tacos-and-tamales impact," but that the national "approach to life will have an increasingly Latin flavor."[70] The presence of "illegal aliens" was also blamed for a great upsurge in social problems, particularly increasing crime rates. In 1977 *Los Angeles Times* reporter John Kendall wrote,

> The image of the illegal alien as a servile person who stays out of trouble at all costs is no longer accurate. There are increasing reports of illegal alien involvement in crime, including street gang activities, narcotics trafficking and usage and organized criminal activities. . . . The solution to the great social problem of illegal immigration depends on passing the necessary federal legislation, providing the resources and giving the problem high priority. . . . It is estimated (by special LAPD divisions) that illegal aliens commit 50 percent of all pickpockets, 30 percent of all hit-and-run accidents, 25 percent to 30 percent of all shoplifts, 20 percent to 25 percent of all burglaries, 20 percent of all auto thefts and 5 percent of all homicides.[71]

That same year the *Los Angeles Times* reported that "as many as 50 Mexican illegal aliens are burglarizing homes in Glendora to Malibu at any moment of any day . . . and the County Sheriff's Department has begun to handle that crime phenomenon as the unique problem that it is."[72] Such newspaper coverage fueled public fear by often pairing immigration and crime rates: "The old problem of illegal aliens has recently been taking on a new face. It's the type of face well known to local, state and federal authorities. It's the grim face of crime staring up from a photograph on a police rap sheet."[73]

Some articles reported that illegal aliens committed crimes in order to sustain their drug habits, while others blamed immigrants for a real increase in communicable diseases and other health problems.[74] "East Los Angeles is fast becoming a potential breeding ground for a host of highly infectious diseases from Mexico," one *Los Angeles Times* reporter wrote. "A mushrooming illegal alien population that immigration and medical officials have discovered is infected with a high incidence of typhoid, dysentery, tuberculosis, tape-worms, venereal diseases and hepatitis, among others."[75] In 1974 the U.S. Public Health Service declared illegal aliens a serious "health problem,"[76] and the County of Los Angeles sued the federal government for remuneration of immigrant health care expenses.[77]

THE GOVERNMENT RESPONDS

Given the myriad public problems attributed to immigrants, many government officials were eager to find an easy solution. Arguing that the presence of "aliens" constituted "a severe national crisis," Attorney General William Saxbe recommended in 1974 that President Ford substantially increase the INS budget and implement a plan to deport Mexican immigrants.[78] Other proponents of immigration control suggested increased use of birth control in Mexico as part of a necessary solution.

By 1975, the federal government was paying attention to the public's cries for immigration control, cries which gained fierce momentum as the United States fell deeper into an economic recession.[79] Many Americans became convinced that Mexican immigrants were taking jobs away from deserving American citizens, and that undeserved welfare benefits were placing a heavy tax toll on the country.[80] In 1977 one *Denver Post* reader summed up these sentiments in a letter she wrote to the editor: "The citizens of this country are deeply concerned about the 13 million illegal aliens allowed to remain in this country, while just as many Americans are unemployed. Also millions of these aliens are collecting government benefits, at the expense of the taxpayers."[81]

Although government officials and others often cited INS immigration statistics, these were later found to be seriously inaccurate. A widely publicized study commissioned by the INS estimated that at that time 8.2 million immigrants resided in the United States (5.2 million of them of Mexican origin). This population, the study claimed, placed a $16 billion tax burden on the American society. Other studies contended that the numbers could be as high as 12 million.[82] These and other such estimates were later revealed to be highly exaggerated, but nonetheless, they were widely disseminated by the news media and policymakers.[83]

Despite the proliferation of mass hostility and anxiety related to the illegal alien "crisis," the federal government did not enact major legislation to halt immigration, even though politicians offered several proposals. Most notably, beginning in 1972, Congressman Peter Rodino repeatedly introduced a bill that would have placed sanctions on employers hiring illegal immigrants. Backed by INS chief Leonard Chapman, the bill was passed twice in the House of Representatives but failed each time in the Senate. In January 1975 President Ford noted that illegal immigration was a "serious national problem" and formed a committee headed by the attorney general to investigate the issue, but little came of it.[84] By 1977, however, many Americans, including President Carter, considered illegal immigration the nation's most pressing social dilemma, and the president formed a six-member Cabinet committee to investigate and propose possible responses and solutions.[85]

THE IMPLICIT PROBLEMS OF RACE AND GENDER

During the 1970s, public discourse about population and immigration policy carried only slightly veiled racial undercurrents. In fact, demographic studies showed that while population control advocates were raising claims of a population explosion, national birthrates had been declining since 1955.[86] In 1972, the same year the Commission on Population Growth and the American Future advocated slower growth, the nation reached the lowest-ever birthrate (2.03), falling below the 2.1 child per family recommendation for zero population growth.[87] Although such statistics indicated that the nation had reached the highly desired replacement-level rate of population growth much sooner than ZPG advocates had hoped, concerns about overpopulation continued, albeit with a somewhat different emphasis.[88]

Despite the significant decline in the nation's birthrates in the 1970s and the fact that birthrates of poor and minority women were experiencing the sharpest drop, the birthrates of poor, non-white population groups were still higher than those of whites.[89] Thus, instead of experiencing a population explosion as ZPG proponents had forewarned, the nation was actually undergoing a population *shift*, with the birthrates among poor whites and non-whites remaining significantly higher than those of their more affluent counterparts.

This drop in the white birthrate was the topic of Dr. Edward C. Hughes's presidential address to the 85th Annual Meeting of the American Association of Obstetricians and Gynecologists in 1975. Concerned with what he considered "the most drastic reduction of birth rate in the history of our nation," Dr. Hughes raised questions about its possible impact on the nation's political and economic situation, and its role in world politics. He asked, "Can this nation with zero population [growth] maintain the leadership in the world and provide the economic and material aid to those countries where population growth probably never can be controlled?"[90] Hughes was not only concerned with the "plummeting" national birthrate in relation to the high birthrates in developing countries within Asia, Latin America, and Africa; he was also interested in the birthrates of the "nonwhite" groups in the United States. He elaborated:

Demographers are interested in the distribution of race in this country in relation to zero population. It appears that the nonwhite population will increase if population growth ceases. Studies indicate that the nonwhite population possesses a predominately greater growth momentum than the white. They claim that if nonwhite and white reach replacement simultaneously, the percent of nonwhite in the total population would increase. The longer it would take to arrive at the replacement level, the larger the percentage would be. It would be 14 percent if replacement occurs instantly, 17 percent in the year 2000. If replacement did not occur until 75 years from the initial date, the percentage would be over 20. Biostatisticians and economists are particularly concerned about approaching negative growth in this country. Will the birth rate decline make for a richer or poorer country in all levels of life and endeavor?[91]

Several scholars in the 1970s, noting such racialized commentary in various public domains, advanced critiques of the population control movement and have suggested that some strains within the movement were primarily focused on maintaining white supremacy.[92] In analyzing a 1972 report of the Commission on Population Growth and the American Future, for example, Ozzie Edwards challenged the report's emphasis on fertility rates and family size. Edwards believed the racial implications of the committee's assertions clearly targeted the reproductive behavior of poor minorities.[93] He wrote that "the implicit notions of the Commission on Population Growth and the American Future are that the composition of the fertility flow should match that of the larger population, thus maintaining current ratios of racial groups and repressing rising proportions of certain groups."[94]

Edwards's perception and accusation were reasonable in the context of the civil rights era, when emerging race-based movements strived to guarantee the civil rights of minority groups in America. Many whites, like Dr. Hughes, worried that a rising non-white population, along with a vibrant civil rights movement, would endanger white America. Population control advocates typically warned that overpopulation would lead to increased social protest, and they referred to social uprisings such as the events occurring in Watts, Los Angeles in 1965, as proof of their doomsday predictions. Civil rights leader Julian Bond criticized Paul Ehrlich's *Population Bomb* as a "theoretical bomb in the hands of frightened racists, as well as over the heads of black people, as the justification for genocide."[95]

At the same time that the civil rights movement was gathering force, the women's movement was becoming a coherent national presence. Women all over the country were actively organizing for reproductive rights, including access to contraceptives and abortion. Unquestionably, the 1970s marked a significant period in birth control politics. The development of the birth control pill during the 1960s and its widespread availability by the 1970s, advances in sterilization procedures and legalization of abortion during the early 1970s, and the passage of the Hyde Amendment in 1977, prohibiting the use of federal funds to pay for the abortions of poor women, render this era an unprecedented period of activism, progress, and reaction regarding reproductive politics.[96]

How did women fighting for reproductive rights fit into the population control effort? According to birth control historian Linda Gordon, "during the 1960s population control was the major, defining part of the politics of reproduction."[97] While overlapping in content to some extent, the population control platform was, in fact, in direct opposition to the reproductive rights platform. Thus, while mainstream feminists lent support (perhaps unwittingly) to population control efforts and the struggle for zero population growth during the first half of the decade, many disaffiliated themselves from the population control cause as they realized that birth control advocates were not necessarily interested in guaranteeing women's rights to control their own bodies.

Although the overlapping discourses of immigration and overpopulation developed across the nation, they were undeniably stronger and more tightly bonded in certain geographical regions. To demonstrate more substantively how the problems of overpopulation and immigration manifested tacit concerns about race and gender in the 1970s, I now turn to the burgeoning concerns with population growth in California—a state with unique demographic characteristics that ignited a powerful movement for population and immigration control during the 1970s.

OVERPOPULATION AND IMMIGRATION IN CALIFORNIA: THE CONVERGENCE OF TWO SOCIAL PROBLEMS

If many experts cast overpopulation as an impending national problem, most identified California as the site of its first and worst incarnation. With its population doubling every twenty years, the state provided the quintessential example of the devastating effects of unmonitored population growth. Experts and others named California the state where the threat of overpopulation was most perilous. During the 1960s and 1970s, the state experienced a 27 percent population increase, twice that experienced by the entire nation.[98] In the introduction of a joint resolution to declare a U.S. policy of voluntary population stabilization, Senator Alan Cranston, a Democrat from California, used his own state as an example to demonstrate the necessity of government action on issues of overpopulation. He advised his fellow senators that "nowhere is this threat of consumption and pollution any greater than in the State of California with its estimated 20,300,000 persons as of this spring."[99]

Its rapid rate of growth made California the focus of discussion about developing a population policy. Prior to the 1950s, significant publicity efforts were necessary to attract people to the state and stimulate population growth. However, increased westward migration after World War II and the post-war baby boom that hit the state beginning in 1945 led the governor to commission committees to monitor the state's growth.[100] By the mid-1950s, the state's rapid population increase was attracting nationwide attention and study.

By 1962, California had overtaken New York as the nation's largest state.[101] Although Governor Edmund G. Brown first welcomed this occurrence "with pride" and called for a statewide celebration, the governor (under pressure from citizen groups such as California Tomorrow) created his own commission in 1966 to consider the state's "population explosion."[102] Comprised of medical professionals, representatives of Planned Parenthood, officials from the state welfare department, and nationally prominent demographer Kingsley Davis (a professor at the University of California, Berkeley), the Population Study Commission was charged with reviewing the state's activities to increase "freedom of choice" in family planning and to investigate discrimination in making these services available in public programs.[103] After surveying 209 county hospitals, Planned Parenthood affiliates, and welfare departments, and reviewing the state's current family planning provisions, the committee proposed more than twenty recommendations for improving the state's services and increasing individual awareness of the population explosion.[104]

In addition to recommending increased welfare funding for contraceptives, public education about family planning, physician involvement in promoting family planning and smaller family size, and increased state funding of demographic centers in universities, the commission suggested that an appointed committee, such as itself, become an ongoing facet of the government. In light of the "continued gigantic flow of migration into California," which is "the main contributor to California's population growth," Kingsley Davis pressed the state government to take the study of the consequences of increased population seriously.[105] Arguing for the development of a formal governmental committee to consider population problems in the state, he asked,

Are conditions of poverty being perpetuated in the state by too high a birth rate among the poor—a birth rate that is certainly higher than it is among less impoverished classes? Is the rising rate of illegitimacy a contributor not only to poverty but to poor child-rearing and swollen welfare roles? Are early marriages primarily a result of premarital pregnancy and the state's abortion laws? Is the passing of mortality as a source of genetic selection, plus the environmental hazards affecting gestation, bringing a serious deterioration of the genetic quality of the population? These are some of the questions that a Population Commission should study.[106]

Although the commission's recommendations were never implemented, the state legislature revisited the population question even more extensively just a few years later, reaching very similar conclusions. By 1970 California's population had reached twenty million, comprising almost 10 percent of the nation's total population.[107] A 1972 article in the *San Francisco Chronicle* reported that "the Legislature is now on notice that California occupies a special and hazardous place in a world that has recognized and is beginning to move against the ills of overpopulation."[108]

The issue of overpopulation—and the role that immigration plays within it—was even more seriously considered by the state legislature in 1971 when the Science and Technology Advisory Council of the California Assembly was asked to research and develop recommendations regarding a state population policy. A formal panel, chaired again by Kingsley Davis, was established to investigate this question. The committee called together a group of distinguished social scientists, demographers, and policymakers to contribute to a statewide symposium held at the University of California, Davis, in March 1971. A number of experts were asked to prepare analyses of the "nature and consequences of population changes in the state."[109]

Based on information shared at the conference, the committee urged the state to develop "deliberate population policies" to control the state's growth, or "California's economic and environmental advantages will inevitably lead us to be the recipient of additional waves of migrants from less favored parts of the nation and from other countries."[110] Toward this goal the committee made thirty-four recommendations, including the elimination of tax deductions for children, increased abortion clinics offering cheaper services, accessible contraceptive education and devices, nationwide uniformity in family assistance programs, and increased state funding for the development of population research.

In addition to the adoption of measures that would deter a natural increase of the population, the commission called for establishing a federal immigration policy. Noting that over one-quarter of the nation's foreign population resided in California, the committee warned that "all evidence indicates that continued migration must be considered as a significant factor influencing not only the state's growth, but also the structure and character of the population."[111] Moreover, "the majority of new foreign residents are from areas which are associated with high fertility and rapid population growth," the committee said, referring to Mexico, Central America, and China, and added, it is "in the interest of the state to press for changes in federal immigration policy."[112]

In response to the report, the Assembly Committee on Environmental Quality held a two-day hearing in September 1972 to "assess the State's role regarding population growth and distribution, demographic and family life education and family planning."[113] As this was the first California legislative hearing dedicated to the issue of the state's population growth and the government's role, participants strongly felt that measures should be taken to develop a state policy on population growth.[114] Many concerned with population growth worldwide paid close attention to the state's treatment of the problem, hopeful that California would set "the pace for the nation" in establishing a population policy.[115] Assemblywoman March K. Fong, who chaired the committee, advocated a twenty-five million cap on state population and spoke in favor of emphasizing "quality" rather than the "quantity" of life.[116] No formal population policy for the state emerged from these meetings, but the committee made several recommendations, including increased funding for family planning services, family planning education in schools, and the establishment of a formal population commission for the state.[117]

By 1975, a dialogue regarding the development of a population policy for California was active within state governmental agencies. Demographer Peter Uhlenberg introduced his paper to the Symposium on California's Population Problems with the somber recognition that "among the most explosive social issues in the United States today is the relative poverty of certain minority populations."[118] Policymakers discussed the increasing numbers of poor people of color in the urban centers of the state, often referring to the "urban crisis" that plagued California and many other states across the nation. Overpopulation was believed to exacerbate the racial crises, and many policymakers argued that until population problems were solved, no other social issue could be alleviated.

With foreign immigration emerging as an expanding component of California's population growth, immigration reform was included under the rubric of population policy discussions, as were the fertility rates of particular immigrant groups. When Frederick Styles spoke at a 1975 Berkeley conference, "Population Growth and Public Policy," he signaled the convergence of these issues. Among the "range of interrelated problems" necessitating attention in the development of a state population policy, he noted that there are not only those of family planning and the availability of contraceptives, but also those concerning the differential fertility among groups and immigration. In particular, Styles pointed out that "increasing at a rate that far exceeds that of any other minority group, the number of Americans of Latino descent in the United States rose from just under 7 million persons in 1960 to approximately 10.5 million in 1970." [119] Although he did not elaborate on the particular ethnic or racial groups whose "differential fertility" was of concern, or what the issues surrounding differential fertility were, Styles's statement indicated that these issues were important to population policymakers during this period.

Clearly, Latino/a growth rates were an important focus. The implications of such concerns for Latinos and people of Mexican origin in California in particular were considerable. [120] By 1975 the Census Bureau reported that the Spanish-surname population in the United States had grown to 11.2 million (7.7 million of which were of Mexican origin), with over half living in the southwestern states. Of this number, the largest portion lived in California, with 3.1 million residing in the state. [121] Historian Albert Camarillo notes that the Mexican population in California grew significantly during the 1970s, with the state's Hispanic or Spanish-origin population, primarily Mexican, almost doubling between 1970 and 1980. [122] This trend was paralleled in the County of Los Angeles during the same period; as the percentage of whites dropped, Mexican Americans comprised over 18 percent of the population. [123]

The nation's rapidly growing Latino population attracted the attention of government officials, who began to shine a media spotlight on the supposed 8.2 million "illegal immigrants" residing in the United States. As demographic projections had not foreseen the rapid growth of this segment of the country's population, this unexpected population upsurge was read by some as having worrisome implications for the country. The growth rate also produced a sizable upsurge of Spanish-surnamed voters, a previously untapped body of political power. Predicted to outnumber African Americans by the year 2000, Latinos were courted for the first time during the 1975 election by the national Republican and Democratic parties. [124] In the multiracial state of California, with Latinos the fastest-growing segment of the population, discussions of immigration and overpopulation were closely and continuously coupled.

CONCLUSION

In this chapter I have documented the coexistence of the distinct but mutually reinforcing ideologies of immigration and population control as expressed in the national landscape during the 1970s. The discourse of both issues relied on rhetoric and imagery of an impending catastrophic situation of world poverty brought about by excessively fertile women and an immigrant invasion from Mexico. Uniting a number of significant actors—demographers, medical practitioners, policymakers, and activists—these "problems" provide the backdrop of a decade that heralded unprecedented social changes. In particular, the 1970s in California provides a unique historical moment during which the crystallization of public interest in the fertility of women of Mexican origin comes sharply into focus.

CHAPTER THREE

"THEY BREED LIKE RABBITS"

The Forced Sterilization of Mexican-Origin Women

Antonia Hernández had just begun her first job as a staff attorney at the Los Angeles County Center for Law and Justice when Bernard Rosenfeld, a resident at LACMC, approached her with data proving that women were being coercively sterilized there.[1] Rosenfeld provided her with information on more than 180 cases of primarily Spanish-surname women who were sterilized during childbirth. All were approached by hospital staff who recommended the procedure during the late stages of their labor, after they had already been administered large doses of Demerol or Valium. Many of the women required emergency cesarean sections, and following their deliveries there was no signed consent form for tubal ligation or any other record of their agreement to the procedure in their files.

Rosenfeld had gone through the medical records of hundreds upon hundreds of Spanish-surname patients; reviewing their indications for cesarean section, he recognized a clear pattern of coercion. The notes on one twenty-three-year-old patient with one child read: "Failure to deliver baby with forceps. Caesarean section needed. Consents signed in markedly distressed handwriting, in English. No medical indication for sterilization." A month and a half later, upon a visit to the Family Planning Clinic to request birth control, this patient was fitted with an intra-uterine device (IUD), which she wore for at least a year before she learned that she had been sterilized.[2] With so many similar cases documented, Rosenfeld believed that the data proved what he had seen with his own eyes during his medical residency: the targeted and coercive sterilization of African American and Mexican women.

Hernández followed up on Rosenfeld's information, locating and talking with many of the women whom he suspected had been coercively sterilized. In an interview with the author, she recalled:

> I remember driving around city terrace. It took a long time. All I can
> tell you is that this case consumed my life. . . . I must have interviewed

a hundred women. I remember driving all over East L.A. with a map looking for addresses of these women. And then I had the difficult job of saying to many of the women, "Do you know you were sterilized?" It was a very painful process. And some of them knew, but they all had the misconception that their tubes were tied but could be untied.

Hernández was often faced with the responsibility of encouraging each woman to take legal action. However, many women who wanted to participate in the lawsuit could not because their statute of limitations had expired; others were worried that if they testified against the hospital, they or members of their family would be deported. In the end, two separate cases were filed against LACMC.

Andrade et al. v. Los Angeles County–USC Medical Center was filed by Richard Cruz, a lawyer most noted for his founding of Católicos Por La Raza, a Catholic Chicano activist organization. Cruz also worked with assistance from the offices of Belli, Ashe, and Choulos, who provided co-counsel and split the costs of the case.[3] Cruz's clients were forcibly sterilized between 1972 and 1973, and because their complaints fell within the statue of limitations, each asked for $2 million in compensation for what they had endured as a result of their sterilization.[4] Their suit charged nurses and doctors at LACMC with battery and claimed that "the government in combination with the University of Southern California and health professionals and administrators accomplished a massive 'push' of unlawful sterilization operations between 1968 and 1974 at defendant hospital."[5] Cruz also argued that there was "no way around the word genocide" when considering the abuses that occurred, and he condemned the medical practitioners on moral grounds.[6] It is unclear why *Andrade* never went to court. Before examining the details of what occurred at LACMC, it is important to understand the context that made sterilization a common practice.

THE ADVENT OF SURGICAL STERILIZATION

Academics and others typically define sterilization abuse as "the misinformed, coerced, or unknowing termination of the reproductive capacity of women and men."[7] The long and well-researched history of sterilization abuse in the United States has demonstrated that practitioners of coercive sterilization have targeted their subjects according to race, class, and gender.[8] As historian Adelaida Del Castillo has noted, sterilization abuse of Mexican-origin peoples for eugenic reasons had occurred previously. Before sterilization was widely available, individual judges would make parole and other conditions of probation dependent upon sterilization. In 1966, for example, Nancy Hernández was sentenced to jail when she refused to agree to be sterilized for a misdemeanor conviction.[9]

During the 1970s, several circumstances directly precipitated sterilization abuse nationwide. For one thing, medical regulations governing sterilization options for most women had become less restrictive. Earlier sterilization was guided by an age-parity formula, whereby a doctor would only sterilize a woman if her age multiplied by the number of her children exceeded 120. In 1970 the American College of Obstetrics and Gynecology withdrew this standard, offering millions of women access to the procedure.[10] The liberalization of medical guidelines for sterilization was coupled with increased availability of funding. Governmental grants to the poor increased substantially after 1965, most notably through passage of the Family Planning Services and Population Research Act in 1970. While in 1965 only $5 million of federal money was available for family planning services for the poor, in 1979 the government distributed $260 million for this purpose.[11]

Government financing for sterilization procedures in particular was substantial. Prior to 1969 the government had prohibited federally supported family planning services from subsidizing sterilization and abortion services. Funds for sterilization became accessible officially in 1971, with Medicaid covering 90 percent of the cost. Most federal funds were offered through the Office of Economic Opportunity (OEO), which was established to fight the "war on poverty."[12] The combination of technical advances in tubal ligation surgery, increased availability of federal funding, and relaxed requirements for the procedures led to sterilization becoming the most popular form of birth control in the United States.[13]

California long held the highest rates of sterilization in the nation, and these developments increased those rates even more.[14] Sterilizations at the Women's Hospital of LACMC exemplified the extraordinary surge in the numbers of women undergoing such procedures. During the two-year period between July 1968 and July 1970, elective hysterectomy increased by 742 percent, elective tubal ligation by 470 percent, and tubal ligation after delivery by 151 percent.[15]

AN "EPIDEMIC" OF STERILIZATION ABUSE REVEALED

Despite the dramatic increase in rates of sterilization through the 1970s, no medical community boards or governmental officials monitored these procedures. No safeguards to prevent widespread abuses were in effect during the first three years that publicly funded sterilization procedures were available, although OEO-funded family planning clinics were asked to refrain from performing the operation until a set of federal guidelines could be administered. Although guidelines were printed in 1972, the U.S. government did not distribute them to clinics until 1974.[16] Within this unregulated environment, many coerced sterilizations occurred without much notice until the case of the Relf sisters captured public attention.

In June 1973, Mary Alice and Katie Relf, two African American sisters in their early teens, were sterilized in a Montgomery, Alabama hospital even though neither of the girls, nor their parents, gave permission for, or even knew about, the operations. The hospital paid for these operations using OEO funds. Although Mrs. Relf signed an "X" on a consent form she could not read, neither she nor her daughters were advised of the specific nature of the "shots" the nurse advised were necessary. Realizing later that their daughters had been unwittingly sterilized, the parents reported the incident to the Southern Poverty Law Center. National objection to the treatment of the Relf sisters forced the federal Department of Health, Education, and Welfare to suspend the availability of federal funds for the sterilization of minors and the "mentally incompetent" until the government enacted regulations. However, coercive sterilization of adults continued unchecked.[17]

One major study in this era, conducted and coauthored by Drs. Bernard Rosenfeld and Sidney Wolfe, and later published by the Ralph Nader Health Research Group in 1973, exposed several reputable teaching institutions for coercively targeting poor women of color for sterilization. The report verified that doctors at some of the nation's most prestigious hospitals pressured women into consenting to sterilization.[18]

Based on medical journal articles, observation, and interviews with medical students and doctors trained in hospitals across the nation, the report revealed an "epidemic of sterilization . . . in . . . almost every major American teaching hospital in the past two years."[19] In most cases, women were not adequately informed of the range of birth control options available to them nor the permanence of the sterilization operation. Moreover, many were unaware that they had been sterilized. In almost every major medical teaching hospital in the country, the number of elective tubal ligations had at least doubled between the years of 1971 and 1973.[20] On finding that most of the victimized women were low-income minorities, the authors of the report charged that doctors and other hospital personnel acted out of racist attitudes regarding "overpopulation" and "ideal family size."[21] Studies also showed that of the many cases of coercive sterilization reported, none documented abuses against white women.[22] In fact, doctors often tried to talk white middle-class women out of sterilization surgery.[23]

While doctors and others targeted African American women in the South, Native American women suffered from rampant sterilization abuse at Indian Health Service (IHS) clinics. Dr. Connie Uri, who interviewed many native women sterilized while under duress or without complete information, became their advocate. The national attention that she brought to these abuses resulted in a study requested by Senator James Abourzek and conducted by the General Accounting Office (GAO). The report revealed that many women had felt coerced into sterilization by the IHS and under threat of losing their welfare benefits if they did not agree to the operation. In the four IHS areas examined in the GAO study, 3,406 sterilizations were performed between 1973 and 1976, an estimated one-quarter of all Native Americans sterilized during those three years.[24] Many of these women were under the age of twenty-one, a violation of the moratorium called by the Department of Health, Education, and Welfare in 1974.

Elsewhere I have argued that although sterilization abuse of women of color was widespread across the nation at this time, institutions in different regions of the country coerced women in numerous ways, using a variety of justifications.[25] The sterilization abuse of women of Mexican origin followed a pattern similar to that of other women of color, but several factors distinguish what occurred at LACMC from other cases. For example, abuses that have received widespread national attention, such as *Relf v. Weinberger* and *Walker v. Pierce*, occurred in the South and targeted African American women receiving public assistance. The case of *Madrigal v. Quilligan*, on the other hand, took place in Los Angeles and involved mostly poor Mexican immigrant women with limited English-speaking ability—none of whom were receiving public assistance. These differences raise unique issues of citizenship, regional racial politics, language, and culture. How these factors shaped the sterilization abuse of Mexican-origin women is best exemplified in the case of *Madrigal v. Quilligan*.

FORCED STERILIZATION AT LOS ANGELES COUNTY MEDICAL CENTER

Prior to the promulgation of the 1974 guidelines, there had been no "official" policy regulating the practice of sterilization at the Women's Hospital at LACMC.[26] Although the Department of Health, Education, and Welfare's regulations were implemented nationwide in May 1974, they remained unenforced at LACMC in December of that year.[27] During the late 1960s, the hospital received substantial federal funds for the development and improvement of the Obstetrics-Gynecology Department, much of which was funneled toward rebuilding the Women's Hospital facility within which these services were housed. During this period several new doctors with prestigious credentials joined the Women's Hospital staff under the newly appointed direction of Dr. Edward James Quilligan.[28] The new staff, well-funded and practicing in upgraded facilities, began at once to promote birth control to their female patients.[29] In addition, several of the doctors were involved in contraceptive studies conducted on LACMC patients and published in esteemed medical journals.[30]

"Birth control" in this case included rampant sterilization abuse at LACMC, yet this was only one aspect of the systematic effort by the hospital staff to reduce the birthrate of their mostly minority clientele. Several other programs reflected the department's attempt to cut the birthrate of the Mexican and African American populations, who made up the majority of the hospital's patients. Bilingual family planning counselors actively visited each new mother prior to her discharge from the ward to ensure her commitment to practice some form of birth control; no woman was released until this was promised. Counselors aggressively recommended IUDs, a long-term method of birth control that women themselves cannot regulate.[31]

Dr. Karen Benker recounted that "the drive to insert IUDs was so great that the women actually did not receive a postpartum check-up or have any of their questions about their baby or their health answered. They were merely placed on the table one after another and an IUD was popped into place."[32] In her affidavit Benker stated that these facts demonstrate "the great emphasis that the department did put on 'cutting the birth rate of the Mexican and Negro population.'"

Doctors implemented the most effective form of birth control during delivery when they terminated the childbearing capabilities of women of Mexican origin by tubal ligation. As was common in teaching hospitals across the nation, LACMC students were encouraged to conduct several surgical procedures to refine their skills. According to Dr. Bernard Rosenfeld, coauthor of the Health Research Group Report and a resident in the Obstetrics-Gynecology Department at LACMC during this period, staff doctors would often congratulate residents on the number of postpartum tubal ligations accomplished within a week's time.[33] Similarly, residents reportedly encouraged interns to press women into agreeing to a sterilization procedure. In one instance, after a patient had refused a resident's solicitations for sterilization, the resident's supervisor remarked, "Talk her into it. You can always talk her into it." In June 1973 a resident told new interns, "I want you to ask every one of the girls if they want their tubes tied, regardless of how old they are. Remember everyone you get to get her tubes tied means two tubes [i.e., two procedures] for some resident or intern."[34] Rosenfeld estimated that 10 to 20 percent of the physicians at LACMC "actively pushed sterilization on women who either did not understand what was happening to them or who had not been given all the facts regarding their options."[35]

Physicians most often approached women for sterilization while they were in the last stages of labor, during their wait in the Active Labor Room, where they stayed until actual delivery. Here women in the most painful stages of labor were attached to fetal monitors and placed in beds side by side. Dr. Karen Benker recalled the scene as one of "crowding, screams of pain, bright lights, lack of sleep by patients and staff, and an 'assembly-line' approach so that many women were literally terrified of what was happening at the time they signed the consents. Of course, this was especially true of non-English-speaking mothers who were left with no explanation of what was happening."[36] Dr. Benker's acknowledgment that non-English-speaking women were "of course" more likely to experience medical mistreatment speaks to the critical importance of language in the sterilization abuse cases that occurred at LACMC. Most residents and doctors were not bilingual; most knew only a few obstetrical-related words. There was "virtually no one available" to interpret for Spanish-speaking women. Often women were sterilized on the basis of one question, "¿Más niños?" (More babies?)[37] While some nurses or translators tried to communicate with Spanish-speaking women, as illustrated below, the doctors apparently took advantage of the women's inability to understand English and manipulated them into consenting to sterilization.[38]

Residents and nurses often approached women to sign consent forms immediately before childbirth. Medical personnel gave women in labor a shot of Valium or Demerol in preparation for the delivery, and they shoved consent forms into the hands of laboring women while they were too groggy to understand or notice that they were signing forms granting permission for their own sterilization.[39] Dr. Benker described seeing this type of coercion "on almost a daily basis": "The doctor would hold a syringe in front of the mother who was in labor pain and ask her if she wanted a pain killer; while the woman was in the throes of a contraction the doctor would say, 'Do you want the pain killer? Then sign the papers. Do you want the pain to stop? Do you want to have to go through this again? Sign the papers.'"[40]

Moreover, hospital staff did not fully explain the irreversible nature of the sterilization procedure. Many women agreed to the surgery believing that their tubes were being tied temporarily and that they could be untied later and their fertility restored. A physician first asked María Figueroa if she wanted tubal ligation as she was being prepared for surgery. She specifically recalled that the doctor told her the procedure entailed the "tying of a woman's tubes" and she could later have them untied. She initially rejected the procedure, but tired from her labor and of the doctor's urgings, Mrs. Figueroa agreed to sterilization if she delivered a boy. As it turned out, she was sterilized even though she delivered a baby girl.[41]

In many instances LACMC patients were not just subjected to a single incident of coercion but were harassed continually by nurses and doctors. Helena Orozco, a plaintiff in the *Madrigal* trial, had repeatedly declined sterilization throughout her prenatal care at the hospital. She had discussed sterilization with her husband prior to labor, and Mrs. Orozco told the nurses, "We decided not to."[42] However, after numerous solicitations from the doctor and nurses, and while crying from intense pain during labor, Mrs. Orozco signed the consent for sterilization because, in her words, "I just wanted them to leave me alone, sign the papers and get it over with. . . . I was in pain on the table when they were asking me all those questions, and they were poking around my stomach, and pushing with their fingers up there. I just wanted to be left alone."[43] Mrs. Orozco also agreed to the operation because "I thought he [the doctor] meant tying tubes only. Then they could be untied later. . . . If they would have put the word 'sterilization' there, I would not have signed the papers."[44] Because she believed the procedure to be reversible, Mrs. Orozco planned to have her tubes untied in three years and did not find out until a year and a half later that she could never again have children.

Hospital personnel also strategically limited communication between laboring women and their husbands. For example, when a patient adamantly resisted sterilization, the doctor would warn the husband that his wife's health was in danger, hoping that the husband would then pressure his wife to submit to the procedure.[45] Such manipulative gender dynamics were apparent in the case of Dolores Madrigal, who refused sterilization from the outset of her stay at LACMC. After Mrs. Madrigal had refused the recommendations of several nurses that she take care of herself and agree to a tubal ligation, doctors talked with Mr. Madrigal in another room, telling him that his wife would die if she had another child.[46] Ten minutes later, a nurse returned to Mrs. Madrigal and informed her, laughing, that her husband had agreed to the sterilization procedure, and again presented her with a consent form to sign.[47]

Women requiring cesarean section delivery were at greatest risk of coercive sterilization. According to Dr. Benker, once it became clear that a cesarean was going to be necessary, the resident was "extremely aggressive" in pushing for sterilization. Many doctors lied to patients, telling them that state law only allowed three cesarean sections and that sterilization was therefore required after childbirth. Maria Hurtado recalled that her doctor "brought someone from outside and explained to her to ask me why I wanted so many children since the State of California only permitted three Cesareans."[48] While unconscious following the delivery of her child, Mrs. Hurtado was given a tubal ligation without her consent. It was not until requesting birth control during her six-week postpartum visit that she recalled a receptionist at the hospital telling her, "Lady, forever you will not be able to have any more children."[49]

Doctors sometimes told patients that they might even die during future childbirths if they were not sterilized after their cesarean.[50] Upon the cesarean delivery of her third child, Consuelo Hermosillo was advised by her doctor that sterilization would be necessary, because a fourth pregnancy would most likely be life-threatening.[51] While medicated, Ms. Hermosillo signed the consent forms, without full comprehension of their content. Likewise, Estela Benavides feared her doctor's warnings that another child delivered by cesarean could be life-threatening, and she consented to a tubal ligation while hemorrhaging during her labor. She made this hard decision, she stated, out of her commitment to continue to care for her existing children.[52]

THE PHYSICIANS' PERSPECTIVE

The physicians' attitudes toward the LACMC clientele, and their perceptions of their own role in providing a panacea for overpopulation, were intricately linked. As authors of the Health Research Group study asserted, "Sometimes the doctors involved held very strong beliefs about population control, others admittedly held strong views about class prejudice—others simply believed all persons on welfare should have their tubes tied."[53] Dr. Rosenfeld recalled once talking to a colleague about coercing patients into sterilization when the other physician said, "Well, if we're going to pay for them, we should control them."[54]

These attitudes were prevalent at LACMC and across the nation during this time. While under general anesthesia in preparation for a cesarean delivery, Jovita Rivera was approached by a doctor who told her that she should have her "tubes tied" because her children were a burden on the government. Ironically, Ms. Rivera was not receiving public assistance, nor were any of the plaintiffs in the *Madrigal* case. However, because physicians and other hospital personnel perceived these women as welfare recipients, they were considered prime candidates for tubal ligation.[55]

The doctors would also make use of patients' racial/ethnic identity and immigrant status to coerce them into sterilization. Many physicians "would express very prejudiced remarks about patients who did not speak English— Mexican American patients" and referred to them as "beans."[56] After four hours in the delivery room in advanced labor, Georgina Hernández was approached by her doctor, who first commented that Mexicans are very poor and cannot provide for a large family, and then suggested that she be sterilized. Although Mrs. Hernández resisted her doctor's urgings and did not recall signing a consent form, she was surgically sterilized during the delivery of her fourth child.[57] Other women were threatened with deportation if they were not sterilized. In a San Diego hospital, "one resident would be so furious if a woman declined (sterilization) that he would say, 'We know you're here illegally and if you don't consent to have a tubal, we'll call the feds [immigration officials] and get you deported.'"[58]

Patients were even roughly handled by some physicians. One doctor slapped a patient and told her to shut up as she cried out in labor pains. Some medical workers expressed moralistic references to the woman's sexual activity. For example, a doctor might observe that if a woman had not had sex, she would not be in pain right now. According to Dr. Benker, these biased attitudes and behaviors were common practice on the obstetrical floor.

The individual experiences of the women involved in the Madrigal trial suggest a range of manipulations of power and privilege that coalesced at LACMC to rob women of Mexican origin of their reproductive liberty. Not only do these incidents demonstrate the ways patriarchal, class-based, and racial ideas were used by hospital personnel to coerce Mexican-origin women into sterilization, they also show how ideological notions impact medical practice. The salient aspects of these ideas are further illuminated by the legal proceedings surrounding the case.

"A CLASH OF CULTURES": THE TRIAL OF *MADRIGAL V. QUILLIGAN*

On June 18, 1975, attorneys for the *Madrigal* plaintiffs filed a class-action civil rights suit in federal district court in Los Angeles, naming USC–Los Angeles County Medical Center, twelve doctors, the State of California, and the U.S. Department of Health, Education, and Welfare as defendants.[59] Three years later, Charles Nabarette and Antonia Hernández began their case in court on May 31, 1978.[60] The lawyers argued that the sterilization of the women without their informed consent constituted a violation of their civil rights and their constitutional right to bear children.

Over the course of the trial, attorneys Hernández and Nabarette tried to establish that the practice of the doctors at LACMC was to approach women during labor and "push" them into sterilization.[61] Moreover, the plaintiffs' attorneys claimed that the doctors acted in accordance with an attitude widespread within the hospital that overpopulation must be remedied through the sterilization of certain social groups who tended toward having large families. In her opening statement Hernández argued, "What we are trying to prove and to show is that the central issue in this case is that there was custom and practice that was not only believed by the individual doctors or the individual defendants, but that it was the overall philosophy of the hospital; that this overall philosophy as taught to the medical students was carried on by all the employee doctors, residents, et cetera, et cetera, at this county hospital. . . ."[62]

The testimony of Dr. Karen Benker most directly captures the issues that Hernández addressed in her statement.[63] While notions of racial abuse and discrimination underlie many aspects of the plaintiffs' case, ideological notions about Mexican-origin women's fertility were most openly addressed in Dr. Benker's testimony. The controversy surrounding that testimony is particularly telling; the defendant doctors' attorney, William Maskey, objected to almost every question or statement she made on the witness stand.[64]

After much dispute, the judge finally decided to allow Dr. Benker to testify. Ms. Hernández began her questioning bluntly: "Did you ever have a conversation with Dr. Quilligan regarding the birth rate of the Mexican and Negro people?"[65] In response, Dr. Benker recounted her memory of her first day of orientation on the obstetrics ward as a medical student in 1970, when she and a group of other medical students met Dr. Quilligan, the head of the ward, in the hallway. Dr. Benker testified that when one of her fellow students commented on the new facilities at the women's building, which were noticeably superior to the hospital's other wings, Dr. Quilligan replied that the department had recently received a federal grant "to show how low we can cut the birth rate of the Negro and Mexican populations in Los Angeles County."[66] When the students appeared surprised by the doctor's remarks, another attending physician referred to the poverty and overpopulation within these populations in an apparent attempt to justify Dr. Quilligan's statement.[67]

While on the witness stand, Dr. Benker recalled several other instances during hospital conferences and meetings when physicians discussed overpopulation and the fertility of Mexican women. In one such incident,

Dr. Quilligan claimed that poor minority women in Los Angeles County "were having too many babies," that this was placing a "strain on society," and that it was "socially desirable" that the women be sterilized.[68]

Over continued objections from the defendants' attorney, Dr. Benker began to testify to the many times she witnessed doctors approaching women during labor to request consent to sterilization. Judge Jesse Curtis, responding to Mr. Maskey's objections, halted this line of questioning, claiming, "This case has taken so long already." The judge stated that the doctors were entitled to invoke social motivations for actively encouraging sterilization as long as they had some medical rationale. In one of his many lengthy orations from the bench during Benker's direct examination, Judge Curtis stated: "Suppose he [a doctor] does favor sterilization in every chance he can get. So long as he does not override the will of one of his patients, I do not see that there is anything objectionable. He may believe that in theory one of the big problems is that some families are too big. He is entitled to that belief. He is just not entitled to overpower the will of his patients."[69]

Furthermore, Judge Curtis recognized the cultural and racially based nature of the discussion occurring in the court, but ultimately deemed it inconsequential. In his words,

> There is confusion in this area which arises from a clash of cultures. The plaintiffs are Mexican-Americans who have a culture the based somewhat foreign to ours [sic]. They just happened to be Mexican-Americans. There could be other people who, I think in this country, come from other ethnic backgrounds who have more or less the same culture, one which highly values the woman's ability to procreate a family, and particularly the size of the family is a matter of great concern, and also has almost a religious significance. . . .
>
> The other cultural aspect is one which exists in this country which has somewhat less regard, let us say, for large families. . . . In fact, there is a big segment of the people in this country, and not only in this country but in the world, who believe that one of the prime causes of our social and economic problems are big families where the parents are not able to socially or economically support them. The people who have that belief have gone out on a program to try to encourage or persuade people who have big families to cut down and to become involved in various birth control procedures. People in that category are just as entitled to their beliefs as the people who feel as the plaintiffs do here. . . .
>
> So, I do not think it is surprising that you might find a doctor who believes that people who are inclined to have big families shouldn't,

and particularly for good medical reasons, undertakes to persuade a person not to have a large family. And if that person agrees and is willing to be sterilized, then I cannot see anything wrong with the doctor having suggested it or having convinced the patient, so long as he does not use his powers, his ability, his circumstances to override what would be a reasonable decision on the part of the patient. What I want to know here is: To what extent the doctors had overridden the wishes of the patients, if they had. And if they have in some instances, what is their medical justification for doing it?[70]

The judge quite simply reduced the conflict to one about cultural difference. On the one side we have a culture concerned about overpopulation. On the other is a culture that "highly values a woman's ability to procreate a family." Judge Curtis essentially absolved the doctors of all responsibility for any coercive actions, arguing that it is within their legal limits to attempt to persuade patients to submit to sterilization. With her examination of Dr. Benker so severely curtailed, the plaintiffs' attorney was forced to call an end to Karen Benker's testimony. The defense attorneys, having successfully attacked the relevancy of Benker's testimony during her direct examination, did not cross-examine her.

"WE ALL KNOW MEXICANS LOVE THEIR CHILDREN": CULTURE AND DIFFERENCE IN THE COURTROOM

The plaintiffs' lawyers agreed with Judge Curtis's assertion that an existing clash of cultures was germane to the abuses that had occurred. Indeed, they argued that the extent of damages to their clients was severe because the plaintiffs were not only physically but also culturally sterilized. To substantiate this cultural perspective, the lawyers called Dr. Carlos Vélez on behalf of the plaintiffs. Vélez was asked "to render an opinion on the probable impact of these procedures and on the cultural and social context in which these woman operate."[71]

A professor of anthropology at the University of California, Los Angeles, Vélez had conducted interviews with the *Madrigal* plaintiffs to ascertain how each experienced her sterilization. Dr. Vélez, testifying about his findings, maintained that for the plaintiffs, procreation is "the core of social identity not only of the women, but interdependently it extends to Mexican males as well, in their ability to sire children."[72] Based on seven months of interviews and fieldwork, Vélez testified that most of the women came from a rural, agricultural cultural subgroup in Mexico, which contributed to their strong desire for many children.[73] All were born in small rural communities, came from large families (a mean number of 7.5 children), and adopted a "subcultural rural strategy," including large families and extensive kinship networks, which were crucial to their lives. Moreover, for women from this cultural subgroup, childbearing "was the means by which their adult status was reinforced and articulated within the domestic group. There these women received prestige and were recognized as valued adults because of the potential and ability to bear children . . . which was reinforced by the continued presence of small children in the household. To be *una mujer* was to have children."[74] As a result of their sterilization and the cessation of their childbearing capacity, many of the women suffered from depression, experienced hardship in their marriages, and lost standing in their community.[75]

Even before Dr. Vélez testified, the court discredited his expertise and its relevance.[76] Specifically, Judge Curtis questioned the necessity of an expert witness on Mexican culture, maintaining that any information such an expert could provide would probably be self-evident. As the judge put it,

> Frankly, I doubt very much whether this witness is going to be able to testify to anything that the Court cannot already take judicial notice of. I noticed when you read his name and what he expected to testify to—if you are paying any real money to get him here, I think it is a waste of money. *The Court knows, and everybody knows, the Mexican people have strong feelings about a big family, and how they have an intense love and affection for children and that sort of thing.* I do not consider his testimony very helpful. . . . I do not anticipate anything that he will tell me that I do not already know. (emphasis added)[77]

Once Dr. Vélez was on the stand, Judge Curtis asked if he would be able to "reduce" the cultural ramifications of the plaintiffs' inability to have more children to "dollars and cents." Here the judge further expressed his sense of the irrelevance of the issue of culture to a legal proceeding.[78]

Many of the plaintiffs' testimonies substantiated Dr. Vélez's claim that sterilization caused intense personal and cultural stigma. For example, one plaintiff was told by her mother, "The more children you have, and the sooner they come one after another, the healthier, happier and better person you'll be."[79] Now that her daughter had been sterilized, the woman's mother implied, she was less likely to be a healthy, happy, or good person. Judge Curtis's willingness to reinforce and trivialize cultural stereotypes ("all Mexicans love their families") points to the significance of racial ideologies in the courtroom. In his testimony, Vélez specifically cautioned that Mexicans are indeed a heterogeneous population and that the plaintiffs represent only one "subgroup" of the total population. The judge's swift and encompassing conclusions summarily dismissed Vélez's cautionary statements and significantly impacted the outcome of the case.

THE DECISION AND THE STERILIZATION REGULATIONS

On June 8, 1978, Judge Curtis handed down his decision in the case of *Madrigal v. Quilligan*.[80] The plaintiffs' lawyers had waived the right to a jury trial, believing that their chances of having a sympathetic judge were greater than finding a jury that would make a fair verdict. The judge thus bore sole responsibility for hearing the plaintiffs' case and making the decision.[81] After noting the difficulty of the case, "for it has involved social, emotional and cultural considerations of great complexity,"[82] Judge Curtis filed his decision in favor of the defendant doctors.

Reviewing every plaintiff's case individually, Judge Curtis concluded that the doctors were acting in "good faith" and with a "bona fide belief" that they were performing the sterilization operation with the knowledge and voluntary consent of each patient. The judge attributed the sterilization of the women to a "communication breakdown" between the women and their doctors rather than to any improper conduct. His decision continued: "There is no doubt that these women have suffered severe emotional and physical stress because of these operations. One can sympathize with their inability to communicate clearly, but one can hardly blame the doctors for relying on these indicia of consent which appeared to be unequivocal on their face and are in constant use in the Medical Center."[83]

Moreover, Judge Curtis expressed his belief that the plaintiffs carried as much responsibility for their involuntary sterilization as did the doctors who performed the surgery. Explaining why he was not convinced that the doctors had acted improperly, he stated,

> The rather subtle but underlying thrust of plaintiffs' complaint appears to be that they were all victims of a concerted plan by hospital attendants and doctors to push them, as members of a low socioeconomic group who tend toward large families, to consent to sterilization in order to accomplish some sinister, invidious social purpose. A careful search of the record fails to produce any evidence whatever to support this contention . . . whenever a sterilization procedure was suggested

or advised, it was done on the initiative of the individual employee. There was no hospital rule or instruction directed to these employees relative to the encouragement of patients to be sterilized and there was no evidence of concerted or conspiratorial action.[84]

During his closing remarks in court, Judge Curtis specifically referred to Dr. Vélez's testimony about the plaintiffs' desire to have large families and acknowledged that "the cultural background of these particular women has contributed to the problem in a subtle but significant way." Continuing on this point, he remarked: "The anthropological expert testified that he would not have known that these women possessed these traits had he not conducted tests and a study which required some 450 hours of time. . . . It is not surprising therefore that the staff of a busy metropolitan hospital which has neither the time nor the staff to make such esoteric studies would be unaware of these atypical cultural traits."[85] Throughout his opinion Judge Curtis made specific reference to the racial thread of the plaintiffs lawyers' argument that the sterilizations were inextricably linked to the women's racial-ethnic culture. However, he manipulated the plaintiffs' evidence to bolster his own argument that ultimate responsibility for their sterilization fell on the women. In essence, Judge Curtis co-opted the plaintiffs' argument that the women's ethnic status was the motivation for the doctors' abuse and used it instead as evidence that, in effect, the plaintiffs' ethnic status was the cause of the women's problems.[86]

Charles Nabarette, co-counsel for the *Madrigal* plaintiffs, said that the court's opinion, if upheld, would result in the coerced sterilizations of thousands of Spanish-speaking women and was a giant step backwards in civil rights litigation. Furthermore, Nabarette added, the judge's decision would be a direct setback for all women who received their health care from public agencies.[87] The Mexican American Legal Defense and Education Fund soon went to work launching an appeal, which I discuss in Chapter Six.

Despite the judgment against the *Madrigal* plaintiffs and the failure to win an appeal, the case actually contributed to the reproductive freedoms of all women.[88] As a direct result of Dr. Rosenfeld's report and public media attention to the alleged abuses, LACMC began to enforce compliance with federal sterilization regulations.[89] Early in the case U.S. District Judge James E. Avery Crary, who first received the case but was later removed, granted a preliminary injunction against the state and ordered California health officials to stop using federal funds for the sterilization of minors. At the same time he ordered them to rewrite existing Spanish-language guidelines at a sixth-grade level. Most important, because of the plaintiffs' legal complaint and organized community political action, revised regulations regarding sterilization were established at the state and federal levels. I analyze these efforts in Chapter Six.

POLICING "PREGNANT PILGRIMS": IDEOLOGICAL UNDERCURRENTS AND MATERIAL ABUSES

There is no question that the language in the hospital and in the courtroom clearly reflected how cultural differences—ideas and attitudes about the birthrates of Mexican and Mexican American women—were central to the abuses that occurred in both venues. This examination of *Madrigal v. Quilligan* demonstrates the correspondence of the forced sterilizations of Mexican-origin women by doctors at LACMC and public attitudes toward procreation among low-income women. However, the relationship between these ideologies and their manifestation in the severed fallopian tubes of Mexican-origin women necessitates further exploration. Primarily, I am interested in asking why physicians targeted the bodies of Mexican-origin women with their surgical scalpels.

Undeniably, certain structural factors existed that facilitated coercive sterilization. To be sure, the absence of any guidelines monitoring physician behavior, the existence of federal funding for sterilization procedures, and a poor, non-English-speaking clientele all facilitated an environment for the abuses. However, trial testimony reveals that hospital and courtroom personnel shared an "understanding" of women of Mexican origin as a high fertility group, a perspective that was fundamental to the abuses that took place.

While images of women of color as prolific "breeders" may have been common in racial discourse in the 1970s, why were such images attributed to Mexican-origin women at LACMC? Where did the doctors get the idea that Mexican women had such high fertility rates? One potentially important source for these beliefs was the social scientific research on Mexican-origin women that was being conducted at the time to understand their "unusually high rates" of fertility.

The results of many of these demographic studies were readily available to the medical community. For example, in 1971, Donald Bogue, a prominent demographer from the University of Chicago, delivered a paper at the annual meeting of the American College of Obstetrics and Gynecology in San Francisco in which he revealed that while "Anglos and Jews" were reproducing at replacement level, most of the national population growth was a result of the behavior of "high fertility remnants," including "the Spanish-speaking population."[90] Professor Bogue's presentation to a prominent gathering of obstetricians is important for two reasons. First, it demonstrates that doctors, and more specifically obstetricians, were being exposed to the results of demographic studies of Mexican-American women's fertility. As Dr. Bogue's statements illustrate, these studies played the dual role of identifying Mexican-origin women's fertility as an issue of public concern and contrasting their fertility patterns with the Anglo norm. Second, the fact that the statements were made at a professional gathering of obstetricians shows that, at the time of the coercive sterilization of Mexican-origin women, the medical establishment considered differences in fertility patterns between racial groups a matter of concern to the practice of obstetrics.

When doctors at LACMC talked about Mexican-origin women bearing many children, they were expressing their concern that if women's fertility were not controlled, their excessive children would place a burden on society. Karen Benker's report and recollections demonstrate the attitudes of USC-LACMC doctors:

> [Mexicanas] weren't really "American" and [they] had come from Mexico pregnant on the bus just so that they could have their baby born a U.S. Citizen so they can't be deported themselves. It was frequently expressed that the poor bred like rabbits and ate up money on welfare, that the women were promiscuous and just having babies because they couldn't control their sexual desires or were too stupid to use birth control. . . . The prevailing attitude was that one or two children were enough for any mother and that any mother who had four or more was an undisciplined and ignorant burden upon the country.[91]

Benker's synopsis of the attitudes of the doctors at LACMC shows how issues of citizenship, legitimacy, welfare dependency, hyper-fertility, overpopulation, and opportunistic Mexican women were all critical elements in their discourse of Mexican-origin women's reproduction. Doctors were not the only ones who believed that women of Mexican origin "bred like rabbits." In fact, their attitudes merged with, perpetuated, and gave legitimacy to a broader public discourse regarding childbearing practices.

The attitudes of LACMC physicians and others, together with the attitudes of many in the general public, show how private actors are the instruments of public policy. A confluence of concerns about overpopulation, illegal immigration, and dwindling social services generated a proliferation of discourse that targeted Mexican-origin women and their prolific childbearing practices as a social problem.

The uproar over undocumented immigrants illegally receiving welfare benefits was one sharp focus of public discourse about Mexican-origin women as illegitimate reproducers. In 1973, 8 to 9 percent of those receiving welfare were found to be "aliens," who reportedly received $100 million a year in welfare benefits and other social services.[92] Concerned that "there are far too many illegal welfare recipients among our citizens," people across the nation called for an end to a "problem . . . so big we don't know where to start."[93] Officials in Los Angeles County imagined this problem so menacing that they commissioned a special report on the impact of welfare payments to illegal aliens. They also initiated a project designed to "weed out" aliens on local welfare rolls. Not surprisingly, results from this study found the actual number of illegal immigrants on welfare was negligible.[94] Ironically, a contemporaneous report had shown that, in fact, state welfare agencies routinely discriminated against Spanish-speaking Californians.[95]

Californians also expressed concerns about the number of Mexican immigrant women who reportedly crossed the Mexican–United States border to have their children; a host of media exposés documenting the lives of these "pregnant pilgrims" flourished in the early to mid-1970s. One emblematic story about the impact of this "problem" on Los Angeles County hospitals depicts many Mexican women allegedly crossing the border illegally, often while in labor, so that their children could be born American citizens, at the U.S. taxpayer's expense. The exposé began:

> A woman in labor groans with pain, and a nurse tries to comfort her.
> "What do you think it will be," the nurse asks, "a boy or a girl?"
> The woman smiles, relaxing slightly. She knows what the baby will be.
> An American.[96]

By 1977, illegal immigrant births at Los Angeles County hospitals were reportedly growing in numbers as the decade progressed. And that was considered only part of the expense of health services provided to illegal immigrants, which "cost taxpayers" $51 million per year. According to one hospital administrator who had surveyed hospitals in other border counties, "every one of them has exactly the same problem," paying for the childbirth of hundreds of undeserving Mexican women.[97]

According to media reports, Mexican women were calculating about their childbearing in other duplicitous ways. While some paid to falsely register their babies as U.S.-born, others reportedly abandoned their newborn babies on the U.S. side of the border.[98] Widely published articles in major newspapers across the nation suggested that, in addition to their high levels of fertility, Mexican-origin women were becoming an increasingly threatening mass of problematic childbearers who required regulation.

This atmosphere of distrust and concern about Mexican-origin women prevailed within LACMC, specifically, and within the medical community, the social scientific community, the border states, and the nation as a whole. Reflecting this situation and in response to it, sterilization abuse in the country's hospitals was rampant. In the media, sensational reports on pregnant Mexican aliens fleeing to the United States were commonplace. Social scientists released alarming data suggesting increases in Mexican American population growth. As a consequence, a wave of negative sentiment toward women of Mexican origin was rising to a crest.

CHAPTER FOUR

"MORE THAN A HINT OF EXTRAORDINARY FERTILITY. . . ."

Social Science Perspectives on Mexican-Origin Women's Reproductive Behavior (1912–1980)

Before judging exaggeratedly high or low fertility . . . it is essential that "the validity of knowledge taken for granted" be always and continually exposed, examined, and brought into question.

CAROLE C. MARKS, "DEMOGRAPHY AND RACE"

In a 1973 article published in the academic journal *Social Biology*,[1] demographer Peter Uhlenberg remarked that "the strikingly high fertility of Mexican Americans relative to the dominant pattern in the United States has received almost no sociological or demographic analysis."[2] Noting that no other racial or ethnic group in the United States has maintained a fertility rate comparable to that of Mexican Americans (not even Native Americans, who were often charged with excessively high fertility rates), Uhlenberg queried social scientists' lack of attention to these distinctive population characteristics. In fact, fertility data for persons with Spanish surnames in five southwestern states were first compiled in 1950.[3] Moreover, as the "high fertility" of Mexican-origin women did not yet exist as a documented statistical certainty, substantive explanatory efforts remained inchoate in the demographic imagination. This was soon to change. Prior to 1970, social science journals hardly mentioned the fertility rates of Mexican-origin women. By 1980, the first large-scale data on the fertility of Mexican-origin women had been collected, and the seeds of a nascent demographic subfield were sown.[4]

This chapter outlines the origins of the social scientific and demographic research on the fertility of Mexican-origin women. It provides an assessment of the production of social scientific knowledge on this topic until 1980 and argues that demographic research during this decade not only established the social and intellectual significance of the fertility rates of Mexican-origin women, but also fundamentally contributed to the construction of Mexican-origin women as a quintessentially "hyper-fertile" population. To present a systematic analysis of the demographic literature on Mexican-origin women's fertility, I first review early publications and other social scientific inquiry into their reproductive behavior. By providing the initial observations, analyses, and questions upon which demographers constructed further research, I detail a long-standing social scientific interest in what came to be described as the "unusually high" fertility of women of Mexican origin. Moreover, I show how this characterization was informed by the racialized assumptions of assimilation and modernization.

EARLY RESEARCH: MODERNIZATION AND ASSIMILATION

During the early twentieth century, local governments in the southwestern United States initiated attempts to document the birthrates of Mexican-origin people because of concerns that these rates were relatively high. Although large-scale national data on Mexican-origin people had not been compiled at the time, a report prepared in 1930 by members of the Mexican Fact-finding Commission used State Bureau of Vital Statistics data on Mexican births to compare levels of Mexican-origin and Anglo-American fertility. Analysis of previously unsegregated data found that by 1930, Mexican-origin births equaled one-sixth of the total births in the state.[5] Data compiled by the Los Angeles County Health Department showed even more drastic statistics: Mexican-origin births rose in proportion from approximately one-twelfth of the total childbirths in Los Angeles County during 1918 to nearly one-fifth in 1927.[6] At the time, Mexican-origin people comprised only 8 percent of the population in Los Angeles, leading one scholar to surmise that "all indications are that in spite of a high death rate, the Mexican rate of natural increase is high because of the large excess of births."[7]

Preliminary social scientific research in the 1930s similarly identified the noticeably high birthrates of Mexican and Mexican-origin women.[8] The first study to focus solely on Mexican-origin women's lives paid significant attention to their reproductive behavior and introduced the enduring construct of Mexican women as hyper-fertile baby machines. Initially published in the journal *Sociology and Social Research* in 1931, sociologist Ruth Allen's ethnographic study of 294 Mexican female farm laborers in central Texas depicted the women she studied as passive, fatalistic, and unquestioning of their life-long service to men.[9] Moreover, Allen claimed that because the women were inept at housekeeping and producing household goods, childbearing became their primary contribution to the family's economic survival. She wrote,

> Since the Mexican woman does not produce services in the home, she must find another method of adding to the economic welfare of the family. Two courses are open. She may bring children into the world and rear them to an age at which they may aid in the production of a money crop, or she herself may go into the fields. It is a generally accepted principle, that a woman must either do field work herself or produce workers to take her place.[10]

As the first and only published sociological study at the time focusing on the lives of Mexican-origin women in the United States, Allen's thesis—that Mexican women bear children to prevent their own toil in the farming fields—received sustained attention. Reprinted more than twenty years later with the new title "Competitive Breeding," Allen's article was included in a book entitled *Race: Individual and Collective Behavior,* appearing within the section "Racial Survival." It was the only article in the book to focus on the Mexican-origin population. More than thirty years later, British population expert Jack Parsons attributed the coining of the term *competitive breeding* to Allen. In his estimation, the term was created to describe Mexican women "who competed with each other to produce large numbers of children to avoid any heavy work in the fields."[11] These early observations were echoed in other contemporaneous social scientific research.

Such remarks often referenced the large families in Mexican-origin communities and were accompanied by assertions that this unique family behavior was a significant marker of cultural and social difference. According to Ruth Tuck's 1946 study *Not With the Fist: Mexican Americans in a Southwest City,* "Throughout Latin America, family life receives a slightly different emphasis than it does in the United States; one is tempted to say, at the risk of raising some inter-cultural storms, that it receives a stronger emphasis. Certainly, the family unit is larger than the American one, which is likely to consist of the parents—in some cases only one—and a child or two."[12]

Other descriptive studies examining the childbearing and large family patterns of Mexican-origin women were published during the early to mid-twentieth century.[13] Many of these studies, which were based on field observations and ethnographic analysis, echoed Allen's depiction of

Mexican-origin women as mothers who capriciously bear children.[14] A book written by University of Southern California professor Emory Bogardus and published in 1934, *The Mexican in the United States,* provides a telling example. Although the author first asserts that Mexican-origin women possess a "maternal instinct," he later contradictorily suggests that they are reckless mothers who do not express sincere concern for their children. Additionally noting that Mexican males tend to desert their wives and children, Bogardus wrote, "The mother may take a somewhat fatalistic attitude. If she be religiously trained, she is likely to view her brood as gifts from God. Her fatalism is illustrated by her belief that one child more or one less does not matter. If a baby dies, it is God's will; there is one less mouth to feed; there will be 'another one along soon.' A high infant mortality rate is not viewed by the mother with alarm."[15] Rife with claims that Mexican-origin women are fatalistic, religiously guided, and callously uninterested in the welfare of their children, Bogardus's portrait clearly depicts these women as vestiges of a traditional, premodern society. Unlike modern individuals who presumably experience childbirth and death in a more rational way, Bogardus discusses the reproductive behavior of Mexican-origin women with distinct modernist condescension.

Scholars have previously argued that early sociological attention to Mexican American family size and gender roles was greatly influenced by the assimilation and modernization frameworks dominating social science thinking in race and ethnic theory during this period.[16] According to Maxine Baca Zinn:

The social science myth of the Mexican family . . . is rooted in two sociological frameworks: modernization and acculturation. Chicano family research has been guided by an ideal construct, postulating on the one hand, the "traditional" Mexican patriarchal type, and on the other, a "modern" egalitarian type. The concept of modernization has not been made explicit in Chicano family literature, but many of its underlying assumptions have guided thinking in this area, most notably the idea that universal evolutionary changes in family structure occur with urbanization and industrialization. . . . like other ethnic families, Chicano families were expected to modernize in the new setting by shedding their cultural traditions. . . . With increasing exposure to American culture, it was expected that Chicano families would take on modern values and that their family structure would move from traditional to modern.[17]

While Baca Zinn aptly outlines the empirical deficiencies that result from such conceptual assumptions, Miller (1978) describes the ideological ramifications more bluntly: "Chicanos must, in effect, think and act as Anglo Americans purportedly do if they are to live viably in the U.S. society."[18] Demonstrating the negative connotations implied in such an attitude, Baca Zinn noted that "the difference between Chicano families and the ideal modern family became, in effect, a culture lag."[19]

Because the transition to smaller family sizes was presumed to indicate social amalgamation, and Mexican-origin communities did not yet exhibit any inclination toward decreasing family sizes, at least one researcher explicitly labeled their reproductive behavior as a discrete social problem. William Madsen's (1964) book, *The Mexican American of South Texas*, clearly attributes the group's inferiority to their holding of different cultural values from Anglo-Americans. Madsen finds particular fault with Mexican American family life, commenting that:

> Today the Anglo value of individualism is in direct conflict with the Mexican value of family solidarity in the Magic Valley. The Anglos believe that equality in the home and self-advancement are necessary to maintain the American ideals of freedom, democracy, and progress. Mexican-Americans believe that putting family above self is necessary to fulfill the will of God. In the process of acculturation, the Anglo ideal of the democratic family is slowly breaking down the Latin family, which is the main stronghold of *La Raza*.[20]

In attributing the inferior position of the Mexican American population in the United States to the conflict between the values of Anglo individualism and Mexican familism, Madsen suggests that Mexican immigrants must alter their cultural values if they truly desire to become successful in American society.[21]

In sum, the foundational social scientific research on Mexican-origin women's reproductive behavior was primarily entrenched within the presupposition of cultural difference and inferiority. Mexican American family size was viewed through the dual lenses of modernization and assimilation. More than fifty years ago, scholars established that the birthrate of Mexican-origin women was abnormally high in comparison with national averages in the United States. Historical investigation of their reproductive behavior also confirmed that their high fertility rates were not only a contemporary phenomenon, but reflected a trend that had endured for over a century.[22]

Sociologists Bradshaw and Bean note that "given the evidently high reproductivity of the Mexican American population, it is surprising that there has been little effort at systematic examination of their fertility."[23] Having shown that the unique fertility rate of Mexican-origin women was not only deserving of, but *necessitated* social scientific analysis, researchers turned their energies toward examining what the possible contributors to this "unusual" fertility rate might be. However, while demographers developed more quantitatively based methodological techniques for the study of the reproductive behavior of Mexican-origin women, the social scientists' analyses of this phenomenon remained guided by the perspectives of modernization and assimilation.

A CULTURE LAG

Social scientists were very interested in the high fertility rate of Mexican-origin women, in part because of the exceptional data their so-called traditional reproductive behavior offered for the study of fertility transition. Some researchers realized that as a recently growing migrant group from a country with one of the highest birthrates in the world, the Mexican immigrant population offered a real-world laboratory for the study of the effects of modernization upon fertility. Presuming the acculturative influences of modernization, Mexican-origin women living in the United States presented an excellent opportunity to measure empirically the impact the transition from Mexico would have on their fertility behavior. The distinctive nature of the women's "exceedingly high" reproductive behavior notwithstanding, Mexican-origin women, as a "pre-modern people," offered a convenient experimental group by which to observe any changes in the fertility patterns of women moving between "pre-modern" and "modern" settings. This was an opportunity to study "fertility transition" firsthand.

In the 1973 article by demographer Peter Uhlenberg, a scholar of the relationship between population and modernization, the author explains how Mexicans residing in the United States offered an ideal sample population for studying the impact of modernity on fertility transition:

The Mexican-American population provides an exceptionally valuable case for observing how various factors influence family size. The foreign-born come from a developing country characterized by a very high birth rate (crude birth rate above 40). They enter a modern, urban, industrial nation with moderately low levels of fertility (crude birth rate under 20). How they are (sic) their descendants adjust their fertility to this new environment reveals much about the social determinants of reproduction.[24]

By directly comparing the birthrates of Mexican-origin and Anglo-American women, Uhlenberg demonstrated "how much Mexican American fertility varies from what is considered ideal in the United States."[25] With almost every facet of the comparison, Mexican-origin women proved to be significantly "deviant" from the purported "American ideal." For example, Uhlenberg found that while the rates of the foreign-born were higher than the native-born during 1910, they were not exceptionally so. By 1960, however, Mexican American women "occupied a unique position," with their rates more than doubling the average number of children per ever-married woman.[26]

Uhlenberg further noted that "the size of completed families for Mexican-born women was similar to that of native-born women in the United States in 1910, which suggests that this group is lagging fifty years behind the dominant society in fertility behavior."[27] Further demonstrating that "Mexican-born women lag even further behind other white women,"[28] Uhlenberg continued,

Women who completed their childbearing by 1910, however, were bearing their children under conditions of much higher infant mortality than now exist. . . . the reproductive level achieved by Mexican immigrants in 1960 was characteristic of all white women in the United States in 1860. Thus, the average family size of first generation Mexican Americans is equal to that of other American families during the early stages of the industrial revolution.[29]

Relying entirely on rates of fertility as a measure of social progress (or modernization), Uhlenberg compared Anglo and Mexican-origin women's reproductive behavior and determined that the latter group was stuck in an "earlier phase" of demographic transition. Based on this evolutionary measure, Mexican American women exhibited a fertility pattern characteristic of a premodern society resistant to forces of change or "modernization." Implicitly assuming this pattern of reproductive behavior as an anomaly to the predictions of demographic transition theory, Uhlenberg remarked that "clearly, the fertility of Mexicans—whether in developing and urbanizing Mexico, or in developed and urbanized North America—does not respond to influences that we customarily regard as anti-natalist."[30] Following

Uhlenberg's lead, subsequent demographic study of the fertility of Mexican-origin women was driven by the primary impetus to determine the roots of and reasons for these deviant reproductive patterns.[31]

THE AUSTIN FERTILITY SURVEY: EXPLAINING THE
HYPER-FERTILITY OF MEXICAN-ORIGIN WOMEN

In 1969 Benjamin Bradshaw and Frank Bean, who eventually became leading experts in this field, were scholars at the Population Research Center in the Department of Sociology at the University of Texas at Austin. Along with Harley Browning,[32] they were the principal investigators of the Austin Fertility Survey (AFS), the first study to deliberately and systematically investigate the factors influencing Mexican American fertility rates. Conducted during the summer and fall of 1969, the AFS generated a sample of 348 Mexican American couples from Austin. The study was partially funded by the National Institutes of Child Health and Human Development of the U.S. Public Health Service and comprised the first publicly published findings based on primary data on the fertility behavior of Mexican-origin women. Moreover, the study was contracted as a report for the Commission on Population Growth and the American Future—the first and only governmental body to consider the need for a national population policy. The purpose of the AFS was to investigate "the social and cultural factors that support high fertility among Mexican-Americans." The study provided a significant sample of Mexican American couples whose fertility behavior could be submitted to reliable quantitative analysis. Almost all of the research conducted on Mexican American fertility during this decade ultimately relied upon the data gathered in the Austin Fertility Survey.

In this, the first-ever systematic demographic examination of the fertility patterns of Mexican Americans, the authors defined the significant social and political implications of the growing population as a justification for their study:

> Because of a high birth rate and continuous immigration, the Mexican-American population has grown rapidly during the last three decades. Mexican-Americans have also begun to mount campaigns for improved civil rights and economic opportunities. Along with other factors, both the increase in size of this population and the rise in political activity among its members have contributed to the

relatively recent recognition of the fact that Mexican-Americans comprise a large and important ethnic group in this country.[33]

By highlighting the data that showed that Mexican-origin women between the ages of thirty-four and forty-four bore approximately 47 percent more children than all other similarly aged women in the United States, the authors stressed how this behavior marked Mexican-origin women as "different."

Bradshaw and Bean emphasized, for example, that the fertility of Mexican American women did not comply with the prevailing socioeconomic explanations for racial differences in fertility rates.

> If changes in factors such as societal economic conditions bear upon secular trends in fertility, the Mexican American population may be less sensitive to such disturbances than the Anglo American population. Whether the relative insusceptibility of Mexican American fertility to such factors owes to discrimination . . . or to cultural orientations in the populations supportive of having large families is a pertinent question for future research.[34]

Contrary to established social scientific knowledge, however, the AFS findings suggested that the cultural context within which Mexican American women bore children was the most salient variable in understanding their fertility. When the authors tested for other possible explanatory variables—such as education, income, and contraceptive use—these variables did not garner significant results. Most surprisingly, no relationship was found between religion and fertility. Although Catholicism was believed to be a primary factor influencing the group's non-use of contraception, the authors admitted that "religious preference and religiosity may be of much less importance than might have been thought."[35]

Although social scientists speculated that socioeconomic status and religious affiliation were the most predictive variables of Mexican-origin women's fertility, AFS's statistical analysis disproved these long-held beliefs. Despite the employment of larger samples and statistical research methods, the results of these studies were similar to those of previous ethnographically based observations: namely, the high fertility rate of Mexican-origin women was a function of some indeterminate yet resilient aspect of Mexican culture. This indeterminate factor was so significant that it was ultimately attributed to racial/ethnic differences, which further rendered the study of Mexican-origin women's fertility sociologically significant.

DIFFERENTIAL FERTILITY AND THE MINORITY-STATUS FERTILITY HYPOTHESIS

Mid-century social scientists were convinced that the study of the reproductive behavior of Mexican-origin women was intellectually important because of the group's "exceptionally" high fertility rate and because of Mexican American population growth in the United States. This sort of study could illuminate the transition process from a "pre-modern" to "modern" culture. The fact that the fertility rate did not show the predicated decline after Mexican women moved to the United States also merited further investigation. Beyond these justifications, however, I believe there is another, more specifically contextual explanation for the burgeoning social scientific interest in Mexican-origin women's fertility during the 1970s. The close examination of this population's fertility rates reflected a general concern over the birthrates of all racial and ethnic groups in the nation and emerged as an important part of demographers' efforts to ascertain systematically the fertility differentials of varying social groups, namely poor minorities.[36] Within this broader area of inquiry, the study of Mexican-origin women's fertility transcended academic curiosity and became politically meaningful. Indeed, as investigation of differential fertility expanded beyond its initial focus on the fertility of African American and religious minorities, Mexican-origin women emerged as an exceptionally critical population to study to establish the impact between race and ethnicity and fertility behavior.

The study of the fertility of Mexican-origin women grew in part as demographers realized the importance of the contributions of racial and ethnic groups to national fertility rates. By all accounts, the nation's rates of growth as a whole had subsided in "virtually every social and economic subgroup" beginning in 1957.[37] However, with increased attention to the nation's changing racial composition, demographers soon realized that trends in the aggregate fertility rate could not be accurately assessed without first investigating the distinct contributions made by the different subgroups of the U.S. population.[38] Hence, the guiding question for demographers during the 1970s was aptly articulated by Robert Roberts and Sul Eun Lee: "What is the effect of minority group status on fertility in contemporary America?"[39]

Previous demographic inquiry, however, found no significant relationship between race/ethnicity and fertility. Solely focused on the African

American population, this earlier research argued that fertility differentials were better explained as a function of social class.[40] The social characteristics hypothesis, which had dominated research on the fertility of racial and ethnic groups in the United States until this time, "contends that fertility, as a major behavioral expression of subgroup norms and values, will vary completely with the degree to which racial-ethnic groups have become socio-economically assimilated into the majority population."[41]

The social characteristics hypothesis was in fact a reiteration of demographic transition theory, the predominant paradigm of fertility change at the time. Developed in the mid-1940s, demographic transition theory "was considered to be the culminating theoretical revelation that clarified the nature of modern population dynamics."[42] Demographic transition theory attributes fertility change to the structural transformation of socioeconomic conditions and proposes that the fertility rates of premodern, or "traditional," countries (such as Asian, Latin American, African, and many southern European countries before the Industrial Revolution) remained high as a necessary ameliorative to the high death rates characteristic of these societies. Simply stated, the theory posits that high birthrates manifest themselves in certain populations to preserve community survival. Demographic transition theory further reasons that, as a result of these conditions, the social institutions in these premodern societies (religious, educational, legal, and so on) must encourage the propagation of large families.[43]

Using the declining birthrate of European countries after industrialization as an ideal prototype, early proponents of demographic transition theory (most notably, Frank Notestein and Kingsley Davis) argued that the fertility rates of modernizing countries remained high during the period of declining mortality, but continued to be high as the modernizing forces (namely, those resulting from industrialization) slowly made their impact.[44] As modernization approached completion, the theory speculated, fertility rates would meet at an even keel with death rates, and equilibrium would eventually be realized. Proponents of demographic transition thus posited that modernization would ultimately change the normative structures of the population, and that:

> Fertility would only fall as a result of the cumulative reinforcing spectrum of effects consequent on full-scale industrialization and modernization: enhanced survival; a growing culture of individualism; rising consumer aspirations; emergence of huge and socially mobile urban populations; loss of various functions of the family to the factory and school; and decline of fatalistic in favor of co-native habits of thought.[45]

The assertions of demographic transition theory are primarily based on the tenets of classic modernization theory that were prevalent in U.S. sociology during the 1950s and 1960s.[46] Modernization theorists (for example, Rostow)—similarly positing a trans-historical, unidirectional, evolutionary model of social development—argued that all societies follow a progressive path of social, political, and economic development from traditional (third world) to modern (Western).[47] Most demographers resolutely adhered to a belief in the interdependence between modernization and population during this period. For example, sociologist Calvin Goldscheider declared that "no study of the determinants and consequences of population processes can proceed very far without analyzing systematically and in detail the links to modernization; no investigation of modernization can be complete without analyzing demographic variables."[48]

Despite its continued prevalence in the field today, a few scholars provide a cogent critique of demographic transition theory. Critics have pointed to the Eurocentric assumptions undergirding the theory. One trenchant critic of the theory, intellectual historian Simon Sretzer, delineates the ideological underpinnings of the argument. According to Sretzer,

> [T]ransition theory in its classic form thereby entailed an unabashedly evolutionary and recapitulationist general theory of the process whereby any country successfully moved from a pre- to a post-industrial state of demographic equilibrium. Although there was nothing historically inevitable in the process, in order to industrialize and modernize a country must pass through the stages of demographic transition, with the appearance of fertility-controlling behavior marking the advent of a final stage, and the general spread of such behavior confirming successful sociocultural adjustment to the conditions of a modernized, economically developed nation.[49]

Anthropologist Susan Greenhaulgh (1996) similarly condemned the ethnocentric focus upon which demographic transition theory is built. In her estimation the presuppositions "that fertility transition is caused by and in turn causes further Westernization and that reproductive Westernization is good for everyone are Eurocentric. Embedded in this second set of assumptions is the problematic notion that Europe and its offshoots are superior to the rest of the world and the source of all significant change."[50]

On the other hand, proponents of the social characteristics perspective maintained that the birthrates of minority groups would more closely approximate that of the U.S. majority (that is, the white population) as their members acculturated and obtained higher class standing. According to the theory, it was not the actual attributes of race or ethnic membership per se, "but rather the social, demographic, and economic characteristics which minority group membership connotes that determine fertility levels, trends and differentials."[51] Accordingly, ending social inequality would result in diminished fertility differentials.[52] Rooted in modernist presumptions that the adoption of European values would indubitably produce modification of fertility behavior (a marker of social progress), the social characteristics paradigm of differential fertility was a quantitatively based reincarnation of the assimilation model of fertility typical of social science research on reproductive behavior published by researchers like Woofter, Bogardus, Allen, and Tuck earlier in the century.

Questioning this line of thinking, in 1969 two researchers at the University of California, Berkeley, Calvin Goldscheider and Peter Uhlenberg, elaborated their classic critique of the social characteristics hypothesis:

> The implicit assumption guiding most research on minority group fertility is that, in the process of minority groups acculturation and assimilation, fertility behavior and attitudes of minority and majority populations will converge. The underlying argument appears to be that fertility changes are features of social cultural change which, for minority groups, represent one aspect of behavioral and cultural assimilation. . . . Indeed, reproductive behavior and fertility norms have been employed as indicators of acculturation. . . .[53]

Positing that such a deduction erroneously underestimated the independent role that race played in the determination of minority group fertility rates, the authors propose an alternative analytical perspective. In their view, the more important demographic question was to determine if the hypothesis was supported empirically: that is, whether the fertility of minority and majority populations were similar when social, demographic, and economic characteristics were held constant.[54]

Skeptical of the predominant assimilationist assumptions undergirding previous research conducted in the social characteristics vein, Goldscheider and Uhlenberg set out to test the social characteristics or assimilationist hypothesis. After reviewing an assortment of previous research and descriptive data on the reproductive behavior of Jews, Japanese Americans, Catholics, and blacks in the United States, the two researchers did not find sufficient evidence supporting the social characteristics argument. Rather, based upon their findings, they posed an alternative explanation for fertility differentials, known as the minority group-status hypothesis. By more explicitly factoring in the cultural and social aspects of minority group membership, this theory affirmed that "under given social and economic changes and concomitant acculturation, the insecurities and marginalities associated with minority group status exert an independent effect on fertility."[55]

Although some scholars questioned Goldscheider and Uhlenberg's methodological design, the minority group-status hypothesis gained support within the discipline as debate and studies over how to build upon such findings ensued.[56] Robert E. Roberts and Sul Eun Lee noted the lack of an explicit sociological definition of minority group status, which, they argued, resulted in an insufficient measurement of the category. They conducted their own quantitative analysis of fertility data to address these shortcomings, but the results nevertheless supported Goldscheider and Uhlenberg's conclusion that "ethnicity has effects on fertility independent of other dimensions."[57]

Additionally, Roberts and Lee found that how the variable *minority group status* is measured produced the greatest variance in fertility rates. By testing three different classifications of minority group status—white/nonwhite, numerical majority/minority, and black/other/Spanish—the researchers found that the latter category produced significantly greater predictive ability than did strictly racial or numerically based definitions of minority group status: "in fact, there is a threefold increase or better in predictive ability in the latter situation. . . ."[58] Their analysis showed that a much more significant test of the hypotheses of the racial/ethnic effect on fertility was obtained by considering the fertility of Spanish-language groups separately. Moreover, Roberts and Lee found significant results regarding Mexican-origin women and their differential fertility, not only in relation to white women, but to women of other minority groups as well. For example, noting the "strikingly" high fertility of Spanish-surname women, they found that the cumulative fertility of Spanish-surname women ages forty to forty-nine in 1960 was consistently higher than that of black and other white women at every level of comparison. These results provided the first recognition by demographers that groups other than African Americans may demonstrate reproductive patterns necessitating demographic analysis. Roberts and Lee emphasized in their research findings,

> The failure to recognize this minority group in the white-nonwhite dichotomy tends to lead to the conclusion of a nonexistent, or minimal, effect of ethnicity on fertility. However, transferring Spanish-surname women from the "white" category to the "minority" category

leads to the alternative conclusion that there is an independent effect of ethnicity on fertility. Separate recognition of the Spanish-surname group explains more variance than the two other classifications of ethnicity.[59]

Thus, the analyses of Goldscheider and Uhlenberg, Roberts and Lee, and others highlighted the fact that the cultural components of race and ethnicity had an impact on fertility behavior. The inclusion of Mexican-origin women as an independent group established race/ethnicity, or culture, as a significant variable in fertility differentials.

Some demographers, however, argued that despite the integration of race and culture in the study of influences on fertility, the minority-status hypothesis did not significantly differ in perspective from the social characteristics hypothesis. Jiobu and Marshall (1977), for example, posited that both the social characteristics hypothesis and the minority group-status hypothesis are entrenched in assimilationist assumptions that prevent a full understanding of racial and ethnic differences in fertility:

This reasoning further leads us to question the "melting pot" idea implicit in the assimilationist *and* the minority status hypotheses. The knowledge that composition cannot fully explain differential fertility coupled perhaps with implicit acceptance of the melting pot notion, would naturally suggest that the fertility differentials must be caused by some type of "aberration" or "pathology" (in this case, tensions and insecurities). In contrast . . . (t)he cultural differences may change over time to facilitate socio-economic mobility without necessarily eradicating key cultural traditions and psychological traits which define a distinct ethnic identity. . . . We recognize that our argument is still a version of the minority status hypothesis. But stating the argument in this way implies very different orientation to the question. . . . we suggest family size differentials should be regarded as resulting from the interplay between structural and cultural assimilation on the one hand, and the history and traditions of particular groups on the other.[60]

Following the research of Roberts and Lee (1974) and the corresponding findings of Bradshaw and Bean (1972), other, subsequent scholars paid more attention to the unique fertility pattern of Mexican-origin women. For example, in his research establishing the important distinction between an "ethnic" effect and a "minority status" effect, Douglas Gurak singled out the fertility behavior of Mexican Americans as a particularly unique exemplar of this ethnic and cultural effect. Gurak noted that:

> Mexican fertility is high at all status levels. . . . it may be due to conformity to strong internal pressures for higher fertility. . . . This pattern is unlikely to be due to minority status itself, since the fertility levels are lower than for Mexico itself. That is, for Mexicans there appears to exist an ethnically rooted tendency towards high fertility that does not appear, for the most part, to result from the common experiences of belonging to a minority. At least it is not necessary to invoke the minority status thesis in order to make sense of findings for this group.[61]

In the end, fertility patterns of Mexican-origin women disproved both the minority-status hypothesis and the social characteristics hypothesis. Indeed, the data consistently showed that the fertility rates of Mexican-origin women were resilient to the forces of modernization, urbanization, and social economic status. Despite social scientific efforts to understand the "abnormal pattern" of Mexican-origin reproduction for over half a decade, any palpable understanding of its specific character, beyond statistically establishing its existence as a marker of racial/ethnic deviance, remained elusive.

CONCLUSION

In this chapter, I have argued that initial demographic research on Mexican-origin women determined that their fertility rate was abnormally high and significantly higher than the North American ideal. Drawing from the models of assimilation described by prior ethnographic studies, demographic research scientifically established that the fertility rates of Mexican-origin women were an indicator of the social integration or acculturation of Mexican immigrants. Mexican-origin women's fertility behavior proved resistant to the forces of modernization. According to a range of social scientists, the group's differential fertility rates were crucial to establishing the impact of race and culture on fertility. Moreover, the terms of demographic research and discourse regarding Mexican-origin women's fertility rates were indubitably tied to discussions of racial and ethnic difference.

At the same time that the "high" rates of fertility of Mexican-origin women became statistically confirmed, these rates did not submit to traditional explanatory models of fertility behavior, and the reproductive patterns of these women became a distinct category of analysis and a focus of further academic consideration. Defying the predictions of modernization-based models of fertility patterns, the reproductive behaviors became even more of an object of academic scrutiny. Emerging during a moment in the nation's history when demographic changes became a pressing political question (with the recognition of a new growing minority in the racial terrain), and race-based claims for full citizenship status were more vibrant than ever, the social scientific work on Mexican-origin women's fertility was shaped by assimilationist assumptions. As a project reliant on preconceptions of normative reproductive behavior, demographic research further reinscribed the deviance of the Mexican-origin population and promoted further scrutiny of their reproductive behavior by scholars and public policymakers.

More recent scholarship has not developed much beyond these traditional frameworks, although very recent studies are beginning to consider a number of different factors, including the mother's age at first birth. Several scholars have also recently pointed to the need to radically transform the way that fertility is studied. In their review of this "first generation" of research about racial and ethnic fertility differentials, Renata Forste and Marta Tienda comment that by attributing "residual racial effects" to abstract categories like "culture" provides little explanatory value. In fact, such tendencies have been "a major roadblock to creative theorizing about the forces that generate fertility differentials along racial and ethnic lines."[62] Antonio McDaniel has similarly called for a "fresh view of fertility patterns."[63] These studies are much needed if we are to develop an understanding of women's reproductive experiences that does not replicate racialized interpretations of their lives.

This is particularly so because, despite its fluctuations in academic discourse, assimilation remains a dominant expectation of racial and ethnic populations in the United States and is commonly referenced to explain changes in immigrant fertility.[64] For example, a 2003 survey conducted by the Center for the Study of Latino Health and Culture at the University of California, Los Angeles, reported that for the first time since the late 1850s a majority of the newborns in the county were Hispanic.[65] However, a more recent, and unexpected, lowering of fertility rates in Los Angeles was interpreted by writers as a sign that the group is assimilating. In October 2004, population forecasts reported that Latina fertility rates in Los Angeles County and in California generally had "plunged."[66] A *New York Times* article published a couple of months later similarly reported that Latinas are "choosing to have smaller families."[67] William Frey, a demographer with the Brookings Institution who is quoted in the article, interprets this as an indicator that Latinos "are like everybody else."[68] If the headlines of the nation's newspapers are any indication of how demographic trends are translated by the general public, fertility rates of the Mexican-origin population will continue to be closely monitored and analyzed.

CHAPTER FIVE

CONTROLLING BORDERS
AND BABIES

John Tanton, ZPG, and Racial Anxiety over Mexican-Origin Women's Fertility

Across the southern border of the United States are 67 million Mexicans. They are poor and Americans are rich. They speak Spanish and we speak English. They are brown and we are white. They want it and we've got it: jobs, prosperity, the Ladies Home Journal-Playboy *lifestyle. As a result we are being invaded by a horde of illegal immigrants from Mexico. . . . The furor has attracted the attention of bigots and bureaucrats as well as concerned citizens who ask: If we are limiting our family sizes so that our children can inherit a better nation, why should we throw open our doors to over-reproducers?*

PAUL EHRLICH ET AL., *THE GOLDEN DOOR: INTERNATIONAL MIGRATION, MEXICO, AND THE UNITED STATES*

So begins the preface to Paul Ehrlich's 1979 book *The Golden Door*, written with his wife, Anne, and Loy Bilderback. Published eleven years after Paul Ehrlich's first treatise, *The Population Bomb* (1968), the new book identified a different problem plaguing the nation—the arrival of super-fertile Mexican immigrants.

In Chapter Two I demonstrated that discussions about population and immigration developed as overlapping discourses throughout the 1970s, particularly in California. Here I argue that as concern about the so-called population problem abated after demographers began issuing reports of a declining U.S. birthrate (which many population control activists attributed to their efforts to change American attitudes about fertility and family size), population control experts identified a new adversary: the Mexican immigrant. Experts described Mexican immigrants as invariably bringing other family members to the United States and engaging in excessive reproduction, thereby depleting the nation's resources.[1] Through publicizing their concerns in the media, advocates such as Erlich invited the public to imagine irrepressible, job-snatching Mexican immigrants whose arrival was thwarting efforts to stabilize the nation's population.

The magnitude of this issue is conveyed throughout *The Golden Door*. The authors documented growing public concern about the contribution of immigration to the nation's population growth, a phenomenon they described as stemming not only from the rising numbers of immigrants crossing the border, but also from their high fertility. *The Golden Door* insisted that increasing rates of immigration spoiled successful efforts to slow population growth through a decreased national birthrate, and encouraged population control activists to deter immigration with even greater fervor.

The public response to *The Golden Door* was so intense in part because it was received by a reading public that the mainstream media had been conditioning for years. For example, a cover headline of *U.S. News and World Report* warned: "Time Bomb in Mexico: Why There'll Be No End to the Invasion of Illegals." The article described the threat of Mexico's high birthrate and the country's lack of jobs. Government officials also contributed generously to public education. A 1974 report of the commissioner of immigration and naturalization stressed the threat of excessive populations invading from the south:

> Latin American nations, including Mexico, Colombia, Guatemala, and the Dominican Republic, which are the principal sources of illegal immigration into the United States, have some of the highest population growth rates in the world. Population in these nations is increasing about 3.5 percent per year, compared to 0.5 percent in the United States, and labor forces in these nations are rapidly outpacing the creation of new jobs.[2]

Recent scholarship has argued that it was primarily during the 1980s and 1990s that "the greening of hate" transpired.[3] However, as this chapter will show, the lobbies concerned about links between population growth, immigration, and nativism were seeded in the 1970s. I specifically focus on how a racializing discourse about illegal Mexican immigrants and their fertility rates took shape during the 1970s in one of the oldest, largest, and most aggressive population control lobbies in the nation—Zero Population Growth, Inc. (ZPG). Many segments of the population control lobby, such as the Sierra Club, considered involvement in halting immigration but were wary of advocating federal legislation for fear of the consequences of its "racial overtones." ZPG believed that immigration presented an impending national disaster necessitating immediate and bold policy action, regardless of its racially charged ideas. The group described this new-found problem as likely to wreak catastrophic social havoc and pressed for an exclusionary national population policy. Largely under the leadership of John Tanton, who became president of the organization in 1975, the board of ZPG expressed a growing conviction that immigration control was a key component of population policy. Although it was only one segment of the population control lobby, ZPG's influence and eventual forays into controlling immigration must be carefully analyzed as a precursor to contemporary nativist efforts.

DR. NO MEETS THE "MODERN-DAY WETBACK": THE ACTIVISM OF JOHN TANTON

Dr. John Tanton, the infamous author of the much-publicized "Witan memo," which decried the catastrophic consequences of continued Latino population growth, is a figure of much interest to scholars of contemporary nativism in the United States. A tireless citizen-activist, Tanton was a leader in several of the nation's most successful population-related lobbying organizations. Scholars have probed the overlapping interests of immigration and English-only reform (heralded by two of Tanton's later groups, the Federation of American Immigration Reform [FAIR] and the U.S. English movement in the early 1990s), but less attention has been paid to the origins of Tanton's population control activism.[4] Well-known for his efforts in immigration reform and the English-only movement in the 1980s and contemporarily (as the founder of FAIR and U.S. English), Tanton's civic activity predates his concern with immigration control.

Long before his days of English-only advocacy, Tanton was centrally involved in several interlocking organizations, including Planned Parenthood, ZPG, and the Sierra Club, promoting what he defined as the overlapping agendas of immigration, population control, and environmentalism. Tanton used each of these platforms to mount his campaign against what he labeled the "modern-day wetback."[5]

Born in Detroit, Michigan, and a resident of the state his entire life, Tanton began his journey into public activism while finishing his medical residency at the University of Michigan. After receiving his degree in 1969, he practiced ophthalmology in a clinic in Petoskey, a resort community in the northern part of the state. Always considering himself a "congenital conservationist,"[6] Tanton formalized his desire "to exist in easy partnership" with the land by joining the Michigan Natural Areas Council and the Nature Conservancy, which preserves land and wetlands around the country.[7]

During an internship at a Denver birth control clinic in 1960–1961 (the first such clinic in any publicly supported hospital in the nation), Tanton became convinced that the growing population was a significant challenge for both conservation and preservation of natural resources. According to Tanton, it seemed logical that "constantly increasing numbers of people would build pressure and create more problems."[8] Additionally, in witnessing the "problems of the poor" during his residency in Denver, Tanton realized that "one way I could express an interest in the population problem was by trying to help people not have kids that they didn't want to have."[9] In the late 1960s, Tanton and his wife, upon returning to Petoskey, acted on this conviction and founded the Northern Michigan Planned Parenthood Federation. With Tanton as chairman, he and his wife worked together to ensure that family planning practices were made available to the community, and they actively promoted their belief in small families.

Tanton held strong views about the necessity of family planning, especially for certain women. He felt that some women should bear children, while others should not. For example, Tanton considered the then-popular family planning slogan "every child a wanted child" inadequate because sometimes children were wanted for the wrong reasons. As a Sierra Club representative addressing the Commission on Population Growth and the American Future (CPGAF), Tanton insisted on more selective criteria for considering a child "wanted." He claimed that "there are many bad and even sociopathic reasons for having many children. In many instances being 'wanted' is simply not enough." Tanton pointed to examples such as a mother with hemophilia who continued to "want children" and thus passed the disease to her sons ("the mother just loves the children, even though they do bleed a lot"), a troubled married couple who bear a child to heal their marriage, and a teenage girl who gets pregnant so that her boyfriend will marry her. Tanton argued that "pathological reasons" for bearing children deserve policy attention, adding, "We need to learn the dimensions of this problem . . . especially if it turns out that the prevention of unwanted births and changes in immigration policy are insufficient to produce a stationary population. If it proves to be necessary to also reduce the number of 'wanted' children, then those children wanted for pathological reasons should receive first attention."[10]

While traveling across the nation to publicize his views, Tanton maintained his involvement in environmentalism. A member of several statewide ecological organizations, Tanton's leadership in the conservation movement led to his appointment to the Michigan Wilderness and Natural Areas Council. He then founded a local Sierra Club chapter and sat on the regional planning committee. Soon thereafter he was appointed to the club's national population committee and was quickly promoted to chairman, serving in this capacity from 1971 to 1975.

When Paul Ehrlich's *The Population Bomb* was published in May 1968 and distributed by the Sierra Club, Tanton was "very much taken by the book," rereading it several times. He was so convinced by its message of impending world chaos through high birthrate that he handed out copies at every opportunity and encouraged Sierra Club leaders to sponsor a conference on population growth that would call for a national population policy.[11] When ZPG was formed that December to promote Ehrlich's prescriptions for population control, Tanton became one of the group's first and most active members.[12]

Soon after, ZPG's national board of directors nominated and elected Tanton to the board. Quickly rising to leadership roles in both of these closely tied organizations, Tanton launched his transition from statewide to national involvement in population issues.[13] He quickly earned a reputation as a prolific speaker throughout Michigan, and he often traveled across the state and the nation, using the speaker's podium to promote his views on family size and family planning.

"STOP AT TWO": THE CALL FOR SMALLER FAMILIES

The primary agenda of ZPG and other population control organizations during the early years of their mission was simple: families should limit their size to two children in order to achieve replacement-level population stability.[14] A father of two himself, Tanton aggressively advocated smaller families. For example, within the Northern Michigan Planned Parenthood Federation, he mounted a campaign for community members to sign a "Pledge of Social Responsibility," by which they promised to have no more than two children.[15] In 1969, working with two community obstetricians who were also concerned about the population problem, Tanton organized a program in the maternity wards of local hospitals in which officials discussed the "social implications of family size with new mothers, in hopes of revising their expectations downward."[16]

Tanton also stressed that eugenic implications of reproduction were equally important. For example, he embraced the idea of family size limits to "improve the genetic character of children within a specific family."[17]

Insisting on the positive correlation between family size and intelligence, Tanton argued that by diligently planning the timing and spacing of births, and the size of families, the "end result" would be more "desirable," eliminating the possibility of children with unwanted characteristics.[18] Foreseeing that others might interpret his mandates as racist, Tanton pointed out that "far from being racist or genocidal," passive eugenics "seeks to improve the potential of minority groups, which will do more for their prospects than any increase in numbers which might be foregone through larger family size and reproduction outside the years of reproductive efficiency."[19]

By 1973, data showed that the national birthrate had indeed dropped.[20] Many population control activists interpreted such statistics as proof that organizational efforts to alter normative American attitudes had been successful, although many were wary about whether the drop would persist. However, just as the news of lowered national fertility rates settled in, the phenomenon of the quickly rising numbers of illegal immigrants "flooding into the country" gained attention.

As we have seen, INS commissioner Leonard Chapman was one of the most ardent critics of this alleged development. He noted the shift in Mexican immigration from single men to complete families, and complained, "The problem [of immigration] is serious. But we are seeing only the beginning of a flood—a human tide that (due to the birthrate in underdeveloped nations) is going to engulf our country, unless something is done to stop, or at least slow it. Without improved controls against illegal immigration, that is absolutely inevitable."[21]

Perhaps exploiting recent concern about overpopulation, Chapman emphasized the links between immigration and excess population in the context of limited resources. He commented in an article in *U.S. News and World Report*,

> We've got a serious national problem with the illegal aliens that are already in this country, and the flood that's coming in every day. It becomes even more serious when we consider the question of how big we want the population of the United States to be. We've got today something on the order of 215 million people in this country that we know about and can count, and we've got an unknown number of additional millions that are here illegally and haven't been counted.
>
> We're approaching the limit on many of our resources. I think there's a fundamental question that the American people should consider. If we decide that we don't want a much bigger population, then

we're going to have to take steps to stop the inflow of millions of illegals who are coming here from every country in the world.[22]

Chapman also noted that the United States had almost succeeded in reaching
zero population growth through replacement-level birthrates and warned
that "as we get closer to that zero growth, immigration will become an even
larger percentage of our population increase."[23]

Many population control advocates ominously pointed out that as the
nation's birthrates dropped, immigration became a larger percentage of
the total growth rate. In 1973, for example, they regularly drew attention
to the fact that immigration constituted 20 percent of the nation's growth
during that year. The *Arizona Republic* expressed one popular opinion in
this way: "With the U.S. birthrate falling and immigration holding steady,
foreign-born persons are becoming a more significant force in America's
population picture."[24]

"IMMIGRANTS GAINERS IN U.S. BIRTH CUT": THE NEW
PROBLEM OF ILLEGAL IMMIGRATION

Over time some members of the population control movement realized that
their efforts to reduce the nation's birthrates were only marginally successful in lowering the rate of population growth. Realization brought definite
frustration. Many activists believed that the United States was absorbing
the unchecked population growth of other, less developed nations. During a
national hearing on immigration, Elaine Stansfield, the president of the Los
Angeles chapter of ZPG, explained, "We environmentalists felt, with relief,
that the U.S. had just barely in the nick of time, begun to limit its population, and government aid to family planning clinics has been of enormous
help. But other cultures and countries have not yet done this, creating an
additional impact on our population as their people immigrate here."[25] The
advocates who had worked so hard to accomplish zero population growth
felt illegal immigration "negate[d] the efforts" of those organizing against
the population problem.[26] John Tanton worried that "couples could come to
regard continued immigration as simply canceling out their reproductive
restraint...."[27]

Convinced that unchecked immigration was undoing efforts to control
overpopulation, Tanton sought to win other organizations over to the side
of immigration control. For example, he informed members of a group

advocating childless families that they might be "surprised to learn the extent to which illegal immigration to the United States is negating their efforts."[28]

Tanton was hardly alone. Don T. Wilson, president of the organization American Residents Abroad in Mexico, complained about the "invasion" of Mexicans into the United States. He claimed that the United States was gaining international notoriety, citing a recent meeting of ecological scholars in Mexico that focused on the United States' "idiotic policy of promoting birth control through planned parenthood while permitting the immigration of 333,000 foreigners annually." U.S. critics of Mexican immigration also emphasized that these immigrants were "taking jobs from American citizens" and populating "our jails, mental institutions and on welfare which cost us millions." According to Wilson, the solution to this problem was simple: "the one million illegal immigrants in the U.S. should be sent home."[29]

Views similar to Wilson's were becoming prevalent in the media and among the general public. Newspaper headlines across the nation read "Population Exploding in Mexico" and "Mushrooming Population Starts to Haunt Mexico." The articles told sad tales of the misery of "Mexico's One Hundred Million."[30]

Many individuals wrote to both ZPG and the Sierra Club, decrying the government's lack of action on illegal immigration and encouraging these organizations to lobby harder for laws restricting immigration and safeguarding the country from the consequences of Mexico's "millions" streaming across the border. Some blamed the lack of family planning services in Mexico for the its rampant overpopulation and asserted that the Mexican government was "more than happy" to take advantage of the United States as an "escape valve" for the nation's impending problems. At ZPG, Tanton was often the magnet for these sentiments. In December 1976, one letter writer claimed that "The apparently easy possibility of immigrating illegally into the U.S. has the unfortunate result of relieving the pressure for family planning in the Caribbean and northern Latin American countries since it makes it possible for these countries to escape the full consequences of their lack of enthusiasm for family planning." The writer urged strategic policy responses: "It is interesting that Mexico only switched its policy from opposition to family planning to putting the 'right' into its Constitution three or four years after we became tougher on immigration."[31]

Angry letters from individuals committed to fighting the problem of overpopulation quite typically assumed an accusatory tone toward the Mexican government, arguing that it deliberately took advantage of U.S. immigration policy. One member of ZPG wrote to the organization's leadership, not naming Mexico, but clearly referring to its "negligent" behavior:

Why [then] should the U.S. continue to absorb multitudes from the segments of the world community which have refused to address the question of population within their own borders? It is unfair to our own country and the growing effort to reduce population here, to continue to permit—legally or illegally—a massive influx which is defeating the progress here in limiting natural population growth. . . . [Why should] the U.S. underwrite religious hangups and ignorance and population apathy by continuing to accept substantial population excesses from indifferent nations. It is an unreasonable and substantial burden.[32]

Douglas Bergalind, a U.S. citizen residing in Mexico, provided ongoing financial support for the population control efforts of both the Sierra Club and ZPG, and maintained a steady correspondence with both organizations, primarily through John Tanton, throughout the 1970s. His correspondence, written as an "insider," argued that much of Mexico's overpopulation could be blamed on the country's cultural predisposition toward large families: "You now have only about 2 children per family in the U.S. and we [in Mexico] are averaging about 6. I know a family that has over 20 children and a man who claims he has over 40 children, thats [sic] machismo. The U.S. had better become adjusted to the idea of accepting many more millions from Mexico because under present conditions it is unavoidable."[33]

Bergalind advanced even more pointed criticism of the Mexican government, suggesting that its passive stance toward population growth demonstrated the country's reliance on the United States as a place to unload its growing hungry and jobless population. Clearly faulting the U.S. government's inaction for the continued problem, Bergalind believed that "Mexico will not start effective birth control until the escape valve of illegal immigration is stopped."[34] Considering the repercussions of continued Mexican immigration and the possible transformation of the U.S. political landscape, Bergalind feared that Mexicans would eventually come to "dominate a large part of the U.S. and influence the political structure."[35] He warned Tanton that, unless affirmative efforts to stop immigration from Mexico were taken, "Mexicans will eventually dominate many cities in the U.S. pushing further north from the border states."[36]

Bergalind recognized the Sierra Club's reluctance to take a stand on immigration because the organization did not want to be associated with policy recommendations that some could interpret as racist. But he wrote to the club's board of directors, urging them to move aggressively on the issue anyway: "I would especially urge a policy for stopping illegal immigration caused mostly by the rapid population increase in Mexico and other Latin American countries and the sloppy U.S. policy for controlling this invasion for the last 10 years."[37] Although the Sierra Club did not adopt a definitive immigration policy at the time, as I will discuss later, this issue has haunted the organization from the 1970s onward.

A SHIFT FROM POPULATION TO IMMIGRATION:
TANTON AND ZPG

Bergalind found a more sympathetic ear with Tanton and ZPG than he had at the Sierra Club. By mid-1970 the issue of illegal immigration was central to ZPG's population control agenda. An article in the ZPG-California newsletter astutely predicted, "During the next few decades, we believe the world will see a new population issue emerge. Instead of family planning, it will be immigration. . . ."[38]

Particularly worried about the "invasion" of the United States by immigrants from Mexico, Tanton "made immigration an issue for ZPG."[39] He became a self-taught scholar regarding Mexican immigration, identifying the Mexican side of the problem as resulting from both uncontrolled reproduction and the Mexican government's inability to provide jobs to all who needed them. Tanton was especially offended that U.S. policymakers ignored international migration when they crafted demographic policies. In response, he decided to devote his future activities to making immigration a central component of population policy.[40]

Tanton avidly sought out experts, conducted research himself, and extensively wrote and circulated his views on the role of international migration in overpopulation. His award-winning paper "International Migration as an Obstacle to Achieving World Stability" received wide readership when it was published as the cover story in the magazine *The Ecologist*. Here, defining the problem of immigration as a problem of "stabilization" affecting the entire world, Tanton wrote:

As certain parts of the globe deal with their problems more effectively than others, they will stabilize more quickly. This will doubtless increase their attractiveness, especially if other regions are not making progress, or are even slipping backwards. This will increase pressures for international migration which, if it is allowed, will tend to destabilize those regions otherwise approaching stability. Thus international migration will have to be stringently controlled, or no region will be able to stabilize ahead of another. If no region can stabilize ahead of another, then it is likely that no region whatsoever will be able to stabilize in an orderly and humane fashion. A more hopeful scenario calls for some regions stabilizing at an early date, and then helping others to do so. Given the demographic and development situation of the world, the control of international migration will be one of the chief problems the developed countries face in approaching equilibrium conditions.[41]

In Tanton's mind, stabilization could not be achieved as long as immigrant populations from poor countries continued to reproduce unimpeded.

As early as 1971, Tanton began advocating that ZPG include immigration reform in its population control platform. Some members warned him that the issue would raise controversy. Mark Horling, executive director of the organization's fundraising arm, the ZPG Fund, wrote to Tanton that his own feelings on the matter were "tentative." Nevertheless, he encouraged Tanton to make more explicit links between immigration and population. Moreover, Horling suggested that Tanton should couch immigration as an issue directly related to population control, as this would make the issue "more palatable" to ZPG members.[42] Others in the organization similarly advised that ZPG could take up the issue of immigration if it were presented in a "reasoned and positive" position.[43]

Richard Bowers, ZPG's founder, urged Tanton not to approve an organizational platform on immigration unless the organization's board of directors could agree on a resolution by more than a 51 percent majority. Like the Sierra Club, ZPG was worried about being labeled racist. Many population control activists in the United States were already being accused of taking "genocidal" efforts to reduce the birthrates of people of color, and they were well aware of the racial implications of a campaign against immigration. Tanton acknowledged the scrutiny a stand on immigration would invite, and recognized that in the country's past the subject "was often highly emotional and divisive," but he refused to be deterred by such arguments.

Other ZPG members were concerned that strong sentiments against immigration might generate antipathy between environmentalists and other social justice activists. One concerned environmental activist who praised ZPG's population control efforts provided a solution: "It is vital that the environmental groups and the social groups *ally* with one another to solve the problems associated with rapid population growth, large families, and high population densities in these cities" (emphasis in original).[44]

However, in the interest of the organization's stability and harmony, some members suggested that as national fertility rates declined, ZPG should develop a platform that would ensure its vitality. Predicting a decrease in ZPG membership because of recent news of the "baby bust," Russell Mills suggested to Tanton that this might be an "ideal time" to raise new issues to bolster support for ZPG—"namely, immigration policy."[45] Noting an "opening of the minds" at ZPG headquarters toward the issue of immigration, Mills advised Tanton to write an article about immigration for publication in the organization's newsletter, the *National Reporter.*[46]

In addition, many members wrote to ZPG's directors supporting the organization's movement toward advocating immigration control. Some went so far as to ask that ZPG call for a halt to all immigration.[47] Tanton urged members to bring the issue of immigration to the ZPG board and welcomed the many new members who joined after reading Tanton's editorials in newspapers. For example, Olga Thornley first appealed to her state representatives to do something about the overpopulation of ethnic families and illegal and legal immigrants. She then wrote to Tanton, insisting that she was "not a racist," but bemoaning the 1965 changes to the Immigration Act, leading to "a free for all." Thornley complained that the "imported Mexicans" brought in by the farmers in her town "always had such huge families." Thornley was "very concerned about it, but did not seem to know where to look for help" until she read a newspaper article by Tanton.[48]

The ZPG newsletter reported that its board of directors began discussing the issue of immigration restrictions "in earnest" as part of its comprehensive population policy in 1973. According to Tanton, "there was a lot of tearing of hair and gnashing of teeth" as some board members realized the need for immigration control to reach zero population growth, but were reluctant to take such a strong stand.[49] Several board members were concerned that ZPG would be viewed as "an 'elitist group' determined to preserve our 'slice of the pie' while urging the rest of the world and succeeding generations to curtail consumption and change their lifestyles."[50] Despite these reservations, the board voted by simple majority to accept Tanton's immigration resolution to Congress calling for a review of the nation's immigration policy. The board also submitted a request to Congress proposing that, in establishing a population policy for the United States, "immigration rates be recognized as a factor subject to regulation, in the achievement of population policy goals."[51] ZPG appointed Tanton chairman of a committee to study the question of immigration and to propose a more definitive recommendation on U.S. immigration policy.[52]

Encouraged by a general public increasingly apprehensive about immigration as well as a growing ZPG membership, the board of directors agreed to tackle the issue of immigration. In the end, ZPG recommended that, in order to reach zero population growth by the fastest means possible, illegal immigration must be halted *and* legal immigration had to be significantly controlled as well. In 1974 the ZPG board of directors, claiming that "immigration poses a serious threat to the achievement of population stabilization," passed a resolution calling for a halt to all illegal immigration and a 90 percent decrease in the numbers of those who legally immigrate.[53]

With Tanton's ascendancy to the post of ZPG president in 1975, immigration became the group's paramount issue. Although membership had dropped to about 8,500, ZPG was "influential beyond its numbers" due to its strong lobbying and public relations efforts.[54] The organization capitalized on this reputation in aggressively pushing for immigration reform. Developing contacts with the Department of Justice (in particular the Immigration and Naturalization Service), ZPG staff members testified in favor of legislation that would penalize employers who knowingly hired "illegal aliens," and they conducted briefing sessions on illegal immigration for members of the House of Representatives and the Washington press corps.

Primarily due to Tanton's insistence, ZPG hired its first full-time staff member for immigration issues in 1977 and began its "official" immigration program. ZPG's primary goal became the dissemination of information about illegal immigration in the United States. Based on its reputation as being willing to tackle controversial issues for the sake of the nation's welfare, ZPG promoted immigration reform nationwide. Seeking funding for its work, ZPG staff asserted in 1977: "The immigration question stands today where population stood ten years ago: surrounded by strong feelings and hampered by a lack of information. Just as it helped breech that earlier barrier, ZPG Inc. now hopes to shed light on the immigration dilemma."[55]

Toward this end, ZPG staffers in 1977 made more than fifty media appearances across the nation and published several articles in nationally distributed magazines to publicize the immigration issue.[56] Tanton was busy establishing communications with prominent scholars, including demographer Kingsley Davis, who agreed to write about immigration issues on ZPG's behalf in national magazines. ZPG held several well-attended press conferences, became a major resource for Washington policymakers and congressional members,[57] and was one of the major sponsors of Senator Bob Packwood's bill (S.R. 1928) to prevent the employment of "illegal aliens."

As Packwood put it, "More than any other group, Zero Population Growth members have an awareness of this problem."[58]

ZPG's anti-immigration line closely followed the apocalyptic tenor deployed in the "population bomb" propaganda earlier in the decade. The organization's campaign to halt virtually all U.S. immigration similarly relied on ideological rhetoric infused with racial inferences, albeit somewhat tempered to deflect criticism. Noting the success of earlier messages about the population bomb, the organization mounted a similar campaign. For example, in a nationwide drive urging immigration curbs in 1977, a letter signed by Paul Ehrlich described illegal immigration as a "human tidal wave" and encouraged members to support ZPG's efforts to sharply curb this segment of the nation's population growth.[59]

The mass-mailed letter aimed to provoke the reader, beginning: "When the small pickup truck was finally apprehended outside of Chicago, 32 people were found crammed inside—men, women, and children—one woman about to go into labor. All were penniless."[60] The three-page letter stressed the terrible impact on the United Stated if these thirty-two immigrants had not been apprehended. It also detailed the depressing living and working conditions they would have faced. Artfully crafted by an outside consulting firm under the direction of ZPG, the letter stressed the "fact" that new immigrants arrived in groups of entire families. Moreover, these immigrant families no longer only crossed the border to return back to Mexico as soon as possible, but now traveled into the "heart" of the nation to settle down and become a permanent part of the population. And, as the letter pointed out, many of the women who arrived were pregnant.

In the letter Ehrlich further claimed that illegal immigrants were "depressing our economy and costing American taxpayers an estimated $10 to $13 billion a year in lost earnings and taxes, in welfare benefits and public services."[61] ZPG projected that, from 1970 to 2000, illegal immigrants and their descendants would add 20 million people ("the size of another California") to the population rolls.[62] Thus, ZPG appealed to the concerns of population control activists, noting that continued immigration would "cancel the benefits of our declining fertility." The Ehrlich letter continued balefully, while congratulating ZPG:

Nine years ago ZPG sounded the alarm. America's population growth was threatening the quality of life of future generations. The problems of urban decay, resource depletion, chronic poverty, environmental degradation could not be solved unless Americans began having smaller families.

Thanks in no small measure to ZPG's educational efforts, America's attitudes about family size began to change. The fertility rate has dropped and we have made important strides toward stabilizing our growth except for the massive hemorrhage of illegal aliens—which in 1976 accounted for an astonishing one-third of our population growth.[63]

Once again, ZPG had sounded the alarm.

IN SEARCH OF THE "INDIRECT EFFECT" OF MEXICAN IMMIGRATION

The truck with Mexican immigrants, including one woman who was "in labor," was iconically important to ZPG's outreach effort. ZPG was strategically reminding potential funders and members that together they could oppose the "hyper-fertile Mexican immigrant," the ever-present tangible threat to the state of the nation, the "menacing" figure who deserved study, containment, and policy attention. This was an issue Tanton himself championed.

Based on his studies of immigration, Tanton argued that the higher birthrates of immigrants was a significant aspect of their contribution to population growth. He was heavily influenced by Kingsley Davis's 1974 article "The Migration of Human Populations"—in particular, its assertion that the fertility rates of Mexican immigrant women were higher than those of U.S. citizens.[64] According to Davis, "the indirect effect of immigration on population growth depends on the fertility of the immigrant women. Insofar as they come from underdeveloped countries, their fertility is high compared with that of native women. In the U.S. in 1970 the number of children ever born to women aged 40 to 44 was 4.4 per women for those of Mexican-origin and 2.9 for all women."[65]

As Tanton focused ZPG on the combination of immigrant and population growth, he repeatedly called attention to this "indirect effect." He expressed his clear frustration that "we know virtually nothing about the fertility of legal immigrants . . . and hence their contribution to population growth."[66] Yet Tanton was certain that a significant differential existed, and his pet project within the area of immigration control became determining the fertility rates of Mexican immigrant women. This led to his severe criticism of most governmental population policy efforts.

Tanton was particularly bothered by the conclusions drawn by the Commission on Population Growth and the American Future, which assumed that immigrants to the United States practiced replacement-level fertility. In fact, he concluded that the commission's recommendations on immigration were baseless. Tanton argued, on the contrary, that because of changes in the Immigration Law of 1965, a larger proportion of immigrants came from less-developed countries (55 percent) with much higher fertility patterns than those of women from developed countries. According to Tanton, the differential fertility of immigrant women, especially Mexican immigrant women, would place a greater burden on the United States than accounted for in the commission's report.[67]

Tanton went to great lengths to determine the rates of fertility not only of Mexican immigrant women, but of all women of Mexican descent. Specifically, Tanton wondered if "there is any indication that the fertility rates of immigrants are rising as an increasing number of immigrants come from less developed countries."[68] While he was chair of the Sierra Club's immigration committee, Tanton asked the group's population officer to seek out any specific data that the U.S. Census Bureau had compiled on the fertility rate of Mexican immigrants and Mexican American women. Tanton wanted to conduct a direct comparison of the rates of native-born women and women of Mexican origin.[69]

Realizing the lack of published data, Tanton also sought confirmation of his argument from leading U.S. demographers. In addition to contacting Kingsley Davis of the University of California, Berkeley, Tanton wrote to Charles Westhoff of the Office of Population Research at Princeton University, requesting information about the fertility rates of this group: "This fertility pattern (native born women and immigrant women sharing similar fertility rates) may have been a valid assumption in the past, but with the shift in origin of the immigrant stream from the developed to the less developed countries, it seems likely that the fertility levels of immigrants will rise towards those of the country of origin."[70]

Much to Tanton's dismay, Westhoff responded that at that point, no such figures were available, which he primarily attributed to the fact that immigrants were not classified as "legal" or "illegal" in the 1970 census, and thus the actual number of births produced by the entire Mexican-origin population in the country could not be determined.[71] Unable to find answers to all of the fertility-related questions he posed, Tanton considered pressing for the inclusion of questions in the 1980 census and all forthcoming Current Population Surveys that would chart the fertility of immigrant women and provide a firm basis for a national population policy.[72]

Despite an absence of good statistical information, Tanton attempted to attract more national media attention to the issue of Mexican women's fertility. Consider, for example, a letter he wrote to Gene Matalene of ABC News. Consulted by the network for a program on illegal immigration, Tanton suggested a historical overview featuring demographic issues, with a focus on the effects of immigration on the United States. He offered several references to the program's producers, including Kingsley Davis's 1974 article "The Migration of Human Populations." Tanton explained the importance of the "indirect effect" of migration to Matalene:

> [Kingsley] Davis . . . states on p. 103 that in 1970 the number of children ever born to women aged 40 to 44 was 4.4 per woman for those of Mexican-origin and 2.9 for all women (in the U.S.). [sic] So it would be less for [U.S. descent] women other than those of Mexican-origin. Add to this that the illegals probably have a higher fertility than their Americanized counterparts, and 800,000 illegals per year probably adds up to much more than 30 million by the year 2000. . . . Incidentally, the TV show "Chico and the Man" highlighted this last week a common phenomenon—the pregnant Mexican girl who comes to the U.S. to deliver, conferring U.S. citizenship on the child . . . and making her an immediate relative of a U.S. citizen. Wild![73]

In citing the popular network television show "Chico and the Man," Tanton shared with Matalene his belief that "the pregnant Mexican girl who comes to the U.S. to deliver" is a "common phenomenon." Tanton portrayed the "girl" as doubly opportunistic: not only does she bear her child in the United States to draw social benefits, she does so also to make herself a relative to a U.S. citizen. Tanton's correspondence with ABC News, along with his expert testimony before Congress and his placement on national boards charged with implementing U.S. immigration policy, demonstrates that Tanton wielded authority in many domains of the immigration arena and that numerous power-wielders sought his advice and listened to what he had to say.[74]

Others shared Tanton's preoccupation with the fertility rates of Mexican Americans and their impact on the social and political culture of the United States. Members of ZPG, especially those from the California chapters, echoed similar concerns. Elaine Stansfield, president of the Los Angeles chapter of the organization, articulated these views in her testimony before the Federal Select Commission on Immigration and Refugee Policy Hearings in Los Angeles. Stansfield asked the members of the Select Commission to assess more comprehensively the impact of Mexican reproduction in national population growth. Decrying the disastrous consequences of immigrant fertility, Stansfield told the Select Commission:

> No one has begun to try to estimate the number of illegals who come in to work, stay and bring their families, and start having their babies here—babies who automatically become citizens. . . . The Health Dept. in California is aghast at seeing diseases they thought had been eradicated, and knowing there are children in school who have never seen a doctor, let alone been inoculated against simple childhood diseases.[75]

Although they had presented a crisis in public health, Stansfield did not blame the immigrants themselves. But she did blame the Mexican government, which she felt, was "happy to have them [immigrants] use the U.S. as an escape valve." However, she worried that, because of overwhelming immigration from Mexico, the United States was "teetering on the brink of chaos which can be prevented if the INS can only be given the powers and regulations of enforcement and control. . . ."[76]

Disappointed by the lack of government action against illegal immigration, Stansfield hoped ZPG would push the issue forward more aggressively. She implored the organization to take explicit measures and expressed great dissatisfaction with its policy recommendations for illegal immigration. Stansfield considered the organization's platform insufficient because it neglected the Mexican "pregnancy culture," which she believed added significantly to the immigration "problem."[77]

In 1978, Stansfield wrote a letter to Phyllis Eisen, director of ZPG's national immigration education and lobbying efforts, concerning a recent brochure delineating the organization's immigration reform platform. Stansfield reiterated California-ZPG's anti-immigration policy, using strident language to claim that residents of the state "see a few things National hasn't." Arguing that the pamphlet circulated by ZPG underestimated the birthrate of Mexican Americans, Stansfield tried to convince Eisen that a more deliberate emphasis on the high fertility rate of immigrants should be a crucial part of the ZPG agenda. In Stansfield's estimation, immigrant birthrates were largely responsible for continued population growth from reproduction as well. She wrote, "there are entirely too many people who don't realize that we have already 'replenished the earth,' so we have mostly here in Calif., Mexican immigrants with a baby-producing culture that won't quit."[78]

Equally frustrated that Mexican immigrants "do not learn English" when they arrive in the United States, Stansfield tied this deficiency to the fact that undocumented workers unlawfully received welfare benefits. She also lamented the "dangerous" illnesses that Mexican children bring with them when they enter the country. Stansfield justified her good intentions by reminding Eisen that "these thoughts come from someone who is fond of latins [sic]." However, Stansfield ended her letter to the ZPG office clearly indicating that her concerns were fueled by racial anxiety and a fear of the changing demographics of the nation. She worried that "WASPS" are "now in the minority" and warned Eisen, "there is bad trouble brewing, and it's not just the using up of our resources by overpopulation, for I see chaos, anarchy and revolution first."[79]

Beyond agitating within ZPG on a national level, Stansfield used her status in the organization to promote her agenda wherever she had the opportunity, even within forums where immigration was not explicitly the focus. For example, during her testimony at White House hearings on families in Los Angeles in December 1979, Stansfield used her speaking time to emphasize the need for better control of the numbers of immigrants coming into the United States, specifically the "Mexican illegals" in California. Stansfield stressed that immigration was germane to family issues in the United States, "not just because of the enormous addition to our already stretched population, but because of a different orientation to large families."[80]

Stansfield's comments, and her influence as a leader, provide evidence of the emergence of a more pointedly racial discussion into the public realm. While earlier in the decade population control advocates were wary of expressing their racial concerns, by the end of the decade such statements were openly admissible in public government forums.[81] Sharing her opinions as a representative of ZPG at national congressional hearings, Stansfield advanced the legitimacy of the problem of the large immigrant family and the "pregnancy culture" of Mexican immigrants as reasonable topics of federal policy concern.

ILLEGAL IMMIGRANTS AND THE POPULATION "SHIFT": THE FEDERATION OF AMERICAN IMMIGRATION REFORM

As public furor over illegal immigration grew more pronounced by the end of the 1970s, immigration control became a more prominent policy issue. By this time, both Tanton and the board of directors realized that ZPG could not be the sole forum for the advancement of national immigration reform. At their yearly meeting in the spring of 1978, the board unanimously approved a proposal to start a program that would help establish a new organization focused on the immigration problem. Convinced that environmental and population groups could not effectively fight to establish immigration reform because of the "hornets' nest" of emotional issues it raised, Tanton had been working on a plan for his own organization for some years. Tanton's brainchild would become the Federation of American Immigration Reform (FAIR), the most influential anti-immigration organization in the nation.[82]

ZPG played a central role in springboarding FAIR into the national limelight, providing the initial funds for getting the organization off the ground. Additionally, while FAIR was being established, the ZPG Fund received FAIR's incoming contributions and provided administrative services. Despite the interdependence of FAIR and ZPG, notes from board discussions indicate that a distinct effort was made to ensure that all FAIR materials would specify that FAIR was not a project of, nor controlled by, the ZPG Foundation.[83]

Nevertheless, FAIR built its membership and fundraising base from ZPG supporters. Many primary funders of ZPG provided substantial monies to jump-start the new organization, and members from chapters across the state of California were among the first to support and join FAIR. ZPG encouraged such relationships. For instance, in their special "Immigration Newsletter," members of the Livermore ZPG chapter were encouraged to join FAIR.[84]

FAIR was deliberately designed to fight the battle against immigration, a project that appealed to population control proponents. Tanton did not believe that the greatest repercussion of continued population growth and natural resource depletion would be to undermine the U.S. standard of living: instead, the most powerful blow would be against "personal liberty." After a lifetime of dedicating himself to the issue of population control through environmental conservation, Tanton now, through FAIR, was ready to press the issue as one of preserving democratic government and individual freedom.

Tanton was clearly embracing and promoting ideas about demographics and immigration that inextricably linked race and politics. In 1980, he predicted that by the year 2000, there would be fifteen million additional legal immigrants and forty, fifty, or sixty million illegal immigrants in the United States. Tanton predicted that immigration would finally alter the very nature of "American" society, tying Mexican immigration to the end of a great democracy."[85]

FAIR's first lobbying action, demonstrating its dedication to protecting the nation from illegal immigration and political doom, was a suit against the Bureau of the Census for the inclusion of "millions of illegal aliens" in the national census.[86] Arguing that the enumeration of "illegal aliens" in the census produced unfair results upon which congressional reapportionments are based, FAIR claimed that this practice resulted in an undue number of seats given to states with large numbers of illegal residents, such as

California, New York, and Illinois. Despite FAIR's ultimate failure with this project, a number of members of congress and others began to pay attention to the organization and its sense of strategy.[87]

CONCLUSION

John Tanton's advancement of an immigration control platform focusing on the fertility of Mexican-immigrant women clearly shows how policymakers and population activists constructed and manipulated a racialized demographics aimed to incite fear in the general public for the advancement of an immigration control agenda. As immigration gained attention as a significant component of late-twentieth-century population growth, the fertility of Mexican immigrants became an issue of public debate. While some prominent leaders within ZPG tried to integrate immigration reform into its population control agenda, eventually John Tanton went even further. He established a separate organization that could fully commit to the issue of immigration. Within FAIR, Tanton could more easily express his concerns and build support for attention to the high fertility rates of women of Mexican origin. He could freely fulminate against the "Latinization" of America and what must be done to stop this development.

Since the foundation of FAIR, Tanton has founded several other interlocking organizations, most of which have been heavily financed by the Pioneer Fund, a foundation committed to eugenic ideals of racial inferiority and superiority. Through these various means Tanton has placed limits upon the physical and cultural impact of immigrants, particularly those from Mexico.

Tanton most recently tried to lobby the Sierra Club to adopt an immigration control policy in 1996–1997 and 2003–2004, when he and other allies ran a well-funded and engineered campaign to force the organization to adopt an immigration reform plank.[88] Although the efforts were unsuccessful, proponents of immigration control were widely labeled as an anti-immigrant faction within the nation's largest environmental organization. Ultimately blamed for staging a "hijacking" of the group's principles, immigration reformers' strategies led to organized resistance within the Sierra Club. Because the effort was made up of several organizations that Tanton founded, including the Center for Immigration Studies, Numbers USA, U.S., Inc., and Californians for Population Stabilization, Tanton was considered the leader of this effort. However, the interests that drive immigration reform have gone beyond the efforts of this individual advocate and have become a central component of debate in the U.S. environmental movement.

CHAPTER SIX

THE RIGHT TO HAVE CHILDREN

Chicanas Organizing Against Sterilization Abuse

Yolanda Nava, representing Comisión Femenil Mexicana Nacional, began her 1973 testimony before the California Commission on the Status of Women with a frank and fundamental point: "Let me begin by stating that contrary to the stereotype of the Chicana at home making tortillas and babies, the Chicana has been and will continue to be an integral part of the work force."[1] Comisión is a feminist group founded in 1970 to focus on the needs and issues relevant to Chicanas. As one of the first and only organizations focusing on Chicana issues and promoting Chicana leadership, Comisión and Latina concerns were being represented before the California commission for the first time.

Slated to speak on the issue of "The Chicana and Unemployment," Nava used her allotted time to challenge the public stereotype of Chicanas as baby machines. Drawing from statistics that she had compiled, she showed that Chicanas were indeed active participants in the workforce but overrepresented in low-paying jobs in the service sector, where they typically received few, if any, benefits. According to Nava and Comisión, Chicanas were relegated to caretaking and service positions in part because of the pejorative social stereotypes that narrowly defined them: "The stereotype of the Chicana as homemaker and 'mother' has left available to her jobs which are similar to those she performs in the home—hence the preponderance of Chicanas as domestic, laundry and cleaning workers."[2]

By identifying Chicanas as workers, not baby-makers, in her opening statement, Nava purposefully sidestepped a long-standing stereotype. Her words provide one example of how Comisión members and other Chicana feminists were aware of the derogatory stereotype about their reproduction circulating in the public domain, and that some openly contested it. In particular, Chicana feminists and activists speculated that sterilization abuse and other compromised health care were directly related to these existing stereotypes. In her classic piece "La Feminista," published in 1974,

Anna Nieto Gómez specifically pointed to the problematics of the breeder concept.

> Sexist racist stereotypes depict the Chicana people as being a sexually irresponsible people. Chicanas are described as "breeders." Sociologists explain this condition as a result of a submissive and animalistic nature and childlike will. . . . Darwinistic doctors who feel that the poor are a burden of the strong play God with the bodies of women. As a result, Chicanas are victims of constant malpractice. They are involuntarily experimented with, and involuntarily sterilized.[3]

Nieto Gomez's contention that social-scientific and medical discourse led to the medical mistreatment of Mexican-origin women reinforced the burgeoning argument that images and ideas of Mexican women as breeders have direct bearing on their reproductive experiences.

As Nava and Nieto Gomez both indicate, by the 1970s Chicana feminists had begun to identify what sociologist Patricia Hill Collins has called *controlling images*, or stereotypes, as a crucial influence shaping their experiences as women of color in the United States.[4] In this chapter, I focus on Chicana activism against coercive sterilization, drawing from their written speeches, public testimonies, and oral history interviews to show how this involved publicly challenging the controlling images of Mexican-origin women. In so doing, Chicanas gave voice to how the stereotype of Mexican-origin women as breeders profoundly limits their social, economic, and political opportunities.

Moreover, their individual and collective efforts also dispel the existing stereotype that women of Mexican origin are simply at home having children by directly demonstrating their involvement in political activism. Chicana activists organized coalitions, circulated petitions, held public forums and rallies, and took other direct action against reproductive abuse at the Los Angeles County Medical Center (LACMC). Newly formed organizations dedicated to Chicana issues, including the Comisión Femenil Mexicana Nacional as well as the Chicana Rights Project of the Mexican American Legal Defense and Education Fund (MALDEF), focused on obtaining legal redress for those forcibly sterilized and establishing regulations to ensure that similar coercions would never happen again. Members of these groups addressed legislative bodies and organized fund-raisers to help support the lawsuits against LACMC (*Andrade et al. v. Los Angeles County-USC Medical Center* and *Madrigal v. Quilligan*).

Through these efforts Chicanas advanced a foundational concept in their reproductive politics: the right of women of Mexican origin to have as many children as they wanted, free from governmental, medical, or social constraint. Although Chicana activists came from a variety of feminist positions and organizational agendas, their speeches, chants, and testimony in legislative hearings echoed a similar refrain.[5] Although Chicana activists wanted to free women of Mexican origin from the breeder stereotype, they also insisted on having the right to bear as many children as they desired.

INDIVIDUAL AND ORGANIZATIONAL ACTIVISM
AGAINST STERILIZATION ABUSE

In December 1976, Consuelo Vasquez, a resident of Ripon, California, and a U.S. citizen, wrote to Governor Jerry Brown after suffering complications from sterilization:

> In 1971 I gave birth to one of my children in a hospital in San Joaquín, California. This was the last of my five children. When I was in the hospital the doctor told me that I needed an operation because I already had too many children. Furthermore, I was told that the operation was needed because I was not healthy and with another pregnancy I could die and leave my children motherless. The doctor would become angered on my refusal to consent to the operation, until finally the doctor frightened me into the operation.
>
> The doctor had reassured me that the operation would be successful and that I would come through it alright. However, I was not alright. Shortly thereafter I began to feel poorly and I went back to the hospital. I was told time and again, that there was nothing wrong with me.

Mrs. Vasquez's repeated returns to the hospital were in vain. On these visits, Mrs. Vasquez cried and pleaded with the doctors to treat her. But, because she could not afford to pay the bill for the delivery of her last child, the hospital refused. When she became unable to walk due to unbearable abdominal pains, her husband had no choice but to take Consuelo to the emergency room, where doctors immediately discovered and operated on a bleeding tumor. Mrs. Vasquez described her condition to the governor:

> The tubal ligation I had received to prevent me from ever becoming pregnant again was not performed properly. The tubes were swollen and twisted. I was immediately operated [on] because of the tumor and they had to remove my appendix since there was something wrong with it, and they also removed my tubes. A year later they performed a hysterectomy because I began experiencing pain. Now I don't have anything. I am empty inside.
>
> I ask you, is what they are doing to me fair? Especially after the way in which I was treated at county hospital? I am willing to pay my bill even if it is a little at a time. I would like you to review my case and if you feel it is justified I would like to have your advice.

The Vasquez family borrowed money from friends to pay for Consuelo's operations, but they still owed the hospital a significant amount. With a collections agency demanding funds, Consuelo wrote to Governor Brown seeking assistance.[6] She sought recourse the only way she knew how. She believed her elected representative would be able to offer help to a person harmed in the public domain. However, there is no record of a response from the governor's office.

In writing to the governor, Mrs. Vasquez emphasized her U.S. citizenship, a fact that she believed was highly relevant to her complaint and her claim for help. As I've detailed in chapter 3 and elsewhere, there were many cases of undocumented Mexican women who were also coercively sterilized, but most feared that if they came forward, they or someone else in their family would be deported.[7]

While Consuelo Vasquez may have felt that she was alone in her appeals for assistance, significant public efforts in response to coercive sterilization had begun to emerge across the state of California and nationwide. Many activists, with a variety of political interests, were driven by the desire to seek redress for the abuses that had occurred and to prevent similar coercion in the future. This work primarily occurred on two fronts: through grassroots activism and legislative reform. In 1977, both efforts coalesced during the public hearings of the California State Department of Health on the new sterilization regulations. In three separate hearings across the state, strong Chicana voices claimed the indisputable right for women of Mexican origin to decide how many children they wanted to have.

ORGANIZING AGAINST STERILIZATION ABUSE

There are a number of accounts of how sterilization abuse at LACMC was exposed. In her interview with historian Virginia Espino, Alicia Escalante, founder of the Chicana Welfare Rights Organization (CWRO), recalled that during a community forum, a member shared her suspicions that she may have been sterilized after having a child at LACMC.[8] Rumors and tales of sterilization abuse and other medical mistreatment at LACMC were not uncommon in Mexican and Chicano communities in Los Angeles. Some of the community members that I interviewed recalled radio ads that ran in both English and Spanish asking women who believed they had possibly been sterilized to contact lawyers.[9]

The practice of coercive sterilization was brought to widespread public attention primarily through a series of articles published in the *Los Angeles Times*.[10] Once the abuse was exposed, a variety of groups responded. Several leftist organizations formed coalitions to show solidarity with what they perceived as a classist and imperialist government sponsoring medical coercion. Groups like the New American Movement, one of the so-called "New Left" organizations comprised of politicized students and intellectuals, and other socialist feminists and Marxist organizers worked together to advance various interventions.

On November 23, 1974, the Committee to Stop Forced Sterilizations (CSFS), "a group of women organizing to put an end to forced sterilization," came together with the Los Angeles Women's Union, the Committee to Free Los Tres, and the Solidarity Band to demonstrate outside of the Women's Hospital at LACMC.[11] "Our Sisterhood Includes All Women . . . Join Us to Fight Forced Sterilization!" their posters and flyers read.[12]

This coalition stressed the connection between population control in the third world and sterilization abuse against women in the United States. Their announcement for the public meeting declared, "We believe that our purpose for birth control is the liberation of women."[13] Isabel Chávez, a member of the Committee to Free Los Tres, and a representative to the Committee to End Forced Sterilization (CEFS), reiterated to the crowd during the rally that the hospital's genocidal tactics were "strategies for eliminating poor people—especially ethnic minorities—by taking away from them the ability to have children."[14] Participants estimated that approximately 250 to 300 people joined the CSFS demonstration on November 23. Protesters held placards reading "*Que Se Ponga Fin a la Esterilización Involuntaria*" (Stop Forced Sterilization) and "*Que Paren las Practicas Experimentales de Medicina con la Gente Pobre*" (Stop Medical Experimentation with Poor People).[15]

The CSFS also produced the informational booklet *Stop Forced Sterilizations Now!*—a bilingual publication that was widely distributed throughout
the community. Again stressing the links between U.S. imperialism and
control of women's bodies, the pamphlet included information, cartoons,
and news articles to provide a critical perspective on sterilization abuse
and other forms of population control. The other group, CEFS, circulated a
petition with several demands, including that LACMC hospital adopt more
stringent guidelines, hire more bilingual staff, and end medical experimentation among poor people.[16]

Activists also organized demonstrations and fundraisers to publicize the
legal efforts on behalf of the sterilized women and to support Dr. Bernard
Rosenfeld, who had exposed sterilization abuse nationwide. Rosenfeld was
the doctor who first contacted the *Madrigal* lawyers with information on
the Spanish-surnamed women who had been coercively sterilized at LACMC.
He was subsequently charged by the hospital with moral turpitude for publicizing patients' medical records. In 1976, the National Coalition Against
Sterilization Abuse held a benefit fund-raiser in Los Angeles to help fund
his defense. Rosenfeld recalled that then-aspiring politician Tom Hayden,
a former leader of Students for a Democratic Society, was in attendance, as
well as Jane Fonda, and that the Chicano band Los Lobos performed at the
event.[17]

Other individuals also helped mount legal efforts on behalf of those forcibly sterilized, and small communities of support developed around each of
the cases and causes. Plaintiffs, lawyers, and witnesses of sterilization abuse
spoke in public forums and at press conferences regarding the legal battles
against the hospital.

At the same time that community activists were staging demonstrations
at LACMC, holding public education forums, and raising funds to support
the campaigns, the lawyers in *Madrigal v. Quilligan* were preparing to go
to trial. In addition to the three lawyers on the case, several other young
Chicano professionals lent their expertise to the effort. Maria Theresa Vélez,
a psychologist who interviewed some of the *Madrigal* plaintiffs, recalled, "I
clearly remember going to Antonia's [Hernández] Lincoln Heights office and
sitting around a table doing stuff—like consulting. She would ask me this or
that and I would give her my opinion or help her—me, Antonia's husband,
some others. . . . We were all part of the *bola*—the second team—and were
all very involved.[18] Over time, many other individuals and organizations
also joined the *Madrigal* effort. In particular, the newly formed Comisión
served as a very important instrument in the case of *Madrigal v. Quilligan*
and the legislative efforts that followed.

"I NEED YOU NOW!": COMISIÓN FEMENIL
MEXICANA—LOS ANGELES CHAPTER

Antonia Hernández, one of the lawyers for the *Madrigal* plaintiffs, recalled her initial communication with Comisión, the group that would become centrally involved in the litigation:

> When we were preparing the case, we decided it was going to be a class action litigation. In order for it to be a class action, we needed to have an institutional organizational client. So I sought out and scheduled a meeting with the national president of Comisión Femenil. I knew some of the Comisión Femenil women, but I needed not only the L.A. branch, whom I knew, but I needed the national branch of the organization. So we went and discussed the case and their involvement as organizational clients.[19]

In 1974, Hernández contacted the board of the Los Angeles chapter of Comisión, and she remembers going to see them and saying, "I need you, now!"[20] The chapter's president, Gloria Molina, was immediately responsive and took the issue to the membership.[21] The group, which held monthly meetings, was receptive but unsure about what they were entering into. Olivia Rodríguez, who joined Comisión's Los Angeles chapter in 1974, remembered hearing that Antonia Hernández would be addressing the body: "When Gloria told us that Antonia was coming to talk about the case, the word 'sterilization' was foreign. I was like what was that? . . . So when she talked to us, it was a little mind-boggling to me how Comisión was going to become part of the plaintiffs for this case."[22] However, once they heard the appalling details of the abuses that had occurred, the members agreed that the organization should be actively involved in the effort and voted to support the case.

Organizers formed a committee within Comisión to take primary responsibility for managing the organization's multiple roles in the effort. With Gloria Molina as chairperson, the committee was responsible not only for negotiating with the court as the plaintiff class, but also for providing research, financial backing, and other support for the *Madrigal* legal team. According to historian Virginia Espino, the Chicana Service Action Center (Comisión's cornerstone project) provided workspace for the organization's efforts on behalf of the *Madrigal* case.[23] Within the Center, Comisión members tracked and called potential plaintiffs, raised funds, and organized community education programs.

Early on, several members of the sterilization committee met a number of the plaintiffs in the *Madrigal* case. One of the roles the groups was initially expected to play was to interact with the possible plaintiffs, listen to their stories, and talk about what had happened to them. Understandably, all were reticent about having such difficult conversations. Evelyn Martínez, chairperson of the legislative committee, remembered the meeting as an emotional one: "I do remember meeting the women who had been sterilized, at least three or four of those women, and they were primarily Spanish speaking. We'd listen to their stories, and I think that motivated us even more to be their voice because for whatever reason, they didn't want to be that lone voice in the courtroom." The *Madrigal* attorneys, who were also present, asked each plaintiff to share her experiences with the Comisión committee. It was the beginning of a process that would have them recounting these painful stories over and over again. Martinez recalled:

For us it was almost a tearful experience because even as young as we were we realized that these physicians were looking at anyone with brown skin or Spanish surnames very stereotypically, that somehow because they didn't speak English, because they were possibly low income, and because they were at that particular hospital that assumption was made, that they were all on welfare, they shouldn't have children—any more children—because the government would have to support them. It was just really, for me it was unimaginable. I mean, how could this be happening? We're Americans, we live in the United States. These kinds of actions—it was really hard to fathom and yet here these women were telling us exactly what had happened to them, and it really brought tears to our eyes. This could have been our mother, this could be happening to our mothers or our aunts. It was just really hard to believe and yet there was the proof sitting right there in front of us. So if you hadn't been there it was like "that sort of thing doesn't happen here," but it did.[24]

It was perhaps for these reasons that when the trial judge ultimately decided that Comisión could not serve as a plaintiff, the organization and its members maintained their commitment to the case by providing support work. Members recorded and transcribed affidavits from those women who agreed to take part in the case, and they also performed other critical tasks. The national arm of Comisión held a fund-raiser with the Mexican-American Bar Association of Los Angeles County and raised three thousand dollars to support the *Madrigal* case.[25] Comisión also provided leadership in moving the legislative aspects of the decision forward.

THE STERILIZATION REGULATIONS AND PUBLIC HEARINGS

Part of the decision in the *Madrigal* trial included early hearings for the affirmative relief portion of the suit against the U.S. Department of Health, Education, and Welfare (HEW) and the California State Department of Health. HEW had recently established federal regulations requiring consent forms in the patient's language and was therefore excused from the case. In October 1975, the federal district court ordered the California State Department of Health to immediately prepare consent forms and counseling materials at an appropriate reading level in both Spanish and English for adoption in all state medical institutions.[26] The Los Angeles Center for Law and Justice and the Coalition for the Medical Rights of Women prepared the model counseling materials and consent forms.[27]

At the same time, in northern California, various activists were organizing to ensure that any new regulations directly administered by the state actually responded to the court's order. The Chicana Rights Project (CRP) of MALDEF along with the Coalition for the Medical Rights of Women (CMRW) filed a petition with the California State Department of Health. Finding the state's first response to the federal court order for new regulations deficient—particularly in meeting the needs of non–English-speaking women—the CRP joined with several other Bay Area organizations to petition the state Department of Health for more strenuous regulations.[28]

In the petition, the coalition urged "the adoption of stringent regulations to insure that every person who is sterilized in California gives her or his uncoerced, informed consent for such an operation."[29] Claiming that medical practitioners "sell" sterilization operations to patients for the purpose of guaranteeing medical students "guinea pigs" on whom to practice their surgical techniques, the petition sponsors argued that the current emergency regulations were "thrown together" to comply with federal mandates and neglected to protect the fundamental constitutional right to procreate. They urged the department to adopt regulations prohibiting nonemergency sterilizations unless the patient gave informed consent at least seventy-two hours prior to the scheduled operation. This informed consent would have to be in the patient's own language and include a review of the pros and cons of all other options to sterilization. They also demanded regulations requiring the presence of an auditor witness, selected by the patient and not a staff member of the health facility, during the signing of consent forms, and declaring the consent invalid if signed while the patient was under duress or under the influence of drugs.

Esther Talavera was co-chair of the CMRW's Sterilization and Informed Consent Project. Part of her efforts included outreach to the Latino community. According to Talavera, educational outreach was crucial in the effort to prevent involuntary sterilization. In her article "Sterilization Is Not an Alternative in Family Planning," published in *Agenda,* the magazine of the National Council of La Raza, she explained that being informed about issues of reproductive health was necessary for the betterment of Latino communities: "We who are informed need to take our knowledge into our communities so that people, especially our youth, can be aware of what can happen to them. . . . If we accept a moral responsibility for 'La Gente.' Someday we may have as many children as we want when we want to have them, for that is an integral part of our decision to determine our destinies."[30] Talavera's statement—that the right to "have as many children as we [Latinas] want" is crucial to larger human rights and social justice— was a central rallying cry in other Chicana efforts to develop sterilization regulations.

The MALDEF CRP, founded in 1974, was formed to concentrate on legal issues impacting women. Although the CRP identified general health care as one of its areas of concern, sterilization abuse quickly became the primary focus. A pamphlet distributed by the group encouraged Chicanas to be conscious of their rights and explained how to recognize possible abuses. By referring to the experiences of four *Madrigal* plaintiffs, the pamphlet pointed to the many ways that a woman could be coerced into sterilization. It debunked many of the myths that doctors had told the women, such as their assertion that there was a maximum number of children that a woman may have. By gearing their educational pamphlet to the women most susceptible to sterilization abuse, the CRP hoped to decrease its incidence.

The CRP also developed a written statement on sterilization abuse emphasizing the right to have children. Sandra Salazar, the project's leader, wrote: "Women in California have a chance to stop forced sterilizations. But we must speak up and not be ashamed to let doctors and government officials know that we value the right to have children and that we value the right to decide how many children we want to have."[31] The right to bear children, as stressed throughout this chapter, was repeatedly voiced throughout this period of activism.

Together, members of CMRW and CRP participated in drafting what eventually became the state's official guidelines for sterilization. The CRP was also centrally involved in negotiations with the California State Department of Health and particularly represented the interests of Latinas.[32]

As a result of these collective efforts, the state agreed to hold three public hearings regarding the proposed regulations. During 1977, organizations and individuals from throughout California traveled to hearings in Los Angeles, San Francisco, and Sacramento to testify about their experiences of forced sterilization and other medical mistreatment. To help ensure that the process of establishing the state guidelines was accountable to and inclusive of low-income women and women of color, the CMRW and MALDEF mounted a letter-writing campaign to the California State Department of Health demanding that at least one of the public hearings occur on a Saturday or at other times when working women might be able to attend. They also requested Spanish-language interpreters at all hearings. At all three forums, health care providers, patient advocates, and activists represented a variety of opinions.

Significant representation at the hearings from the women's movement was the cause of some tension. In particular, groups such as the California chapter of the National Organization of Women (NOW) opposed lengthy waiting periods between the signing of consent forms and the actual operations. Concerned that a waiting period would be used to deny women who wanted sterilizations from having them, NOW opposed any waiting period, steadfast in their argument that women should have access to whatever reproductive procedures they wanted, without limitations.

Comisión had in fact attempted to sway NOW members in advance of the hearings. Over several discussions, Comisión board members—including Gloria Martínez, Evelyn Martínez, and Antonia Hernández—presented information from the LACMC case to persuade them to modify their position. Evelyn Martínez recalls this effort:

> We were trying to get support of the other women's organizations, feminist organizations, and I think we were also a little surprised that the support we just assumed would be there because we were all struggling for women's rights wasn't there. Again, it was like somebody threw cold water in your face. Wait a minute. We've all been struggling together for certain issues like equal pay and other things. Now why all of a sudden is this not an issue we can all stand together on? We found quickly that NOW was the group that said, "No, when we go in and want sterilization procedures, we don't want to wait 48 hours, we want it on demand." But that is what happened here. Women were being sterilized without their consent, consent forms being shoved in front of them in the middle of

labor, in English, a language they didn't understand and read, and they were just totally against that process. . . . Even to this day when I think of NOW, I always think of their not supporting this issue and we were always expected as Latinas to just jump on their bandwagon.[33]

Although NOW defended their concern that women might not have immediate access to the procedure if they desired it, they did agree to research the issue and consider changing their position—but they never did. Gloria Molina sums up the episode in this way:

They got more caught up in the remedy we were proposing than in the dilemma of the problem. We were in conflict right away, and we were sort of shocked because we really expected to be embraced by the feminist organizations and instead were rebuffed and basically told to find other solutions. . . . They didn't have a problem with the consent forms, they did have a problem with the counseling. At that time there was a feeling that counseling was to prevent someone from wanting to be sterilized, which is not what the counseling was supposed to be about. It was supposed to be about letting them know what it meant, educating them, and they didn't have time for that. They didn't want the thirty-day waiting period or the three-day waiting period. They just were not willing to compromise on any of it, and I've got to tell you that it was a real tough situation, feeling that here we are, feminist women together working on these issues and here's a group of women . . . who don't seem to understand our issues and aren't sympathetic.[34]

Because NOW and Comisión held fundamentally different stances on the right to have and not to have children, a lasting tension was born between the two groups.

Although they did not find the support from mainstream feminists that they had expected, Latina activists, along with other women of color, continued to fight for a woman's right to have children. Chicana spokespersons from grassroots, professional, advocacy, and health organizations each articulated the threat that sterilization abuse constituted to Mexican American communities. Many, if not all, referred to the sterilization abuse of women of Mexican origin as genocide, and some accused the state outright of being complicit in this genocide of the Chicano community. Elisa Sánchez, president of the Mexican American Women's National Association (MANA), told the hearing officers: "As minority women we are too painfully aware that this abuse has reached genocidal proportions. . . ."[35] Accordingly, each of the Latina representatives who spoke urged state officials to enact legislation that would guarantee the reproductive freedoms of Mexican-origin women and other women of color.[36]

For many, it was the first time they had ever spoken before such a body. Evelyn Martínez recollected her experience at the Los Angeles hearings:

> It was the first time I ever testified before any kind of jury, so I have to admit I was a little nervous. I wasn't sure what the reception would be from the elected officials. For me it was quite an intimidating process, but at the same time all we had to do is think back to the meetings we had with these women, and it gave me the courage and the strength to say, "It's our duty to speak up on their behalf and on behalf of other women who should not have experienced that kind of tragedy." I was nervous, no doubt about it. I'm glad Gloria was sitting next to me. I think we gave each other strength and courage.[37]

Despite their inexperience, their message rang loud and clear.

Comisión's president, Gloria Molina, most clearly faulted state governmental officials for the reproductive abuses committed against women of Mexican origin. During her testimony at the Los Angeles hearing, she told the committee that Chicanas desired to make their reproductive decisions without interference from the politicians, hospitals, and doctors who "felt it their responsibility to regulate the size of the Mexican family. We strongly advocate that it is each woman's right to decide the number of children she will bear."[38] Concha Saucedo, an employee at the Mission Neighborhood Health Center in San Francisco, also emphasized that this period of fighting for Latinas' reproductive rights was fundamentally about the right to have children. Speaking on behalf of the La Raza Mental Health Network of Northern California, the Mujeres Latinas Nation, and thirty other Latino health workers, she emphasized that "for Chicanos the issue is the assurance that our right to procreate will be respected and protected."[39] Other Latina spokeswomen testifying at the hearing repeatedly demanded the right to decide how many children they want without state interference. With this refrain, Latina women were defining access to reproduction as a basic human right.

In the end, the new regulations issued from the California State Department of Health acknowledged the input of those at the statewide hearings and were designed to ensure that a patient choosing sterilization would be supplied with sufficient information to make a decision under "legally effective informed consent."[40] The guidelines required that surgical sterilization candidates be formally advised that federal benefits, such as welfare, would be available to them whether they underwent sterilization or not. The guidelines also required that patients be thoroughly informed about the procedure, its risks, and permanence, and that sterilization candidates had to receive counseling on other forms of birth control. Moreover, the guidelines established a seventy-two-hour waiting period following consent and placed a federal ban on sterilization of girls under the age of eighteen.[41]

The MALDEF CRP would also spearhead the appeal of *Madrigal v. Quilligan* to the Ninth Circuit Court of Appeals. On October 19, 1979, the CRP filed their appeal, along with the Los Angeles Center for Law and Justice (which had filed the original case) and the Western Center for Law and Poverty. Carmen Estrada, a MALDEF attorney, stated that in the case of *Madrigal v. Quilligan,* the court "failed abysmally to recognize the helplessness" of the plaintiffs. Moreover, argued Estrada, the case pointed to "a much larger series of problems that amounts to abuse and neglect of women who do not speak English and depend largely on county hospitals for medical care."[42] Comisión also submitted an *Amici curiae* brief in the appeal, requesting that the *Madrigal* decision be reversed.[43] However, when the appeal was unsuccessful, MALDEF decided not to take the case further, perhaps in part because the legislative effects of the case had been so successful.

CONCLUSION

The combined individual and organizational efforts taken to stop sterilization abuse marked an unprecedented moment in Chicana history. First, the courage and strength of the ten plaintiffs who were willing to take action against LACMC, the state, and the country, must be recognized. Women who were taken advantage of because of their underprivileged status in society essentially challenged the medical establishment and the state government head on. Despite their understanding that such a case would not likely result in financial compensation, ten women were willing to come forward to discuss issues of great personal pain. Their willingness to address the court about the abuses they had experienced and the repercussions that involuntary sterilization had on their emotional well-being, their families, and their personal lives cannot be emphasized enough. By speaking out publicly during a time when the reproduction of women of Mexican origin was so openly reviled, these women who were coercively sterilized, along with their advocates, pushed for expanded discourse—nationally and within the Latino community—on reproductive health and sexuality. As a result, a very private issue became a matter of intense public debate. Their bravery inspired others to join together to change social policy so that others would not be similarly abused.

The efforts to halt sterilization brought health professionals, lawyers, community activists, and concerned Chicano citizens and their allies together, perhaps for the first time, to fight for the basic right of women of Mexican origin to have children. Members of Comisión Feminil Mexicana Nacional, the Chicana Welfare Rights Organization, the Chicana Rights Project of the Mexican American Legal Defense and Education fund, the Chicana Nurses Association, as well as other Chicana and Chicano health activists all played a critical role in organizing against forced sterilization. The public marches, the hearings, and the overall efforts to publicize the abuses were spearheaded by this Chicana leadership.

Moreover, this project brought Chicana activists further perspective on where and how they needed to mobilize. At the conclusion of the *Madrigal* trial, Georgina Torres-Rizk, a lawyer for the *Madrigal* plaintiffs, stated,

> It is minority women who must take it upon themselves to insure that their right to determine whether or not to bear children be preserved in order to halt the genocidal practices which are occurring in the name of "family planning" in this country. As minority women gain awareness of the problem and initiate organizational momentum, they themselves must begin to control the policies and administration of such governmental programs.

Torres-Rizk also noted that the case and surrounding activism "resulted in a growing awareness among Chicanas and their special needs and problems of this country and the understanding that they themselves are the most qualified to address themselves to these issues."[44]

As her statement highlights, at a time when their reproduction was under increased scrutiny by social scientists, the medical community, and others involved in population control efforts, Chicana activists directly responded to images circulating in public arenas about women of Mexican origin as breeders and developed a counter-discourse that stressed their unequivocal right to have children.

CHAPTER SEVEN

"BABY-MAKERS AND WELFARE TAKERS"

The (Not-So) New Politics of Mexican-Origin Women's Reproduction

Gobernar es poblar translates "to govern is to populate." In this society where the majority rules, does this hold? Will the present majority peaceably hand over its political power to a collection that is simply more fertile? . . . Can homo contraceptivus compete with homo progenitiva if borders aren't controlled? Or is advice to limit one's family simply advice to move over and let someone else with greater reproductive powers occupy the space? . . . Perhaps this is the first instance in which those with their pants up are going to get caught by those with their pants down!

On October 9, 1988, the *Arizona Republic* published the above confidential memo intended only for participants in a private study group concerned with the demographic changes occurring in the United States. The study group, convened by John H. Tanton, previous president of Zero Population Growth (zpg) and founder of both the Federation of American Immigration Reform (fair) and U.S. English, included distinguished academics, politicians, and lobbyists.[1] Having been a citizen-activist for over two decades, Tanton yearly assembled friends, contributors, and colleagues to discuss and develop strategies addressing what he considered to be the most pressing national matters of the day.

Inspired by *Population Change and California's Future* (1985), by Leon Bouvier and Philip Martin, Tanton dedicated that year's annual meeting (and the memo highlighting the meeting's talking points) to the "noneconomic consequences of immigration to California, and by extension, to the rest of the United States."[2] The lengthy WITAN memo outlined the impact of immigration on areas such as politics, culture, religion, race and class relations, and conservation.

Filled with racial anxiety and xenophobia reminiscent of the eugenic panic expressed at the turn of the century, the memo has since been called a "frank revival of race suicide theory."[3] In each section of the document, Tanton expressed his concern that the high fertility rate of Mexican immigrants threatened the assimilation of Mexicans in the United States and questioned the demographic impact of the migration. He was most worried about the cultural transformation that could occur across the nation as a result:

> Will Latin American migrants bring with them the tradition of *mordida* (bribery), the lack of involvement in public affairs, etc.? . . . How will we make the transition from a dominant non-Hispanic society with a Spanish influence to a dominant Spanish society with non-Hispanic influence? Is apartheid in Southern California's future? The demographic picture in South Africa now is startlingly similar to what we'll see in California in 2030. . . . Will there be strength in this diversity? Or will this prove a social and political San Andreas Fault? As Whites see their power and control over their lives declining, will they simply go quietly into the night? Or will there be an explosion?[4]

Tanton's semiprivate musings with his close colleagues forebode a more public nativist activism that was to become amplified at the turn of the twenty-first century. Occurring particularly, but not exclusively, in California, this era has been widely referred to as the most significant contemporary mobilization of nativist expression in recent times. Driven by what Javier Inda has called "racialized nativism," by the turn of the century, the hyper-fertile Mexican immigrant woman once again gained infamy as a social problem necessitating public action and governmental intervention.[5]

Set within a context of increasing government concern, during the 1990s the emergence of a formal structure around the study and containment of the fertility of Mexican-origin women was at hand. During this period, there were several notable developments in public opinion and governmental action directed at the reproductive patterns of Mexican immigrants.

1. Attention to the fertility of women of Mexican origin increased in the news media and public debate. Once a fact significant only to demographic specialists and some in the population and immigration control movements, the reproductive behaviors of Mexican-origin women was now a matter of general public interest. Among nativists,

the fertility of Mexican immigrant women had become deserving of the title "the most pressing matter of the day."

2. The fertility of Mexican-origin women had also now come under the consistent purview of the state (government). Differential fertility of immigrant women was a public policy issue.

3. There was a corresponding growing intelligence around the topic of Mexican-origin women's fertility; research studies, data, and reports, most of which were ordered or funded by state and federal government entities, were being conducted.

4. Increased public debate and discourse about Mexican-origin women's hyper-fertility occurred on many levels, from grassroots and membership organization groups to governmental debate and federal legislation hearings.

5. Legislation and other policies designed to limit the reproductive health care options of immigrant women was under development.

Most broadly stated, by the turn of the twenty-first century the reproduction of Mexican-origin women had become an established object of state purview and policy development. As such, their fertility gained legitimacy as an identifiable social problem to be remedied and a subject of public debate throughout the 1990s. Moreover, public concern was growing at the same time that legislative and social efforts to limit the reproductive autonomy of low income and immigrant women were being enacted. This chapter largely examines the parameters of this debate within the state of California, although parallel conversations and national policy increasingly echo these trends.

POPULATION, FISCAL, AND IMMIGRATION CRISIS: THE RETURN OF THE PREGNANT PILGRIM

While social analysts' attentions were directed to the increase in California's population during the 1970s, policymakers portended even more disastrous consequences for the state at the close of the twentieth century. Despite alarmists' warnings, however, California's population increase during the 1970s was minimal in actual numbers relative to the exponential growth of subsequent decades. By the end of 1989, the state had grown by 6.2 million to a total population of 29.5 million, a number higher than in any previous decade. In 1993 the State Department of Finance estimated that the total population of California was 31.3 million, doubling that of 1960.[6] Simultaneously facing tremendous growth and the largest state deficit in American history during the 1990s, many policymakers identified population expansion and the state's demographic transformation as the primary cause of its financial crisis and social ills. According to several analysts, much of the state's debt was attributable to an ever-growing number of residents reliant upon public services.

A widely publicized California Department of Finance study, *An Analysis of the 1990 Census in California*, reported that "for the first time in California's history, population growth, combined with demographic change, worsens rather than strengthens the economy."[7] According to the report, the state's budget woes boiled down to a few basic demographic phenomena: namely, the number of state residents using social services (such as welfare recipients, prisoners, students, and the elderly) was increasing at a rate substantially greater than the number of working-age Californians who pay taxes. According to Tony Quinn, the principal author of the report and analyst for then-governor Pete Wilson, "A growing 'user' class translates into greater need for social services at a time when the 'earners' who pay for them through taxes are dwindling."[8]

Fearing a dangerous decline in the generation of tax dollars and a growing state deficit,[9] many policymakers tried to ascertain exactly who comprised this "user class." Conservative social analysts quickly identified the primary culprit of the supposed resource drain: a 1993 report determined that it was, in fact, unprecedented numbers of immigrants arriving from less-developed nations who were depleting the state's social, economic, and natural resources.[10] Convinced that illegal immigrants were to blame for the state's fiscal crisis, some analysts advocated a quick and deliberate end to this so-called flood of immigration.[11]

To buttress their argument for population control, many state policymakers drew upon research studies that confirmed higher fertility rates among immigrant women. Assisted by increased data collection about their reproductive patterns, social analysts transformed the high fertility of Mexican-origin immigrant women from being merely suspect (as it was during the 1970s) to being a statistically verifiable culprit of the state's population increase late in the century. For example, in 1992 the California Department of Finance published data that calculated fertility rates of 1.74 for Anglos, 2.48 for blacks, 3.33 for Hispanics, and 2.15 for Asians. Given these apparent distinctions in racial fertility rates, the report concluded that the diverse racial character of the state's population is the primary reason for its anomalous growth:

Although between 1950 and 1980 fertility between California and the nation did merge, a sharp divergence began during the 1980's. While the nation's fertility was flat, fertility in California rose sharply. The majority of this divergence was due to California's greater race/ethnic diversity and the fertility differences among these groups.[12]

The proliferation of this new body of demographic research confirming the previously suspected higher fertility rates of immigrant women, coupled with data documenting the substantial cost of large-scale immigration to the state, fueled fears that led to the most significant contemporary mobilization of nativist expression in recent times.

Similar to the backlash experienced with the arrival of the European immigrants during the beginning of the twentieth century, the anti-immigration movement in California during the 1990s manifested nativist attitudes toward immigrant invasion and fiscal and cultural degeneracy.[13] These attitudes were not only readily visible in organized nativist circles, but among governmental officials and within national policy. For example, in a 1993 letter to President Bill Clinton published in several national newspapers, Governor Pete Wilson detailed his plan to end the "flood of illegal immigration" and warned readers to "make no mistake, our quality of life is threatened by this tidal wave."[14]

Bemoaning the "drain" on state resources caused by needy immigrants and their families,[15] anti-immigrant forces in California successfully initiated and fueled a series of restrictive proposals designed to deter undocumented immigrants by eliminating the free social services purportedly attracting them to the state.[16] The most restrictive manifestation of these anti-immigrant efforts was Proposition 187. Placed on the state ballot in November 1994, the referendum's provision barred undocumented immigrants from receiving public entitlements and services, including non-emergency health care, welfare, and public school education.[17] Contending that newly arriving immigrants and their families unduly rely on public services, the proponents of this "save our state" initiative claimed that such strong and deliberate measures were necessary to halt the "illegal alien invasion" that was overtaking California.

Some scholars have acknowledged that immigrant women and their children, in particular, are being targeted when measures such as Proposition 187 are drafted. Anthropologist Leo R. Chávez contends that such efforts at immigration control focus on restricting the reproduction of immigrant communities rather than on acknowledging and rewarding the productive work of immigrant labor.[18] Tamar Diana Wilson has further noted that a host of initiatives targeted at immigrants, such as the militarization of the border, the development of state legislation (e.g., Proposition 187) designed to deny undocumented workers and families social services, calls for the abrogation of the Fourteenth Amendment, and proposals for welfare reform "are related to the desire to re-separate the processes of production and re-production among the now more permanent Mexican labor force working in the U.S."[19]

In addition to contributing to the end of social reproduction of Mexican-origin communities by separating reproductive and productive labor, these policies also directly impact the way in which women experience access to and negotiation of reproductive health services.

THE CRIMINALIZATION OF PREGNANCY: THE ATTACK ON PRENATAL CARE

Some illegals come here simply to have a child born on U.S. soil. That, of course, renders the child eligible for a host of public benefits. . . . The 14th Amendment to the Constitution was never intended to be a reward for illegal immigration; it's time to change it.[20]

The above comment by Governor Pete Wilson was made amidst efforts to repeal the Fourteenth Amendment to the U.S. Constitution, which grants automatic citizenship to any child born within the borders of the United States. In 1995 members of Congress once again proposed legislation abrogating birthright citizenship, arguing that if newborns were not guaranteed U.S. citizenship (and thus a right to a host of social services), Mexican women would no longer illegally cross the border.[21] While introducing immigration reform legislation he co-authored, Elton Gallegly (R-California) informed his fellow congressional members that a measure denying birthright citizenship to illegal alien children was included to "discourage pregnant aliens from entering this country illegally in order to have their babies delivered free of charge and become U.S. citizens eligible for an array of benefits."[22]

The debates surrounding the issue of birthright citizenship (which I discuss in greater detail later in this chapter) illustrate the set of assumptions operating within contemporary discourse about the reproductive behavior of women of Mexican origin. According to such accounts, undocumented immigrant women from Mexico illegally cross the border to gain two benefits available in the United States: publicly funded prenatal care, and delivery and citizenship status for their children, which ensures access to social services. Moreover, as Gallegly's comments indicate, there is widespread belief that "pregnant aliens" crossing the border to secure citizenship benefits for their American-born children is a common occurrence, one necessitating government intervention—indeed, a social problem that someone should do something about.[23]

Efforts to eradicate the Fourteenth Amendment were being advanced to alleviate this problem at the federal level, and corresponding attempts have been made in the state of California since the mid- to late 1990s. Within debates over the fiscal cost of immigrants to the state of California, the expense of providing health care services to undocumented immigrants arose as a particular area of contention. At the very beginning of his tenure in 1991, Wilson asked President Clinton to reimburse California for the $534 million it had purportedly expended for the provision of health care to undocumented immigrants.[24] Additionally, while all health care to undocumented immigrants was being considered for revocation, Wilson touted the provision of reproductive health services to undocumented immigrant women as one of the most serious problems facing California. When asked to delineate his main gubernatorial concerns in 1993, Wilson instantly raised the issue, expressing the problem this way: "We are required to provide prenatal care, obstetrics, delivery, and postnatal care to illegals. I asked the Legislature for the same kind of care for working-poor mothers—women who are not eligible to receive Medicaid and [they] cannot give me the funding because we are spending almost $3 billion on various services for illegals."[25] Referring to a 1992 state study that reported that births to undocumented immigrants represented 40 percent of all publicly funded births in the state, Wilson repeatedly argued that provision of prenatal care services cost California taxpayers $3 billion a year.[26]

The provision of prenatal services to immigrant women gained substantial public attention, aided in no small part by Wilson's identification of it as a top governmental priority. Proponents of Proposition 187 customarily cited the report from 1991 stating that two-thirds of newborns at Los Angeles County hospitals were born to undocumented women; this statistic became a benchmark of the initiative and of Wilson's efforts to pass it. One concerned citizen's letter, published in the Los Angeles Times in 1995, read: "Illegal-immigrant advocates who claim that illegals come here for jobs must not have seen the latest statistics out of County-USC Hospital: Close to 70 percent of all births there are to illegal immigrants, and more than 40 percent of those babies immediately exercise their 'rights' as U.S. citizens and are signed up for the cradle-to-grave government goodie bag known as welfare." [27]

While the controversy surrounding Proposition 187 undeniably focused attention on the public funding of undocumented immigrants' reproductive health care, Wilson took aggressive steps to stop providing these services to immigrant women even before the initiative went to vote. Estimating that discontinuation of the services to undocumented immigrants would save the state $92 million a year, Wilson simply eliminated this item from the 1994 state budget. [28] Although these proposed budget cuts were never passed by the state legislature, Wilson proposed the same cuts in subsequent years. [29]

The upsurge of public attention incited by Wilson's efforts to end pre-natal care to undocumented immigrant women was well covered in the media. Dozens of accounts in major metropolitan newspapers attested to the "widespread" phenomena of Mexican women illegally crossing the border to deliver their children on U.S. soil. Such stories, which relied heavily on interviews with medical providers in border area hospitals, recounted the "common knowledge" that pregnant women from Mexico illegally crossed the border to guarantee a U.S. birth certificate (and thus the social services afforded to U.S. citizens) for their child. [30] According to Sally Super, the head nurse in a maternity ward five miles from the border, "We know the big magnet to come across [the border] is the U.S. birth certificate. All you have to do is ask them." [31]

Proponents of ending the availability of these services readily reported stories of Mexican women who surreptitiously planned migration to the United States around an upcoming delivery. For example, in February 1994 the San Diego Union-Tribune ran a multi-article series titled "Born in the USA." [32] Together the articles accentuated the problematic nature of the is-sue, running under headlines such as "Births to Illegal Immigrants on the Rise: California Taxpayers Finance Soaring Numbers of Foreigners' Babies" and "Blockade at Border Hasn't Cut Births." The latter article detailed the efforts of a hospital in El Paso, Texas, to measure whether strict enforcement of the border resulted in a measurable decrease in the number of Mexican immigrants "abusing" medical services. Despite reports that enforced bor-der control provided no decline in the number of undocumented immi-grant deliveries at the hospital, the newspaper story ended with the follow-ing vignette:

The afternoon of April 29, as they patrolled the Rio Grande, [two bor-der patrol] agents were flagged down by migrants who led them to a riverbank. Her feet still wet from the crossing, Sara Hernández Nuñez was in labor and unable to move. The agents called for help, but before paramedics arrived, they had to take matters into their own hands. They delivered a healthy boy—by birthright, a U.S. citizen.[33]

This series of articles, along with several others published in major metropolitan newspapers in southern California, brought widespread attention to pregnant women of Mexican origin as a bona fide public problem. The issue was sometimes presented as approximating organized crime in its clandestine yet organized nature. One nurse manager of the maternity ward at Sharp-Chula Vista Medical Center in San Diego surmised, "We believe there's an underground out there, where people are coached on how to get into the system."[34] The prevalence and nature of this imagery—i.e., a trail of women who come to the United States to "drop their babies"—in the mainstream media helped feed negative opinion in the larger public domain.

In addition to Proposition 187, other measures were undertaken to counter the perceived pandemic. In San Diego County, officials from the Department of Health discontinued Spanish-language television ads promoting Baby Cal (the state-funded perinatal services available to low-income women) on public radio in the border region, fearing that the program would encourage soon-to-be mothers from Mexico to deliver and raise their children in the United States.[35]

Scare tactics were sometimes used to discourage pregnant, undocumented women from seeking health care for themselves and their unborn babies. At the McAllen Medical Center in Texas, private security guards wearing green uniforms resembling those of the U.S. Border Patrol were posted at the hospital entrance to frighten and thereby dissuade undocumented immigrants from seeking care.[36]

The most assertive and widespread reaction to the perceived problem, however, was voter approval of Proposition 187 in California by a 3:2 margin in November 1994. While the initiative eliminated a host of social services, Wilson's very first action on the day following the election was to issue an executive order barring the continuation of prenatal services to undocumented immigrant women.[37] By mandating that medical practitioners report patients unable to provide documentation of their citizenship status to the immigration authorities, the passage of Proposition 187 had immediate repercussions for undocumented women seeking prenatal care. Although the governor's executive order was almost immediately suspended until its constitutionality could be determined, in the months following this decree many undocumented women stopped their prenatal appointments for fear they would be reported to immigration by clinic personnel.[38]

"EL NIÑO HYSTERIA"

While Proposition 187 was immediately enjoined by court order and eventually overturned in 1998, Wilson maintained efforts to deny reproductive health services to Mexican immigrant women and was vastly assisted in his cause by an overhaul of federal welfare law in 1996. Initiated and signed by President Clinton, the Personal Responsibility Work Opportunity and Reconciliation Act (PRWORA, P.L. 104-193) was passed on August 22, 1996. While this reform of the country's welfare system had many repercussions in its own right, it also had significant ramifications in terms of the availability of services to immigrants as states were ultimately granted the power to decide whether undocumented and documented immigrants were eligible for welfare benefits.[39] In its original configuration, which fundamentally legislated a dramatic reduction in legal immigrants' eligibility for welfare, the elimination of public benefits accounted for half of the federal savings expected to be generated by the reformed welfare law.[40]

Speculations that immigrants' benefits were at the center of these relatively recent welfare reform efforts are confirmed not only by the elimination of immigrants' eligibility for public services, but by the outright admission of many policymakers that welfare reform and immigration control are fundamentally connected. Consider, for example, the following statement by Congressman Michael Bilirakis during congressional deliberations on the welfare reform bill:

> Let me speak for a moment about illegal aliens. Illegal immigration is breaking our treasury, burdening California, and trying America's patience. It is wrong for our welfare system to provide lavish benefits for persons in America violating our laws. I am proud that the Personal Responsibility and Work Opportunity Act ends welfare for illegal aliens. It ends eligibility for Government programs for illegal aliens. It ends the taxpayer-funded red carpet for illegal aliens. Our plan is to send a clear message to those who jump our borders, violate our laws, and reside in America illegally: Go home.[41]

Bilirakis's testimony clearly shows how the denial of services via welfare reform was in many ways consistent with removing the lure that attracted undocumented immigrants to the United States.[42] In fact, although one widely cited study argued that the availability of public benefits was unduly influencing immigrants' decision to migrate to the United States,[43] other research debates the strength of the social service magnet purportedly luring immigrants across the border.[44]

In California, Governor Wilson proclaimed the new federal welfare legislation "an act of vindication" and a victory for his efforts to terminate state aid to undocumented immigrants. Five days after the law was signed, he issued an executive order eliminating public services to those not able to provide proof of legal citizenship. While Wilson's edict ended undocumented immigrants' access to a range of public benefits, only prenatal care restrictions immediately fell prey to his mandate, which was consistent with his past course of action.[45] The following week, Wilson's office ordered county government and health care agencies to cease providing prenatal care to women unable to provide proof of legal citizenship.[46] Arguing that the new federal welfare law mandated that the state discontinue benefits to "illegal aliens" as quickly as possible, Wilson issued emergency regulations in November 1996, ending prenatal care services by the first of the following month.[47] Similar to the passage of and mandates following Proposition 187, the mere publicity of Wilson's edict led to a sharp decline in patients seeking prenatal services.[48]

In the end, a policy to end prenatal care for undocumented immigrant women was prevented by the organized response of immigrants' rights groups, civil rights lawyers, and concerned health practitioners. Responding to the Department of Health Services' promise that such measures would be "imminently" enacted, a coalition of immigrant rights groups filed an unsuccessful restraining order blocking Wilson's efforts. Several counties, including San Francisco County, promised continued provision of prenatal care to undocumented immigrant women despite the termination of state funding.[49] State and local medical associations also condemned Wilson's plans, arguing that the denial of prenatal care to undocumented immigrant women would actually result in greater taxpayer expenses due to greater infant mortality, birth complications, low birth weight, disability, and emergency room deliveries.[50] The implementation of the state's plan to deny prenatal care to immigrant women was challenged continuously over the next two years by a series of court rulings and remained derailed throughout Wilson's tenure.[51] When Gray Davis replaced Wilson as governor in 1999, he modified Wilson's proposed state budget, allocating $60 million for prenatal care for undocumented immigrant women, and eventually signed a budget bill authorizing a state-funded prenatal care program for undocumented women.[52]

CONCLUSION

Although eventually squashed, Proposition 187 and Wilson's subsequent efforts to deny prenatal care to undocumented immigrant women served as important and lasting political catalysts, attracting and focusing public attention on the problem of undocumented pregnant immigrants. At a time when California was facing greater population growth and financial strain than ever before, the heightened attention directed toward undocumented women of Mexican origin placed them in the spotlight as easy targets of blame. Then-governor Wilson's role in promoting the eradication of prenatal care for immigrant women points to a much broader movement within which such actions were nurtured and condoned. These ideas about undocumented Mexican women were further propagated and legitimized through their integration into state policy issues and substantive legislative efforts to discourage Mexican immigrant women from reproducing. Indeed, public discourse about pregnant, undocumented Mexican women was an integral component of legislative efforts to end state funding for their prenatal care, which in effect did prohibit some women from receiving prenatal care and other reproductive health services.

Moreover, the discourse surrounding the politics of the fertility of women of Mexican origin took place in and between multiple social sites—from the rhetoric of governmental officials to that of organized nativists, to more underground efforts such as the circulation of nativist propaganda. Consider the following excerpt from a flyer distributed in student mailboxes, over e-mail, and to the general public during the months when the Proposition 187 controversy raged: "America has a serious problem. Low-life Mexicans are streaming into our society and polluting our cultural landscape. . . . These vermin are popping up from the sewers of Mexico and siphoning money from our welfare system. They keep insisting that American taxpayers pay for their unrestrained breeding habits." [53]

Written in 1995 by a group identified only as Students Against the Brown Peril, this chilling statement determinedly identifies the growth of the Mexican population as a result of the "breeding" habits of Mexican-origin women. The authors propose that a necessary corrective is to "sterilize Mexican illegals" and "send the smelly, dirty little rats back to Mexico where they belong." [54] Unabashedly constructing Mexican women as prolific and burdensome "breeders," the authors of this nativist propaganda conjure a historical legacy of coercion regarding the reproductive behavior of Mexican-origin women.

The actual impact of legislation and discourse on the reproductive health of Mexican-immigrant women is not always explicit or measurable, but it does appear that these efforts have discouraged their and other immigrants' pursuit of health care services. Several studies have documented the decline in immigrant usage of social services since the late 1990s, partially attributable to the chilling effect of welfare legislation. Fix and Passel's analysis of the 1995 and 2000 Current Population Surveys revealed significant declines in legal immigrants' use of all major benefit programs between 1994 and 1999 nationwide. In particular, use of Temporary Assistance for Needy Families decreased by 60 percent, and Medicaid usage decreased 15 percent. Moreover, low-income, working-age noncitizens exhibited a much larger decline in Medicaid usage rates than their counterparts with citizenship.[55] Their data suggest that these changes cannot be attributed to individuals' completion of the naturalization process or increased incomes, and must be considered part of the legislation's efficacy in deterring immigrant usage of social services.[56] Moreover, Grace Chang's research with immigrant women has demonstrated that women often consume these images themselves, constructing themselves in opposition to such myths and images. In so doing they can often serve as gatekeepers and promoters of the very images that constrict their lives.[57]

These changes also impacted the delivery of health care services to pregnant immigrant women. In a 2000 study, Lisa Sun-Hee Park and her colleagues found that the Personal Responsibility and Work Opportunity Reform Act of 1996 served to directly limit immigrants' use of pregnancy services in California. Interviews with government officials, health care providers, and immigrant advocates showed that even though legal challenges to the implementation of welfare reform guaranteed that immigrants would still receive Medi-Cal coverage for pregnancy-related services, "the policy implementations of welfare and immigration reforms have created a chilling effect that has discouraged the use of Medicaid by immigrants who are legally eligible in California."[58]

One community clinic director shared her experiences with a client:

There was one woman who had come in asking, can we assure that she is going to be able to access Medi-Cal during her pregnancy and also after her pregnancy. I am guessing that she was concerned about public charge issues. She was saying that we have to be able to assure her that she would be able to be eligible for Medi-Cal and [that] it would not have any negative repercussions. Otherwise she was going to have an abortion. She was asking us to tell her what to do.[59]

Thus, even if legislation such as Proposition 187 is ultimately not implemented, it still creates a context within which Mexican immigrant women make reproductive choices. This goes beyond a decline in the number of low income, pregnant immigrant women utilizing prenatal care; when faced with losing her welfare relief or being deported if she bears another child, many women choose to limit their childbearing.

The picture of immigrant (read: Mexican) women at the turn of the twenty-first century was at the front and center of several significant political reforms being proposed at this time. Proposition 187, Governor Wilson's efforts to deny prenatal care to immigrant women, attempts to repeal the Fourteenth Amendment to the U.S. Constitution, and current welfare reforms, then, can be considered part of a much longer historical trajectory of the social construction of women of Mexican origin as hyper-fertile breeders needing restriction and requiring containment. I have shown here that in its most recent forms, such interests have developed a formal structure of intellectual and governmental inquiry for the study, analysis, and containment of immigrant women's fertility.

EPILOGUE

LEGACIES: JOSEPH RODRÍGUEZ

Just over thirty years after the case of *Madrigal v. Quilligan* was tried, reporter Fransizka Castillo wrote an essay about the anniversary of the case, published in *Latina* magazine. Included to celebrate Hispanic Heritage Month, the four-page spread focused on the valiant efforts of Antonia Hernández and Comisión Femenil, the Chicana professionals who undertook the fight, rather than specifically detailing the abuses that occurred at Los Angeles County Medical Center.[1] Although Rodríguez originally pitched the story to make links to current coercive sterilization in Peru, she was ultimately forced to eliminate most of the details of the abuse that occurred at LACMC because *Latina* editors thought it would be too depressing for the magazine's readers. I met Joseph Rodríguez through Fransizka. He is the son of Helena Orozco, one of the plaintiffs in the *Madrigal* trial. Having been unable to locate any of the *Madrigal* plaintiffs over the ten years of research I had done on the case, I was eager to talk to Joseph, and he was immediately forthcoming.

When we met in a pizza place in Pico Rivera, California, just miles from LACMC, I learned that Joseph had also been born at the hospital, before his younger brother, who would be his mother's last child. He was fourteen years old and living in La Puente when, according to Joseph, his mother began going to a lot of meetings. Although reticent to discuss it, she eventually told him that she was going to participate in a suit against the doctors at LACMC and that she might have to go to trial. She explained that the doctors had "done something bad" to her and that she might have to testify before a judge. Joseph clearly remembered that one of his mother's greatest concerns was that she did not want to be publicly recognized. "She told me that she didn't want to show her face on camera. She would cover it when the press was outside the courtroom. I don't know why she did that."[2]

Frank Cruz, a young Chicano reporter—the only newsperson who covered the trial in its entirety—similarly recollected that the *Madrigal v. Quilligan* plaintiffs refused to be publicly interviewed. He encouraged them to speak on camera of their experiences at LACMC, stressing that it could help people see how horrible these events had been. A few eventually agreed to be interviewed, but only when Cruz promised that the camera would focus on him rather than on them. Like Helena Orozco, all of the plaintiffs in *Madrigal* participated in the lawsuit despite the public humiliation they feared. Moreover, most clearly recognized that it was unlikely that the case would result in any financial remuneration, even if the case was won.

When the case was eventually lost, however, young Joseph saw his mother's emotional and mental health decline. He blames her sterilization for the "downhill slope" that characterized his family's life from then onward.

It was one bad thing after another. First they sterilized her under duress, trying to lie, and then they go to court with many of them thinking they might make this right, and then all of a sudden the doctors get away with what they did. Now she can't have any more children, but nothing happened to the people who did this to her and the others. It was just one bad thing after another. Her life turned for the worse.[3]

I was curious about how a young boy would understand such an event in his mother's life, and asked Joseph directly why he thought his mother was coercively sterilized. He thought for a moment, and said, "Deep down they probably just didn't want any more Mexicans having babies."[4] Surprised at his blunt response, I asked him to explain. A youth during the Chicano Movement, Joseph saw a clear connection between the social activism he witnessed and the abuse his mother faced:

In the '60s and in the '70s, or at least when I was a child, I sensed like it was like a Chicano uprising. All the injustices that were done to the Mexican American culture, the Mexican culture, we'd had enough. I just think that the system or the Anglo people wanted to do something to stop the Mexicans from having so many babies and this was just another one of their vicious ideas of doing wrong to the Mexican people, just another way to hurt us.[5]

Joseph spoke at length on the repression of Mexican Americans that he continues to see in the United States today. He told me that he wanted to speak about his mother's story because he feels that similar abuses are occurring now. As I've documented in this book, the reproduction of women of Mexican origin is being subjected to public scrutiny now more than ever before.

ILLEGAL IMMIGRATION: THE NATIONAL DEBATE

No sooner did news headlines announce that Latinos had become the largest ethnic group in the nation than immigration reform became the number one public policy issue in the United States. As the House and Senate debated, activists across the nation organized the largest pro-immigration marches the nation had ever seen.

At the same time that national debate over immigration policy is at a height, census figures reveal that fertility is in fact the major factor in Latino population growth. Just days after pro-immigrant marches occurred across the country on May 1, 2006, the Census Bureau reported that birthrates contribute more to Latino population growth than does immigration from Mexico.[6] The politicization of Mexican-origin women's fertility continues to be a central aspect of contemporary nativism and mainstream efforts to curb immigration policy.

ANCHOR BABIES, THE THREAT TO AMERICAN MEDICINE, AND THE FOURTEENTH AMENDMENT

More recent incarnations of the construction of Mexican-origin women's hyper-fertility as a social problem now include more directly criminalizing their progeny. In particular, politicians and immigration reformers have new concerns about Mexican women birthing children on U.S. soil. Claims that Mexican women come to the United States to gain birthright for their children have led to proposed legislation that would overturn the Fourteenth Amendment, which grants citizenship to all children born in the United States.

The term "anchor babies" (sometimes referred to as "jackpot babies") has been coined to refer to children born to undocumented mothers in the United States. Although critics point out that U.S. citizenship makes one eligible to sponsor the legal immigration of relatives, sponsorship is not allowable until after one is twenty-one years of age. Nevertheless, the newly born child becomes the U.S. "anchor" for an extended immigrant family.

For many proponents of immigration restriction, so-called anchor babies represent a fundamental example of the failure in current U.S. immigration policy. In the past decade or so, Congress has yearly considered measures that would change the U.S. Constitution's promise of birthright citizenship. In February 2005, Congressman Nathan Deal (R-Georgia), along with eighty-seven cosponsors, proposed H.R. 698, the "Citizenship Reform Act," to deny citizenship rights to children born of undocumented immigrants. This legislation was referred to a subcommittee in March 2005.[7] Similar legislation continues to be promoted.

Immigration concerns have once again moved from being primarily those of nativists and their sympathizers to entering mainstream American medical policy. An article by Madeleine Pelner Cosner, "Illegal Aliens and American Medicine," in the spring 2005 issue of the *Journal of American Physicians and Surgeons* blamed childbearing immigrants for forcing many hospitals to close. Cosner identified this as an escalating problem, writing that "Illegal aliens' stealthy assaults on medicine now must rouse Americans to alert and alarm."[8] Her language positions illegal immigrants as a disease, attacking the medical system and, therefore, the health of the nation.

The most menacing aspect of this illegal illness, according to Cosner, is the pregnant immigrant: "American hospitals welcome anchor babies. Illegal alien women come to the hospital in labor and drop their little anchors, each of whom pulls its illegal alien mother, father, and siblings into permanent residency simply by being born within our borders."[9]

At the same time, recent studies show that Mexican immigrants face serious health deficiencies and disparities. Erosion of prenatal care access continues. In 2001, a federal appeals court reversed a 1987 ruling requiring the government to provide prenatal care for undocumented immigrants. The ruling resulted in the denial of prenatal care to 13,000 undocumented immigrants in New York state that year.[10]

Mexican-origin women and other Latinas face a host of reproductive health disparities and are among those who most often report dissatisfaction with their health care providers. The fact that racial stereotypes impact medical treatment and help perpetuate health care disparities was recently acknowledged by the National Institute of Medicine. An extensive report cites evidence that "bias, prejudice, and stereotyping on the part of health-care providers may contribute to differences in care."[11]

CONTROLLING IMAGES

As I have detailed throughout this book, the links between the controlling image of Mexican-origin women as "breeders" and social policies that shape women's reproductive realities can significantly impact people's lives and, in fact, negatively affect entire communities. Although I have focused on sites where the discourse about Mexican-origin women's fertility and reproduction has originated and fermented, these are only examples of what can happen when such ideas become part of more encompassing political projects and social legislation. Individual attitudes that Mexican women "breed like rabbits" and legislation that focuses on "anchor babies" both identify the reproduction of Mexican-origin women as problematic.

Saying that Mexican-origin women are the problem is utilizing the classic move of placing blame upon individual behavior rather than identifying and eliminating the real, ongoing inequities in access to social service providers and health care. Operating with this sort of mentality gears policy toward changing the behavior of individuals rather than aiming for changes within the larger system, such as redistribution of resources, leaving ample room for individual coercion and the implementation of abusive policies.

Moreover, controlling images belie the realities of the reproductive politics of women of Mexican origin. First, the stereotype of baby-makers eclipses the actual obstacles many women of Mexican origin have faced while trying to bear and rear healthy children in the United States. As I have shown throughout this book and elsewhere, the reproduction of women of Mexican origin has been fundamentally shaped by the context of racial and class domination within which they bear children.[12] In addition, women of Mexican origin have had severely limited access to safe, affordable prenatal care and other resources required to raise healthy children. The condescending and classist identification of Mexican women as hyper-fertile baby machines obscures how social pressures within the United States may have infringed on the rights of women of Mexican origin to have as many children as they may want. In addition, the stereotype of women of Mexican origin as careless "breeders" disregards the efforts of activists who have worked hard to achieve a wide range of safe, affordable, health care options for their communities.[13]

The activism of Chicana feminists in the 1970s in response to sterilization abuse was indeed a direct forebearer to contemporary Latina reproductive rights organizing. Assertions of the right to have children continue to be at the center of Latina reproductive health agendas. Today several organizations, such as the National Latina Institute for Reproductive Health, as well as local, community-based groups direct their efforts toward improving the reproductive health of their communities. These efforts are needed more than ever.[14]

With the nomination of ultraconservative Judge Samuel Alito to the Supreme Court in 2006, and the abolition of virtually all abortion procedures in South Dakota (with increasing numbers of similarly draconian laws being passed in many other states), all women are facing more limited reproductive options than those of the previous generation. While the reproductive freedom of all women is in jeopardy, circumstances are particularly stark for low-income women of color. Reproductive justice organizing must be informed by reexaminations of the way we think about having children in the United States. Moreover, we must increase our efforts to enable those women who want to have multiple children to do so, free of government-imposed barriers and racialized stereotypes that limit their ability to experience true reproductive justice.

NOTES

CHAPTER ONE

1. Trial transcript, 828, *Madrigal v. Quilligan* (C.D. Cal., 7 June 1978) (No. CV-75-2057-EC). Trial transcript and other case pleadings are available in the Carlos Vélez-Ibañez Sterilization Archives, Chicano Studies Library, University of California, Los Angeles (hereafter referred to as Vélez Archives).

2. The first line of the complaint reads, "This is a suit against State officials and others acting under color of state law to redress the violation of the plaintiffs' constitutional right to procreate and their constitutional right to due process of law." Plaintiffs' First Amended Complaint, *Madrigal v. Quilligan* (C.D. Cal., 25 November 1975) (No. CV-75-2057-EC), p. 1, Vélez Archives.

3. Plaintiffs' Proposed Findings of Fact and Conclusions of Law, *Madrigal v. Quilligan* (C.D. Cal., 22 June 1978) (No. CV-75-2057-EC), Vélez Archives.

4. Antonia Hernández, Charles Nabarette, and Karen Benker each reported to me that several other staff members corroborated Dr. Benker's story. Although willing to speak "off the record," they feared retribution and the permanent loss of a job in medicine if they were involved in the case. Hernández, Nabarette, and Benker interviews.

5. National Council of La Raza (NCLR), *Beyond the Census.*

6. U.S. Bureau of the Census, Census 2000 Redistricting Data.

7. U.S. Bureau of the Census, March 2002 Current Population Survey.

8. National Center for Health Statistics, *Births of Hispanic Origin, 1989–1995.*

9. For example, see Melissa Healy, "Latina Teens Defy Decline in Birth Rates," *Los Angeles Times,* 13 February 1998, sec. A, p. 1.

10. "Family Disunification," *National Review,* 9 March 1998, p. 20.

11. Daniel P. Moynihan's 1965 report is infamous as a classic example of victim-blaming. See Moynihan, "The Negro Family: The Case for National Action." See also Baca Zinn, "Family, Feminism, and Race in America," for commentary on the significance of Moynihan's report and a critique of the deficiency model upon which it is proposed. See also Briggs, "I Like to Be in America," chap. 6 of *Reproducing Empire.*

12. See Briggs, *Reproducing Empire;* Gutiérrez, "We Will No Longer be Silent or Invisible."

13. López, "Agency and Constraint."

14. López, "An Ethnography," 243.

15. Perea, *Immigrants Out!* For a succinct but thorough review of nativism in the United States, see Feagin, "Old Poison in New Bottles."

16. "Immigrant Bashing: Beware Statistics Bearing Bias," *Arizona Republic,* 3 November 1993, sec. B, p. 6.

17. See Lindsley, "The Gendered Assault on Immigrants"; Wilson, "Anti-Immigrant Sentiment and the Problem of Reproduction/Maintenance in Mexican Immigration to the United States"; and Inda, "Biopower, Reproduction, and the Migrant Women's Body." See also Chávez, "Immigration Reform and Nativism," for his argument that Proposition 187 targeted "reproduction while ignoring production" as a means of deterring the maintenance of family systems yet continuing the exploitation of immigrant labor. This tactic, Chávez explains, accounts for the proposition's goal of halting services that would specifically impact the health, education, and well-being of immigrant women and their children.

18. Hondaganeu-Sotelo, "Unpacking 187."

19. Montejano, "On the Future of Anglo-Mexican Relations in the United States." See also Perea, *Immigrants Out!* for various analyses of anti-immigrant sentiment, organizing for English-only legislation, and other forms that these xenophobic postures have taken.

20. Hanson, *Mexifornia,* xii.

21. Ibid., 10–11.

22. Huntington, *Who Are We?*

23. Chang, "Undocumented Latinas"; Hondaganeu-Sotelo, "Women and Children First" and "Unpacking 187"; and Chávez, "Immigration Reform and Nativism."

24. Irving, *Immigrant Mothers,* 3.

25. Spector and Kitsuse, *Constructing Social Problems;* Gusfield, *The Culture of Public Problems;* Nathanson, *Dangerous Passage.*

26. Spector and Kitsuse, *Constructing Social Problems.*

27. Goode and Ben-Yehuda, "Moral Panics."

28. Gusfield, *The Culture of Public Problems,* 8.

29. Andrade, "Social Science Stereotypes of Mexican American Women," 238.

30. I provide further analysis of sociological research on Mexican-origin women's fertility in chapter 4.

31. Ginsburg and Rapp, "The Politics of Reproduction," 332. Ann Anagost similarly notes that "population is first and foremost a discursive category" ("A Surfeit of Bodies," 39).

32. Purvis and Hunt, "Discourse, Ideology," 497.

33. Omi and Winant, *Racial Formation in the United States.*

34. Ibid., 55–56, emphasis in original.

35. Omi and Winant note, "A vast web of racial projects mediates between the discursive or representational means in which race is identified and signified on the one hand, and the institutional and organizational forms in which it is routinized and standardized on the other" (ibid., 60).

36. Kuumba, "Perpetuating Neo-Colonialism Through Population Control"; Collins, "Shifting the Center," 45–65, and "Will the 'Real' Mother Please Stand Up?"; Williams, "Babies and Banks"; Roberts, "Who May Give Birth to Citizens?"; See Davis, "Racism, Birth Control, and Reproductive Rights," for one of the first published analyses of reproductive rights that included a racial framework; see also Shapiro, *Population Control Politics*; and Ginsburg and Rapp, *Conceiving the New World Order*.

37. See Davis, "Racism, Birth Control, and Reproductive Rights" and "Surrogates and Outcast Mothers: Racism and Reproductive Politics." Also see Mullings, "Households Headed by Women"; Collins, "Will the 'Real' Mother Please Stand Up?" 272–273; Solinger, *Wake Up Little Susie*; Silliman et al., *Undivided Rights*.

38. Roberts, *Killing the Black Body*, 8.

39. Collins, *Black Feminist Thought*, chap. 4; Mullings, "Images, Ideology, and Women of Color."

40. Collins, *Black Feminist Thought*, p. 85, and "Shifting the Center." See also Roberts, *Killing the Black Body*, 10–20.

41. Mullings, "Images, Ideology, and Women of Color"; Collins, "Will the 'Real' Mother Please Stand Up?"

42. Castañeda, "Engendering the History of Alta California, 1769–1848." Also see Castañeda, "The Political Economy of Nineteenth Century Stereotypes of Californianas."

43. "Perils of the Mexican Invasion," *North American Review* (May 1929): 616.

44. George Horace Lorimer, "The Mexican Conquest," *Saturday Evening Post*, 22 June 1939, p. 26; cited in Ruiz, *From Out of the Shadows*, 28.

45. Montejano, *Anglos and Mexicans in the Making of Texas, 1836–1986*, 180.

46. Quoted in Stern, *Eugenic Nation*, 208–209.

47. For a thorough discussion see Stern, *Eugenic Nation*.

48. Ruiz, *From Out of the Shadows*, 38; Sanchez, "'Go After the Women'"; Deutsch, *No Separate Refuge*.

49. Sanchez, "'Go After the Women,'" 255.

50. Ibid.; also see Deutsch, *No Separate Refuge*.

51. Ruiz, *From Out of the Shadows*, 38.

52. Sanchez, "'Go After the Women,'" 258.

53. Andrade, "Social Science Stereotypes of Mexican American Women," 229; Baca Zinn, "Mexican American Women in the Social Sciences."

54. Zavella, "Reflections on Diversity Among Chicanas, 73–84; "Talkin' Sex"; and "'Playing with Fire.'" See also Segura and Pesquera, "Beyond Indifference and

Antipathy" and "Chicana Feminisms"; Gonzales-López, *Erotic Journeys*; Hurtado, *Voicing Chicana Feminisms*.

55. Hurtado, *Voicing Chicana Feminisms*, 10.

56. Collins, *Black Feminist Thought*.

CHAPTER TWO

1. Gordon, *Women's Body, Women's Right*, 387.

2. Shapiro, *Population Control Politics*; Hodgson, "Orthodoxy and Revisionism in American Demography," 541–569; Gordon, *Women's Body, Women's Right*; and Greenhaulgh, "The Social Construction of Science." While population concerns have been relevant throughout history, the topic has not often entered formal political discourse. One notable exception is the report *Problems of a Changing Population*, submitted to President Roosevelt in 1938 as a study of the *decreasing* rates of population growth and its possible consequences given the nation's continued economic stagnation. See Westhoff, "United States," 740–742, for a discussion. As Westhoff notes, "the committee was especially sensitive to the problems of differential fertility—the negative relationship between rates of production and the level of cultural-intellectual development" (741). However, discussion about U.S. population growth in the second half of the century marks a significant transition from fears of *underpopulation* of certain groups to concerns about *overpopulation* of others.

3. Piotrow, *World Population Crisis*, xi.

4. Piotrow, *World Population Crisis*.

5. Wilmoth and Ball, "Arguments and Action in the Life of A Social Problem, 332.

6. Hartmann, *Reproductive Rights and Wrongs: The Global Politics of Population Control*, 104. A long historical link existed between demographers and issues of population control. According to Linda Gordon (*Women's Body, Women's Right*), "In the 1940s the OPR became a center for eugenicist demographers. Kingsley Davis, Frank Notestein, Dudley Kirk, and Frank Lorimer all worked there" (389).

7. Population Council, *Population*, 5–6.

8. Because my focus is the development of a population policy for the United States, I do not discuss population control efforts in underdeveloped countries or "early" U.S. interest in these issues further. For detailed analyses of U.S. population efforts in the third world, see Symonds and Carder, *The United Nations and the Population Question, 1945–1970*; Piotrow, *World Population Crisis*; Demerath, *Birth Control and Foreign Policy*; and Johnson, *World Population and the United Nations*.

9. The groups of individuals involved in creating the discourse about population growth and policy during this period have been referred to as "the population establishment" or "population coalition." For an interesting analysis of the various interest groups involved in the population movement in the United States during the latter half of the twentieth century, see Bachrach and Bergman, *Power and Choice*.

10. Population control did enter into formal government discourse with the publication of the Draper report in 1958, which considered its implications for economic growth. See Lader, *Breeding Ourselves to Death*, 15; and Hartmann, *Reproductive Rights and Wrongs*, 105–106. Although this was the first time that government was willing to introduce family planning through legislation, I contend that population policy has always been of national interest, although perhaps not explicitly expressed as such.

11. Quoted in Westhoff, "United States," 734.

12. Recognized legally as Public Law 91-572.

13. The bill provided $382 million for services and research over three years and received bipartisan support. However, funds were not made available to programs that offered abortions. For an informative history of this bill, see Population Crisis Committee, *The Family Planning Services and Research Act of 1970*, 20–24; and "President Signs Birth Curb Bill," *New York Times*, 27 December 1970, sec. A, p. 1.

14. Recognized legally as Public Law 91-213.

15. Ogg, *Population and the American Future*, 3. Note the curious alteration in the wording of the commission's statement in the final document versus that of the *Interim Report*: "examine the probable extent of population growth and internal migration in the United States between now *and the year 2000; to assess the problems this will pose for our* government, our economy, and our resources and environment; and to make recommendations on how the Nation can best *resolve these problems*" (my emphasis), as cited in the Commission on Population Growth and the American Future, *Interim Report*, 6.

16. Rockefeller founded the Population Council in 1952. For a concise insider's account of the selection of the members of the Commission on Population Growth and the American Future and the internal struggles within the commission, see Westhoff, "Commission on Population Growth and the American Future."

17. Hartmann, *Reproductive Rights and Wrongs*, 104.

18. Ibid., 447.

19. Browning and Poston, "Population and the American Future." Many of the resulting manuscripts were published as individual reports and are introduced and reviewed throughout this book as they become relevant.

20. "A Presidential Panel Supports Abortion on Request," *New York Times*, Box 164, Folder 26, Sierra Club Papers.

21. Robert D. Semple Jr., "Nixon Turns Down Birth Curb Plans," *New York Times*, 6 May 1972, Box 164, Folder 24, Sierra Club Papers; Harry F. Rosenthal, "Nixon Rejects Population Panel Advice," *Washington Post*, 6 May 1972, Box 164, Folder 28, Sierra Club Papers.

22. Westhoff, "United States," 732.

23. Bachrach and Bergman, *Power and Choice*.

24. Paul Ehrlich borrowed his book title from a 1954 publication of the Hugh Moore Fund, which was one of the earliest post–World War II treatises on overpopulation. Other similarly apocalyptic treatises on the "population explosion"

during this period include Hauser, *The Population Dilemma;* Day and Taylor Day, *Too Many Americans;* Appleman, *The Silent Explosion;* and Paddock and Paddock, *Famine—1975!*

25. Ehrlich, "World Population," 3.

26. For an uncritical consideration of the work of the Hugh Moore Fund and the Campaign to Check the Population Explosion, see Lader, *Breeding Ourselves to Death.*

27. Quoted in Hartmann, *Reproductive Rights and Wrongs,* 106.

28. Critchlow, *Intended Consequences,* 4.

29. Ibid.; Hartmann, *Reproductive Rights and Wrongs,* 106.

30. See Barnett, "A History of Zero Population Growth, Inc.," Box 4, Folder: History, Tanton Papers. This was, in fact, the peak membership of ZPG in this decade. It is also significant to note that a survey of the membership determined that it was "almost entirely white" and that two out of five members were full-time students. Moreover, such a significant portion of its membership was from California that the organization relocated its offices to Menlo Park to better stay in touch with the heart of membership.

31. Carden, "Zero Population Growth Expands Goal" *Christian Science Monitor,* 17 April 1973, Box 180, Folder 5, Sierra Club Papers.

32. Commission on Population Growth and the American Future, *Interim Report,* 2.

33. Ibid.

34. See Blake and Giménez, "Coercive Pronatalism and American Population Policy," for an analysis of the various forms pro-natalist pressures took during this period.

35. "Campaign Aims to Cut Size of U.S. Families: Group Says It Wants to Persuade Couples to Produce No More that Two Children," *Los Angeles Times,* 11 August 1971, Box 2, Folder: Reports and Proposals, 1974–1978, Tanton Papers.

36. Wilmoth and Ball ("The Population Debate in American Popular Magazines, 1946–1990") provide a comprehensive review of the population debate in popular American periodicals between 1946 and 1990.

37. Rummonds, "The Role of Government in Population Policy."

38. Letter from Robert B. Carleson to "All County Welfare Directors," 20 October 1972, Box 164, Folder 24, Sierra Club Papers.

39. Ibid. In a personal communication with a social worker in Los Angeles County during this period, all staff were told to make special efforts to encourage women with "too many children" to utilize family planning services.

40. Wood, "Presidential Address."

41. "AMA Policy on Human Reproduction, Including Population Control," in Veatch and Draper, "Population Policy and the Values of Physicians," 377–408. In 1965 the AMA appointed an ad hoc committee to review "the earlier positions of the AMA on contraceptive practices and to prepare, for review by the Board, statements on this and other subjects related to reproduction" (Buxton, "The Doctor's

Responsibility in Population Control," 113). The American Nurses Association also passed a resolution in 1966 supporting family planning.

42. Legislators and other population policy advocates also considered physicians to be a significant group within the population establishment and often courted their support. For example, see "Address of Senator Joseph D. Tydings before the American Medical Association," 4 May 1970, Box 1, Folder: Michigan Population Commission, Tanton Papers.

43. Anderson, "Obstacles to Population Control."

44. Buxton, "The Doctor's Responsibility," 114.

45. Ibid.

46. Ibid., 116. Citing an article printed in *The New York Times Magazine* (1966), Buxton notes the need for medical practitioners to

penetrate into the home as though a plague were raging, all the adults dead and the children moaning in their cribs for help. The "unavailable mother"— unwed, indigent or surviving on welfare payments, socially deprived, economically deprived, intellectually deprived . . . unable to supply the needs of a newborn child, already burdened with children she has rejected—the unavailable mother produced the unreachable child. (115)

47. Kaplan and Chez, "The Economics of Population Growth," 136.

48. Wulff, "Presidential Address." While societal interest in the population problem waned after 1973, the issue remained salient for obstetricians and gynecologists throughout the decade. See Hellman, "Fertility Control at a Crossroad"; Hughes, "The Greatest Show on Earth/Presidential Address"; and Randall, "The Obstetrician-Gynecologist and Reproductive Health"; all of them focus on this continuing crisis in medical care.

49. Commission on Population Growth and the American Future, *Population and the American Future*, 114–117.

50. Keely, "Immigration Composition and Population Policy."

51. Commission on Population Growth and the American Future, *Population and the American Future*, 114.

52. Ibid., 115.

53. For a more thorough review of U.S.-Mexican relations during the Bracero period (1942–1964) and the poor working and living conditions of the *braceros,* see Acuña, *Occupied America.*

54. "A Final Report on Population," *San Francisco Examiner,* 2 April 1972, sec. 1, p. 2.

55. Fernández and Pedroza, "The Border Patrol and the News Media Coverage of Undocumented Mexican Immigration During the 1970s," 3.

56. Ibid., 21.

57. Gallup Organization, "The Gallup Study of Attitudes Toward Illegal Aliens."

58. Gutiérrez, *Walls and Mirrors,* 185.

59. Ibid., 188.

60. Clarence La Roche, "The Alien Tide," *San Antonio Express*, 28 January 1973, Comité de México y Aztlán (COMEXAZ) News Clipping Service (hereafter referred to as COMEXAZ Clippings).

61. Immigration Commissioner Leonard F. Chapman stated in 1975, "The stereotyped image of the illegal alien as a little fellow working in the fields of the Southwest is out of date. They're now in heavy industry, light industry, construction work, driving taxis, working in clothing factories and restaurants. And they're making good money" (quoted in "On Illegal Aliens," *El Paso Times*, 19 January 1975; in COMEXAZ Clippings). See also "Wetbacks: A New Breed; Alien Hordes Push North," *San Antonio Express*, 18 December 1973; "Illegal Aliens Now Make Big Money in Cities," *San Antonio Express*, 15 March 1975; COMEXAZ Clippings.

62. Corwin and McCain, "Wetbackism Since 1964," 69–70.

63. Quoted in John Kendall, "Illegal Alien Entries Held 'Out of Control,'" *Los Angeles Times*, 9 January 1977; and L. H. Whittemore, "Can We Stop the Invasion of Illegal Aliens?" *El Paso Times*, 29 February 1976, COMEXAZ Clippings.

64. Corwin and McCain, "Wetbackism Since 1964," 95–96.

65. For a discussion of the problem of Mexican overpopulation in mainstream news media, see Ramon Villalobos, "Birth Rate, Lack of Milk Serious Mexican Problems," *El Paso Times*, 26 November 1972; C. L. Sulzberger, "Mexico's Top Problem," *San Antonio Express*, 5 March 1973; Harold K. Milks, "Mexico's Baby Boom of 35,000 a Week Negates Efforts to Hike Living Standard," *Arizona Republic*, 15 May 1974; James Reston, "Mexico's One Hundred Million," *Denver Post*, 31 August 1975; "Mexico's Population Booming," *San Antonio Express*, 3 November 1975; all in COMEXAZ Clippings.

66. James Reston, "Mexico's Population Explosion Worsens Immigration Problem," *Arizona Republic*, 2 September 1975; COMEXAZ Clippings.

67. "Solutions Discussed for Alien Problems," *Arizona Journal*, 9 June 1975; COMEXAZ Clippings.

68. "Population Control Tied to Illegal Alien Problem," *Denver Post*, 18 September 1977, COMEXAZ Clippings.

69. "The Newest Americans: A Second Spanish Invasion," *U.S. News and World Report*, 8 July 1974, pp. 34–36.

70. Ibid.

71. "L.A. May Have 1 Million Illegal Aliens by 1981," *Los Angeles Times*, 30 January 1977.

72. Officials quoted in the article also commented that "Some of those [aliens] arrested have been in the United States less than 12 hours" (Patt Morrison, "Illegal Aliens Blamed for Increasing Crimes," *Los Angeles Times*, 30 January 1977; COMEXAZ Clippings). Also see James Quinn, "Illegal Aliens Blamed for Rise in Burglaries," *Los Angeles Times*, 19 September 1976; COMEXAZ Clippings.

73. Dick Merkel, "New Breed of Alien Turns to Crime," *San Antonio Express*, 30 May 1976; COMEXAZ Clippings.

74. Dick Merkel, "Many Steal to Support Drug Habits," *San Antonio Express,* 31 May 1976; COMEXAZ Clippings. Merkel writes: "They [aliens] commit crimes, burglary, theft, armed robbery to support their habit and others get directly involved in drug trafficking. . . . State health officials also cite the high incidence of tuberculosis and other communicable diseases among illegal aliens as an increasing health problem."

75. Mike Goodman, "Epidemics a Barrio Specter," *Los Angeles Times,* 16 September 1973; "Heavy Border Traffic Hampers Tuberculosis Detection in City," *El Paso Times,* 10 October 1974. See also "'Illegal Aliens' Fears Spawn Health Peril," *Denver Post,* 30 September 1973; Frank del Olmo, "U.S. Refuses to Repay County's Alien Health Bill," *Los Angeles Times,* 15 August 1974; Harry Nelson, "U.S., Mexico Will Share Data on Venereal Disease," *Los Angeles Times,* 10 April 1975; Phil Kimball, "VD Rate Called 'Disgrace'; EP Slightly Above Normal," *El Paso Times,* 13 February 1976; "Mexico 'Exporting' TB Into Texas," *El Paso Times,* 26 May 1976; COMEXAZ Clippings.

76. "U.S. Failing to Solve Illegal-Alien Problem," *Denver Post,* 7 October 1974, COMEXAZ Clippings.

77. Bruce Keppel, "County to Sue U.S. Over Aliens," *Los Angeles Times,* 20 July 1977; COMEXAZ Clippings. The article reads: "Los Angeles County will sue the federal government to recover its cost of providing services to aliens residing here illegally, the supervisors decided Tuesday. . . . A 'high incidence of tuberculosis' among undocumented aliens requires special efforts to check the spread of TB."

78. "A Plan to Deport 1 Million Aliens," *San Francisco Chronicle,* 21 October 1974, Box 1, Folder: Tax Law Changes, Tanton Papers.

79. Fernández and Pedroza, "The Border Patrol."

80. For typical expressions, see Robert S. Allen, "Illegal Aliens Take Heavy Toll on Nation's Economic Problems," *El Paso Times,* 19 March 1973; and "Illegal Aliens Causing Unemployment in U.S.," *Denver Post,* 27 December 1974; COMEXAZ Clippings.

81. Laura E. Taggart, "Aliens and Jobs," *Denver Post,* 15 May 1977; COMEXAZ Clippings.

82. "Study Finds 8 Million Aliens Here," *New York Times,* 7 November 1975, Box 4, Folder: People and Topics to Bring Up With Them, Tanton Papers; and "Illegal Aliens Called Tax Burden," *San Francisco Chronicle,* 1 December 1975; "Illegal Tax Bill Claimed," *Arizona Journal,* 3 December 1975; COMEXAZ Clippings.

83. These statistics, and the methodology employed, were highly criticized and determined to be scientifically indefensible. The results were based upon a "Delphi panel," which is an averaging of estimates provided by national "experts." See Ehrlich et al., *The Golden Door,* 378–379, for how the method was employed; it was later found to be grossly inaccurate.

Ehrlich et al. provide a telling account of how and why Chapman sensationalized these faulty statistics, and their subsequent misuse, in their book *The Golden Door* (esp. 178–182, 185–186). A Labor Department study conducted interviews with 793 illegal aliens and determined that 77 percent paid taxes and only 0.5 percent had received welfare payments. Researchers concluded that illegal aliens actually paid more in taxes than they reaped in governmental social benefits. See "Illegal Aliens Keep Up Kin, Pay U.S. Tax," *Denver Post,* 20 November 1975; "Illegal Aliens Pay Tax, Study Shows," *Arizona Journal,* 20 November 1975; Frank Del Olmo, "Illegal Aliens: No Quick Solution Seen," *Los Angeles Times,* 10 December 1975; COMEXAZ Clippings.

84. "The Rising Flood of Illegal Aliens," *San Francisco Chronicle,* 17 August 1975; COMEXAZ Clippings.

85. For one analysis of Carter's policy on undocumented Mexicans, see Corwin and McCain, "Wetbackism Since 1964."

86. Chase, *The Legacy of Malthus,* 412.

87. "Census Estimate at Century's End Cut by 20 Million," *New York Times,* 18 December 1972, Box 164, Folder 28, Sierra Club Papers; "Birth Rate at Record Low," *San Francisco Chronicle,* 4 March 1972, Box 180, Folder 9, Sierra Club Papers.

88. "National Birth Rate Plunges in 1972," n.d., Box 164, Folder 23, Sierra Club Papers.

89. "A Million Fewer Babies," *San Francisco Chronicle,* 4 March 1972, Box 164, Folder 23, Sierra Club Papers; "Birth Decline Held Largest for Minorities," *Los Angeles Times,* 18 June 1974, and "U.S. 'Fertility Gap' Trend is Reversed," COMEXAZ Clippings. Also see Sweet, "Differentials in the Rate of Fertility Decline: 1960–1970," for a complete discussion of the study covered by the latter two articles.

90. Hughes, "The Greatest Show on Earth," 743.

91. Ibid., 742.

92. Littlewood, *The Politics of Population Control;* Chase, *The Legacy of Malthus;* and Shapiro, *Population Control Politics.*

93. Edwards, "The Commission's Recommendations From the Standpoint of Minorities."

94. Ibid., 467.

95. Julian Bond quoted in Littlewood, *The Politics of Population Control,* 60.

96. Birth control historian Linda Gordon characterizes this moment of reproductive rights activism as "more complex" and "widespread" than previous birth control movements because it focused not on a single issue, but on contraception, sterilization, and abortion (*Women's Body, Women's Right,* 398).

97. Ibid., 395.

98. Lena Baker, "Population Growth and the Future," *San Francisco Chronicle,* 25 February 1972, Box 164, Folder 23, Sierra Club Papers.

99. *Congressional Record,* 92nd Cong., 1st sess., 2 June 1971, p. 7965.

100. In 1942, Governor Culbert L. Olson created a seven-member California Population Commission that was primarily responsible for coordinating the development of state population statistics and estimates, as well as disseminating this information to private agencies and the general public. I have identified two reports published by this commission (1942, 1943). According to the California Population Commission (*Annual Report, 1942*), migration contributed to 81–86 percent of the state's growth during this time.

101. "Just What Will We Celebrate?" *San Francisco Chronicle*, 10 January 1962, and "Big Boast from the Coast: Tops in Population, California Claims, and in Problems, Too," n.d., Box 80, Folder 35, Sierra Club Papers.

102. "'Slurbs' Assailed by Californians," *New York Times*, 14 January 1962; "Politics, Planning, and the Spreading Slurbs," *San Francisco Chronicle*, 15 January 1962; "Southland's Dismay Prophesy," undated news clipping; all in Box 80, Folder 35, Sierra Club Papers. See also D. B. Luten, "The Dynamics of Repulsion," *The Nation*, 30 January 1967, pp. 133–138, Box 80, Folder 35, Sierra Club Papers, for the evolution of Governor Edmund G. Brown's sentiment on the growth of the state.

103. Edmund G. Brown, "Charge to the Population Study Commission," 11 August 1966, in California Population Study Commission, *Report to the Governor*.

104. California Population Study Commission, *Report to the Governor*.

105. Ibid., 74.

106. Ibid., 76.

107. California Assembly Committee on Environmental Quality, *Report on the State's Role*, 4.

108. "California's Growth," *San Francisco Chronicle*, 16 February 1972, sec. 1, p. 11.

109. Many of the papers presented at the symposium are compiled in a monograph (Davis and Styles, *California's Twenty Million*). According to the editors, the compendium of the papers constitutes "the most comprehensive treatment of the state's population problems so far published" (vii).

110. Dr. Emil Mrak, Council Chairman, to Bob Moretti, Speaker of the Assembly, 21 December 1971 in California Assembly Science and Technology Advisory Council, *California Population Problems and State Policy*.

111. Ibid., 4.

112. Ibid., 26.

113. California Assembly Committee on Environmental Quality, *Report on the State's Role*, i.

114. The full text of the hearings is available in California Assembly Committee on Environmental Quality, *Report on the State's Role*.

115. Letter from Mrs. Otis Chandler, member, President's Commission on Population Growth and the American Future, to March K. Fong, California Assembly Committee on Environmental Quality, *Report on the State's Role*, 100.

116. "Problems of Population," newspaper clipping, 9 September 1972, Box 164, Folder 28, Sierra Club Papers.

117. It should be noted that while California continued to be the nation's fastest growing state, the 1970 census reported that the state's rate of growth had fallen sufficiently to reflect the national average (Jack Rosenthal, "California's Rate of Growth Drops Sharply After 7 Decades of Rapid Rise," *New York Times*, 18 September 1972, sec. C, p. 17). Dr. Kingsley Davis attributed this decreased birth rate to the state's newly liberalized abortion law ("Birth Rate Drops in California," *Washington Post*, 29 July 1972, sec. A, p. 4).

118. Davis and Styles, *California's Twenty Million*, 93.

119. Styles, "Introduction."

120. Gutiérrez, *Walls and Mirrors*, 1; also see Boswell, "The Growth and Proportional Distribution of the Mexican Stock Population"; and Bean and Tienda, *The Hispanic Population of the United States*, 36–103, for similar assertions. See also "Spanish-Surnamed Individuals in U.S. Put at 11.2 Million," *Los Angeles Times*, 26 August 1975; "Census of Spanish Origin Population Shows Most Live in Southwest Area," *El Paso Times*, 23 March 1976, COMEXAZ Clippings.

121. "Spanish-named Population Heaviest in California," *San Antonio Express*, 21 January 1973, COMEXAZ Clippings.

122. Camarillo, *Chicanos in California*.

123. Ray Hebert, "L.A. County Latin Population Grows 113 Percent," *Los Angeles Times*, 18 August 1972, COMEXAZ Clippings.

124. The Democratic Party launched a campaign to register Latino voters. See Charles Overby, "Mexican-Americans' Votes Being Sought," *El Paso Times*, 7 November 1975, COMEXAZ Clippings; Lucia Mount, "U.S. Hispanics a Growing Political Power," *Christian Science Monitor*, 16 December 1975, Box 4, Folder: People and Topics, Tanton Papers.

CHAPTER THREE

1. Rosenfeld had first gone to the Southern Poverty Law Center, which funded some of the initial case costs and legal advice. See Elizabeth Shalen, Esq., to Kent Russel, Esq., 11 May 1974; and Morris Dees to Mr. Melvin Belli, 17 December 1972, Box 15, Folder 4, Ricardo Cruz/Católicos por La Raza Papers (hereafter referred to as Cruz Papers).

2. Bernard Rosenfeld, Notes on Medical File, File 72, Notes, personal papers of Bernard Rosenfeld, in author's collection (hereafter referred to as Rosenfeld Papers).

3. Kent A. Russel to Ricardo Cruz, 18 June 1974, Box 15, Folder 4, Cruz Papers.

4. Mike Goodman, "Women Ask $6 Million From County in Sterilization Claim," *Los Angeles Times*, 21 November 1974, Rosenfeld Papers.

5. "First Amended Complaint for Damages," *Virginia Andrade et al. v. Los Angeles County, University of Southern California Medical Center, et al.*, 6 November 1975, No. C126404, p. 4, Rosenfeld Papers.

6. See, for example, Richard Cruz Testimony at California State Hearings on Proposed Sterilization Regulations, Los Angeles, 113–122, RG 5, Box 54, Folder 9, MALDEF Papers.

7. Clarke, "Subtle Sterilization Abuse."

8. Although heavily concentrated on the early part of the century, the most comprehensive account of sterilization abuse during the twentieth century is Reilly, *The Surgical Solution*. For late-twentieth-century sterilization abuse historiography,

see Donovan, "Sterilizing the Poor and Incompetent"; Littlewood, *The Politics of Population Control*; Shapiro, *Population Control Politics*; and Davis, *Women Under Attack*. This was not the first occurrence of massive sterilization abuses in the United States. During the late nineteenth and early twentieth centuries, sterilization of the "unfit" was advocated for achieving racial purity and race progress. For discussions of sterilization during this period, see Haller, *Eugenics*; and Chase, *The Legacy of Malthus*. Puerto Rican women also suffered a disproportionate amount of sterilization abuse; see Ramírez de Arellano and Seipp, *Colonialism, Catholicism, and Contraception*; and López, "Agency and Constraint."

9. "Cruel and Unusual?" *Newsweek* 67 (13 June 1966): 46; "Criminal Justice: Jail or Sterilization?" *Time Magazine* 87 (3 June 1966): 46.

10. Shapiro, *Population Control Politics*.

11. Ibid.

12. A 1967 study conducted by the Office of Economic Opportunity (OEO) determined birth control to be the most "cost-effective" method of poverty prevention. In 1968, the OEO sponsored a county-by-county study designed to ascertain how many indigent women were provided with family planning services; a total of 5.3 million were found to be "in-need," with only 85 percent of those receiving services. See "Birth Control Effectiveness," *Science*, 12 May 1967; U.S. Office of Economic Opportunity, *Need for Subsidized Family Planning Services*; and Hern, "Family Planning and the Poor." Advocacy for birth control as an effective way to treat poverty grew during the 1960s. See Shepard, "Birth Control for the Poor"; and "Welfare Birth Control," 157.

13. Gordon, *Women's Body, Women's Right*; Petchesky, *Abortion and Women's Choice*; National Center for Health Statistics, *Trends in Contraceptive Practice*.

14. Reilly, *The Surgical Solution*.

15. Health Research Group, *A Health Research Group Study*.

16. Historians of sterilization abuse have noted the "spurious political considerations" that deterred the implementation of federal sterilization regulations. Most suggest that because 1972 was an election year, the White House purposefully suppressed the regulations, fearing that it would hinder Nixon's re-election. See Littlewood, *The Politics of Population Control*; Shapiro, *Population Control Politics*.

17. The case of *Relf v. Weinberger* (later merged with a similar suit by the National Welfare Rights Organization) aimed to force the federal government to establish stringent guidelines to regulate doctor behavior and protect patients from possible abuse. The case was crucial in establishing the requirement of informed consent and federal regulations regarding sterilization that were implemented in April 1974. See *Relf et al. v. Weinberger et al.*, Civil Action No. 73-1557, U.S. Dist. Ct., Washington, D.C., 15 March 1974.

18. Robert Kistler, "Women 'Pushed' Into Sterilization, Doctor Charges: Thousands Victimized at Some Inner-City Teaching Hospitals, Report Claims," *Los Angeles Times*, 2 December 1974, pp. 1, 3, 26–28; and Les Payne, "U.S. Sterilization Abuses Disclosed," *Los Angeles Times*, 5 January 1975.

19. Pointing to class differentials in medical care, "Such abuses ... historically have found fertile climates in the nation's giant, core-city teaching complexes such as the USC–Los Angeles County Medical Center, where medicine is high volume, often impersonal—and practiced on patients who are generally poor, frightened and uneducated." See Health Research Group, *A Health Research Group Study;* and Kistler, "Women 'Pushed' Into Sterilization," 1.

20. Health Research Group, *A Health Research Group Study.*

21. Hernández, "Chicanas and the Issue of Involuntary Sterilization."

22. Gordon, *Women's Body, Women's Right.*

23. Roberts, *Killing the Black Body.*

24. Dillingham, "Indian Women and IHS Sterilization Practices"; "Sterilization of Native Americans"; and "Sterilization Update."

A full copy of the Abourzek Report, released in November 1976, can be found in RG 5, Box 910, Folder 5, MALDEF Papers.

The in-depth research of Dr. Connie Uri, which investigated beyond those four Indian Health Service areas, indicate that even more Native women were sterilized. For narrative accounts of sterilization abuse of Native American women, see Joan Burnes, "Shocking Sterilization Statistics Surface," *Indian Country Today,* 24 August 1994, p. 8; "Sterilization of Native Women to IHS Charged," *Akwesasne Notes* (Early Winter 1974): 6–7; Larson, "And Then There Were None," 61; and Lou, "The Sterilization of American Indian Women," 43, 51, 57, 100. See also Richard M. Harley, "Indian Women Plan to Sue U.S. in Sterilization Cases," *Christian Science Monitor,* 27 May 1977, p. 6, for an account of legal action taken on behalf of Native women who were coercively sterilized.

25. Gutiérrez, "Policing 'Pregnant Pilgrims.'"

26. Not until 22 February 1974 was it specified that "patients will not be approached for the first time concerning sterilization when they are in active labor" in a memo dispersed to all staff by Dr. Quilligan. Deposition of Roger Freeman, 12, *Madrigal v. Quilligan* (No. CV-75-2057-EC) (29 June 1977), (Vélez Papers). I am indebted to Carlos Vélez-Ibañez, who graciously shared personal collected materials (Vélez Papers) from the *Madrigal* case that are not available in the Vélez Archives.

27. Robert Kistler, "Many U.S. Rules on Sterilization Abuses Ignored Here," *Los Angeles Times,* 3 December 1974, sec. 1, pp. 3, 24–26. Dr. Quilligan told a *Los Angeles Times* reporter that he did "not recall" the guidelines distributed on 18 April 1974.

28. The information in this section is based on Karen Benker's "Statement on Sterilization Abuse," n.d., Vélez Archives (hereafter referred to as Benker Statement).

29. Although definitive statistics are unavailable, it was reported by the head of Obstetrics/Gynecology, Dr. Quilligan, that the "predominate race" that frequented LACMC was Mexican American (trial transcript, 740).

30. Selected publications from doctors eventually named as defendants in the *Madrigal* trial include Brenner et al., "Ectopic Pregnancy Following Tubal Sterilization Surgery," *Obstetrics and Gynecology* 49(3) (March 1977): 323–324; Bernstein

et al., "Clinical Experience with the Cu-7 Intrauterine Device," *Contraception* 6(2) (August 1972): 99–107; E.J. Quilligan, "Contraception After Pregnancy," *Journal of Reproductive Medicine* 21 (5, Suppl.) (November 1978): 250–251; Tyler et al., "Long-term Studies of Oral Contraceptives and IUDs at the Family Planning Centers of Greater Los Angeles," *Journal of Reproductive Medicine* 8(4) (April 1972): 162–164; Tyler et al., "Present Status on Injectable Contraceptives: Results of Seven-Years Study," *Fertility and Sterility* 21(6) (June 1970): 469–481; and Zuspan et al., "Discussion (On Current Concepts of Contraception)," *Journal of Reproductive Medicine* 21 (5, Suppl.) (November 1978): 257–271.

As "experts" in the field, several doctors also provided public testimony regarding contraceptive usage. See "Statement before the Subcommittee on Intergovernmental Relations, House Committee on Government Operations," 12 June 1973; Mishell et al., "The Need for Development of New Methods of Contraception," Statement, 2 May 1978; in *U.S. House of Representatives Select Committee on Population and Development: Research in Population and Development: Needs and Capacities*, vol. 3, Hearings, 2–4 May, 1978 (Washington, D.C.: U.S. Government Printing Office, 1978), 374–380; Mishell et al., Population Control Statement on IUDs, Submitted to the U.S. Congress, House, Committee on Governmental Operations, Subcommittee on Intergovernmental Relations, 12 June 1973.

31. See Gordon, *Women's Body, Women's Right,* 423–424, for a succinct discussion of the problematic uses of the IUD.

32. Benker Statement, p. 2.

33. Rosenfeld documented his personal observations while a resident at LACMC, and his accounts were used by the attorneys for the Southern Poverty Law Center in the Relf case against HEW over the adoption of sterilization guidelines. Rosenfeld was also scheduled to serve as a witness in the *Madrigal* case but did not testify out of fear of retribution. See *Madrigal v. Quilligan,* trial transcript, 1445, 1449. His contract was not renewed at the Women's Hospital because of his involvement in unveiling sterilization abuses there.

34. Health Research Group, *A Health Research Group Study,* 7–8.

35. Narda Zacchino and Kris Lindgren, "Plaintiffs Lose Suit Over 10 Sterilizations," *Los Angeles Times,* 1 July 1978, sec. B1.

36. Benker Statement, p. 5.

37. Ibid.; see also "Deposition of Dr. Karen Benker," 6 September 1977, 32, Vélez Papers.

38. Juan Nieto, an intern at LACMC, reported that he had experienced similar treatment—"particularly of Mexican-Americans"—at a hospital in Colorado where he completed his medical training. Suggesting a pattern of abuse of Mexican-origin women throughout the Southwest, Nieto was sure that Spanish-speaking patients "had no idea the procedure urged on them was permanent" (Bernard Rosenfeld, interview notations, Rosenfeld Papers).

39. Ibid.

40. Benker Statement, p. 3.

41. Georgina Torres-Rizk, "Sterilization Abuses Against Chicanas in Los Angeles," 2 December 1976, pp. 1–2, RG 9, Box 95, Folder 4, MALDEF Papers.

42. Trial transcript, 18. Mrs. Orozco testified that doctors almost cheered when she finally signed the consent (19).

43. Trial transcript, 370. All of the following quotes from the women involved in the *Madrigal* case were taken directly from the court transcript. During the trial the women all testified in Spanish, with their words translated by a court translator, then transcribed by the court reporter.

44. Trial transcript, 383.

45. Benker Statement, 4.

46. Trial transcript, 453.

47. Ibid., 454. Preferring the husband's decision regarding sterilization over the woman's is also evidenced in Dr. Quilligan's admission in the situation of another patient; although Mrs. Melvina Hernández was sterilized without her knowledge, he said, "We wouldn't have done it without the husband's permission" (Goodman, "Women Ask $6 Million," *Los Angeles Times*, 21 November 1974, sec. 1, pp. 1, 25). However, the doctors would also lie to the husbands, telling them that their wives would die unless they were sterilized, or that they were signing forms to consent for a cesarean-section delivery only. Gabriel Acosta, fearing for his wife's life, believed that he was only signing a consent to an emergency cesarean section. See Diane Ainsworth, "Mother No More," *Reader*, 26 January 1979, pp. 1, 4–9.

48. Trial transcript, 406.

49. Ibid., 416.

50. Benker Statement, p. 3.

51. "He told me, in these words: 'Lady, the limit for cesarean are three by law. So, you have to decide whether you want to risk the next one, because I think the next one you can die because you are rated here in the history as a patient of high risk'" (trial transcript, 665).

52. The words of Mrs. Benavides clearly reflect that she was fearing for her life: "They told me the reason was that if I got pregnant again the baby would probably be in the same position, and something else could happen serious. . . . I thought maybe I could die. . . . I thought if I had another child something could happen to me." Moreover, she testified that her only concern was for the daughters she already had: "The only thing I thought about was the girls. That is why I asked the question, that if I accepted that operation, I want it to be all right for my girls" (trial transcript, 126–129).

53. Kistler, "Women 'Pushed' Into Sterilization," 1.

54. Ibid.

55. The actual versus the perceived welfare status of the plaintiffs proves problematic in the case. In fact, the defendants opposed the plaintiffs' case as a class action because they are supposed to represent "a class of persons receiving medical and/or other aid from federal or state governmentally funded sources." Because this is not "uniformly true" of all the plaintiffs (many did receive aid after their

sterilization), the case was never considered a class action suit. See "Affidavit of Nancy L. Menzies," 13 July 1977, RG 5, Box 946, Folder 10, MALDEF Papers.

56. Deposition of Dr. Karen Benker, 6 September 1977, Vélez Papers.

57. Torres-Rizk, "Abuses Against Chicanas," 2; and "Interview of Georgina Hernández," 9 May 1978, 10, Vélez Papers.

58. Kistler, "Women 'Pushed' Into Sterilization," 2.

59. Robert Rawitch, "11 Latin Women File Suit on Sterilization: Claim They Were Coerced or Deceived Into Having Operation at Medical Center," *Los Angeles Times*, 19 June 1975, sec. 1, pp. 1, 3.

60. A third lawyer, Georgina Torres-Rizk, served as a lawyer on the case from its beginning until just before the trial.

61. Trial transcript, 789.

62. Ibid., 828.

63. See Vélez-Ibáñez, "Se Me Acabó la Canción," 84–86, for a more detailed description of the "paternalistic behavioral environment of the courtroom and the racial and class discrepancies between the plaintiffs and defendant doctors."

64. In particular, Mr. Maskey attempted to severely limit Dr. Benker's statements by stringently confining her testimony to the time period that Dr. Benker was at the hospital when the plaintiffs' sterilizations took place, a period of just seven days in June 1971.

65. Trial transcript, 795.

66. Ibid., 797.

67. Ibid.

68. Ibid., 802.

69. Ibid., 827.

70. Ibid., 823–825.

71. Carlos Vélez-Ibáñez Deposition, *Madrigal v. Quilligan*, 4 November 1977, p. 34, Vélez Papers.

72. Vélez-Ibáñez, "Se Me Acabó La Canción," 80.

73. See Vélez-Ibáñez, "Se Me Acabó La Canción," 78–84, for a more in-depth review of his extensive fieldwork.

74. Ibid., 79.

75. The plaintiffs' lawyers called additional expert witnesses to corroborate Vélez's analysis. Dr. Terry Kupers, a psychiatrist, completed psychological examinations on the plaintiffs and testified to their depressed state, low self-esteem, and ravaged marriages (trial transcript, 930–994).

76. Vélez-Ibáñez, "Se Me Acabó La Canción."

77. Trial transcript, 392–394.

78. Ibid., 394.

79. Terry A. Kupers, "10 Lose Their Fertility—And Their Case," *Los Angeles Times*, 28 September 1978, sec. C, p. 7, Vélez Archives. Interestingly, in a letter to the editor, someone took issue with this, saying that these ideas are "refuted by a wealth of medical, psychological, sociological, and economic information, although it may

well be part of a particular folklore. Worldwide, as income and education improve, the trend is towards smaller family size, a demographic fact that knows no cultural or ethnic barriers" ("Letters to the Editor," *Los Angeles Times*, 7 October 1978, Vélez Archives).

80. *Madrigal v. Quilligan*, Opinion, Vélez Archives. Further discussion of the court's opinion is taken from this document unless otherwise noted.

81. According to Antonia Hernández, this decision was based on the understanding that the jury selection process, especially in federal court, did not result in juries that were representative of the population as a whole. Hernández interview.

82. Zacchino and Lindgren, "Plaintiffs Lose Suit."

83. *Madrigal v. Quilligan*, Court Opinion, 19 (C.D. Cal., 30 June 1978).

84. Ibid.

85. Vélez-Ibáñez, "Se Me Acabó la Canción," 86–87.

86. Judge Curtis's co-optation of the plaintiffs' argument of "cultural difference" harkens back to feminist discussions of the testimonies of historians Alice Kessler-Harris and Rosalind Rosenberg in the sex discrimination suit brought forth by the Equal Employment Opportunities Commission in 1979. As Ruth Milkman reminds us, feminist and other scholars must be cautious of the way arguments about cultural difference can be co-opted. A similar examination of the "difference dilemma" with regard to racial and ethnic thinking necessitates further exploration.

87. News release, 10 July 1978, Item 80, Vélez Papers.

88. Based on the contention that Judge Curtis erred in his application of the law to the case, the decision was taken to the Ninth Circuit Court of Appeals. The appeal claimed that Judge Curtis abused his judicial authority in his decision by unilaterally overlooking the testimony of several key witnesses for the plaintiffs. When the appeal was denied, lawyers involved with the case decided not to take the appeal to the U.S. Supreme Court. See Zacchino and Lindgren, "Plaintiffs Lose Suit"; and Narda Zacchino, "10 Women Will Appeal Ruling On Sterilization," *Los Angeles Times*, 8 July 1978, sec. A, p. 26.

89. Ainsworth, "Mother No More," 1, 4–9.

90. Bogue, "Demographic Aspects of Maternity and Infant Care." It is also significant to note that as a demographer, Bogue was committed to using social scientific tools toward world population control.

91. Benker Statement, 5.

92. See "The Aliens Who Get Welfare Aid" and "Aliens Reportedly Get $100 Million in Welfare," *Los Angeles Times*, 27 January 1973, COMEXAZ Clippings.

93. Robert M. Lewis, "Illegal Welfare Recipients," *Arizona Republic*, 7 September 1975; and "Aliens Reportedly Get $100 Million," COMEXAZ Clippings.

94. See Frank Del Olmo, "Few Aliens on Welfare Illegally, Study Indicates," *Los Angeles Times*, 1 July 1975; "A Ruling on Aliens and Welfare," *San Francisco Chronicle*, 25 December 1974; and "Study of Alien Welfare Ruling on County's Finances Sought," *Los Angeles Times*, 27 December 1974; COMEXAZ Clippings.

95. Jim Wood, "Report On Bias Against Latinos in Welfare," *San Francisco Chronicle*, 2 July 1972, COMEXAZ Clippings.

96. See Steve Kline, "Aliens: Victims or Victimizer?" *San Antonio Express*, 23 August 1977, COMEXAZ Clippings. The tone of every article I have read that mirrors these issues is similarly anecdotal at the beginning. See also "Pregnant Pilgrims Make Trips to U.S. Hospitals," *El Paso Times*, 23 November 1972; "Mexico's Pregnant Women Wish to Give Birth in the U.S.," *El Paso Times*, 15 June 1975; "Hospital Told to Refuse Alien Births," *Arizona Republic*, 1 November 1975; Phil Kimball, "Juarez Mothers-To-Be Using El Paso Hospitals Have Financial Impact," *El Paso Times*, 1 August 1975; and Tom Kuhn, "Aliens Give Birth at State's Expense," *Arizona Republic*, 27 April 1975; COMEXAZ Clippings.

97. Kuhn, "Aliens Give Birth."

98. "False Registration of Alien Babies Alleged," *El Paso Times*, 12 May 1977; "Born on Border, Twins Left Behind By Mexican Mother," *Los Angeles Times*, 8 July 1977; COMEXAZ Clippings.

CHAPTER FOUR

1. In 1969 *Eugenics Quarterly* (1953–1968) changed its name to *Social Biology*. The journal was previously called *Eugenical News* (1939–1953).

2. Uhlenberg, "Fertility Patterns Within the Mexican American Population."

3. Bradshaw and Bean, *Some Aspects of Mexican American Fertility.*

4. This surge of scholarship was enabled by an influx of government funding for research about national population growth during the late 1960s, also detailed in chapter 2. See Demeny, "Social Science and Population Policy"; Hartmann, *Reproductive Rights and Wrongs.*

5. Mexican Fact Finding Committee, "The Mexican Family."

6. Ibid.

7. Woofter, *Races and Ethnic Groups in American Life.*

8. Ibid. See also Bogardus, *The Mexican in the United States.*

9. Allen, "Mexican Peon Women in Texas."

10. Allen's ethnocentric measurement of a household's productivity reflects clearly modernist assumptions of women's central role as homemakers. She writes:

The Mexican woman on the central Texas farms is unproductive in an economic sense, and, consequently, the home over which she presides is unproductive. Of the 269 women who lived on farms, only eight did any canning or preserving of food and no one of these did an amount that an American housewife would consider worthy of note. . . . Home production for the typical Mexican farm wife consists of inexhaustible supplies of tortillas, when the ingredients are available; peppers from her little patch dried for the winter, and some making of clothes. ("Mexican Peon Women in Texas," 191)

11. Jack Parsons, "Human Competitive Breeding," Tanton Papers.

12. Tuck, *Not With the Fist*.

13. Bogardus, *The Mexican in the United States*; Murray, "A Socio-Cultural Study of 118 Mexican Families"; Clark, *Health in the Mexican American Culture*; Madsen, *The Mexican American of South Texas*.

14. Additionally, Allen's work typifies the exclusive social scientific focus upon Mexican *women's* reproductive behavior, demonstrating the gendered nature of this research inquiry. All discussion of the reproductive patterns of Mexican-origin people is exclusively focused on the behaviors of Mexican women; men are rarely mentioned, if at all.

15. Bogardus, *The Mexican in the United States*, 24–25. This characterization of Mexican-origin fathers as "child deserters" is common in these early social scientific depictions. For example, Bogardus writes that "The father views large numbers of children carelessly. Again, the attitude is quite primitive. If the children become too numerous and the burden of feeding these hungry mouths too heavy, the father may desert." Tuck likewise describes the husband of one of her informants as a "pregnancy deserter" (*Not With the Fist*). Such comments deserve further examination for their part in the effective construction of "good mother/bad father" duality.

16. Montiel, "The Social Science Myth of the Chicano Family"; Mirandé, "The Chicano Family"; Miller, "Variations in Mexican American Family Life"; Baca Zinn, "Chicano Family Research"; Ybarra, "Empirical and Theoretical Developments in the Study of Chicano Families"; Zavella, *Women's Work and Chicano Families*.

17. Baca Zinn, "Chicano Family Research."

18. Miller, "Variations in Mexican American Family Life," 271.

19. Baca Zinn, "Chicano Family Research."

20. Madsen, *The Mexican American of South Texas*.

21. While most commentary about this behavior was largely based upon the personal speculation of ethnographic social scientists, a few scholars boldly questioned Mexican Americans about their beliefs regarding family size in order to ascertain their attitudes. For one of the most deliberate attempts to conduct direct investigation of Mexican American attitudes about family size, see Clark, *Health in the Mexican American Culture*.

22. Bradshaw and Bean, "Trends in the Fertility of Mexican Americans: 1950–1970."

23. Bradshaw and Bean, *Some Aspects of Mexican American Fertility*, 143–144.

24. Uhlenberg, "Fertility Patterns Within the Mexican American Population, 30.

25. Ibid., 32.

26. Ibid.

27. Ibid., 31.

28. Ibid.

29. Ibid., 31–32.

30. Ibid., 33.

31. Kazen and Browning, "Sociological Aspects of the High Fertility of the U.S. Mexican-Descent Population."

32. Also curious about the phenomenon of Mexican-origin women's reproductive behavior, in 1966 Browning completed an exploratory field study of Mexican American women's attitudes with colleague Phyllis Kazen. Rather than "document the facts of high fertility for this group," the purpose of Kazen and Browning's study was to "uncover the social factors that help to explain why [Mexican American] fertility is so high" (ibid., 2). Conducting in-depth ethnographic interviews with twenty families in Austin, Kazen and Browning's study provided the groundwork necessary to "generate propositions and hypotheses that can be used in larger and more representative surveys" (ibid., 4).

33. Ibid., 143.

34. Bradshaw and Bean, "Trends in the Fertility of Mexican Americans: 1950–1970," 696.

35. David Alvírez, who served as the field director for the AFS, published a paper in 1973 specifically considering the impact of religion upon Mexican American women's fertility behavior. Utilizing data from the Austin Fertiliy Survey (AFS), he conclusively established that religion does not have a significant impact upon Mexican American fertility patterns ("The Effects of Formal Church Affiliation and Religiosity").

36. Earlier in the century similar concerns led to investigation of the differential fertility rates of different classes; see Notestein, "The Differential Rate of Increase"; Osborn, "Characteristics and Differential Fertility."

37. Recently published studies have demonstrated that the baby boom characterizing the years between 1948 and 1958 had subsided, with the crude birthrate decreasing by approximately 30 percent (Sweet, "Differentials in the Rate of Fertility Decline).

38. In their book *Postwar Fertility Trends and Differentials in the United States,* demographers Ronald Rindfuss and James Sweet write that "knowledge of such subgroup differences facilitates the understanding of the composition of aggregate fertility rates as well as of the dynamics of changes in those rates" (xi).

39. Roberts and Lee, "Minority Group Status and Fertility Revisited."

40. For example, Anne and Everett Lee concluded that:

Even today the higher Negro fertility can be explained in terms of education and socio-economic level. Whenever Negroes and whites are equated in these matters, no matter how roughly, Negro fertility seldom appears much higher than white and it is often lower. In particular, the decrease in fertility of Negroes is especially sharp, and this is an area in which the improvement of Negroes can hardly be doubted. . . . Still, the struggle to rise will be harder for Negroes and, as they become more middle class in orientation and enter more generally in competition with whites for white collar or supervisory jobs, they may try to counter-act some of their disadvantages by deferring or limiting childbearing. ("The Future Fertility of the American Negro, 231)

41. Bean and Marcum, "Differential Fertility and the Minority Group Status Hypothesis."

42. Hodgson, "Demography as Social Science and Policy Science."

43. For a cogent and comprehensive historical review of the development of demographic transition theory, see Hodgson, "Demography as Social Science and Policy Science."

44. Hodgson (ibid.) also provides a lucid account of the development of the thinking of Davis and Notestein regarding demographic transition theory (see especially 11–27). For classic formulations of demographic transition theory by these authors, see Davis, "The World Demographic Transition," and Notestein, "The Differential Rate of Increase."

45. Sretzer, "The Idea of Demographic Transition and the Study of Fertility."

46. Hall, "New Ethnicities."

47. The corresponding value judgment attending modernization theory is evident in the categorization of certain countries as "modern" and others as "less-modern."

48. Goldscheider, *Population, Modernization, and Social Structure.*

49. Sretzer, "The Idea of Demographic Transition and the Study of Fertility."

50. Greenhaulgh, "The Social Construction of Science: An Intellectual, Institutional, and Political History of Twentieth-Century Demography."

51. Goldscheider and Uhlenberg, "Minority Group Status and Fertility."

52. Goldscheider and Uhlenberg submitted that "It may be deduced from this interpretation of minority group fertility that when the social, demographic, and economic characteristics of minority and majority populations are similar— through standardization and statistical controls or at some time in the future—differences in fertility should be eliminated" (ibid., 361–362).

53. Ibid., 361.

54. Ibid., 361–362.

55. Although I will not develop this point here, it is important to note that having "proven" the independent effect that minority group status bears upon rates of fertility, the authors proffered an explanation for this phenomenon utilizing social-psychological reasoning. Particularly focusing on minority groups that exhibit lower fertility rates than the Anglo norm, Goldscheider and Uhlenberg ("Minority Group Status") hypothesized that minorities (who are notably assumed to desire acculturation) attempt to counteract the insecurities they feel as a result of their social location as a socioeconomically disadvantaged minority in the United States by purposefully limiting their childbearing.

56. Criticisms leveled at the Goldscheider and Uhlenberg study varied from a lack of definition of what constituted a "minority" group to failure to control for

confounding variables such as the wife's age at marriage and the husband's education level. Most notably, Roberts and Lee critiqued Goldscheider and Uhlenberg's
emphasis upon cumulative, rather than current, fertility and their failure to control
for factors previously found to significantly influence fertility (such as employment
status and the age of the woman at the time of first marriage) ("Minority Group Status and Fertility Revisited").

57. Roberts and Lee, "Minority Group Status and Fertility Revisited."

58. Ibid., 519.

59. Ibid., 517.

60. Jiobu and Marshall, "Minority Status and Family Size."

61. Gurak, "Sources of Ethnic Fertility Differences."

62. Forste and Tienda, "What's Behind Racial and Ethnic Fertility Differentials?" 110.

63. McDaniel, "Fertility and Racial Stratification," 134.

64. Ochoa, *Becoming Neighbors in a Mexican American Community.*

65. Dean E. Murphy, "New Californian Identity Predicted By Researchers:
Most Newborns in State Are Now Hispanic," *New York Times,* 17 February 2003,
sec. A, p. 13.

66. Beth Barrett, "Population Forecast Falls," *Daily News of Los Angeles,* 5 October 2004, sec. N, p. 4.

67. Mireya Navarro, "For Younger Latinos, a Shift to Smaller Families," *New
York Times* (online edition), 5 December 2004, 1.

68. Ibid.

CHAPTER FIVE

1. Letter from John A. Harris to Bruce Rubridge, 10 August 1975, Box 4, Folder:
Board Communications, Tanton Papers.

2. Immigration and Naturalization Service, "Report of the Commissioner
[Leonard Chapman]," iii.

3. Bhatia, "Green or Brown? White Nativist Environmental Movements."

4. Crawford, "Hispanophobia"; Stephancic, "Funding the Nativist Agenda";
and Tatalovich, "Official English as Nativist Backlash."

5. "Petoskey Doctor Leads 3-Way Fight Against Overpopulation," *Grand Rap-
ids Press,* 9 July 1975, p. 9, Box 1, Folder: Personal, Tanton Papers.

6. Crawford, "Hispanophobia," 152.

7. "John H. Tanton Oral History," p. 8, Box 10, Folder: Oral History, Tanton
Papers.

8. Cited in Tom Damman, "Doctor No," *Detroit News Magazine,* 8 February
1981.

9. "John H. Tanton Oral History," 10, Box 10, Folder: Oral History, Tanton
Papers.

10. John H. Tanton, "Statement at the Commission on Population Growth and the American Future Public Hearings," 15 April 1971, Washington, D.C., in Commission on Population Growth and the American Future, *Statements at Public Hearings*, 53–57.

11. Letter from John H. Tanton to David Brower, 10 October 1968, Box 2, Folder: Population Committee Correspondence, 1968–1970, Tanton Papers.

12. "John H. Tanton Oral History," 12, Box 10, Folder: Oral History, Tanton Papers. For background on the popularity of ZPG, see "A New Movement Challenges the U.S. to Stop Growing: ZPG," *Life*, 17 April 1970, p. 32.

13. "John H. Tanton Oral History," 11–12, Box 10, Folder: Oral History, Tanton Papers.

14. By 1975, ZPG realized that fewer than two children per family was needed to achieve zero population growth, and they altered their population policy prescriptions accordingly. Under the advisement of Deborah Oakley, a demographer at the University of Michigan, and after thoughtful consideration, ZPG adopted a "new demographic goal" of 1.5 children per family. See letter from Carl Pope, Chairman, Population Policy Committee, to ZPG Board, September 1975; memorandum from Debby Oakley to Carl Pope, 10 September 1975; Box 5, Folder: Population Policy, Tanton Papers.

15. See Box 1, Folder: Pledge of Social Responsibility, Tanton Papers.

16. John H. Tanton to Frederick Jaffe, 19 December 1969, Box 1, Folder: LTH Program, Tanton Papers.

17. Tanton, "The Case for Passive Eugenics," 24 April 1975, pp. 1–4, Box 5, Folder: Writings, Tanton Papers.

18. Ibid., 3.

19. Ibid., 4.

20. Sweet, "Differentials in the Rate of Fertility Decline"; Jack Rosenthal, "Census Estimate At Century's End Cut By 20 Million," *New York Times*, 18 December 1972, Box 164, Folder 28, Sierra Club Papers; "Birth Rate at Record Low," *San Francisco Chronicle*, 4 December 1972, Box 180, Folder 9, Sierra Club Papers; "A Million Fewer Babies," *San Francisco Chronicle*, 4 March 1972, Box 164, Folder 2, Sierra Club Papers.

21. Cited in Huss and Wirken, "Illegal Immigration."

22. "How Millions of Illegals Sneak Into U.S.: An Interview with Leonard Chapman," *U.S. News and World Report*, 22 July 1974, pp. 27–30.

23. Ibid., 30.

24. "Immigrants Gainers in U.S. Birth Cut," *Arizona Republic*, 24 February 1974, COMEXAZ Clippings.

25. Elaine Stansfield, director of ZPG-LA, "Testimony at Senate Commission on Immigration and Refugee Policy Hearings," Box 3, Folder: Immigration 1979–1980, ZPG Records.

26. Letter from Tanton to NON members, 31 May 1975, Box 4, Folder: Letters, 1971–1975, Tanton Papers.

27. Tanton, "The Great Escape," 29 March 1973, Box 1, Folder: Tanton Miscellaneous Letters, Tanton Papers.

28. Letter from Tanton to NON, 31 May 1975, Box 4, Folder: Letters 1971–1975, Tanton Papers.

29. Letters from Don T. Wilson to Tanton, 14 September 1972 and 7 April 1973, Box 1, Folder: Tax Law Changes, Tanton Papers.

30. Ramón Villalobos, "Birth Rate, Lack of Milk Serious Mexican Problems," *El Paso Times*, 26 November 1972; C. L. Sulzberger, "Mexico's Top Problem," *San Antonio Express*, 5 March 1973; Harold K. Milks, "Mexico's Baby Boom of 35,000 a Week Negates Efforts to Hike Living Standard," *Arizona Republic*, 15 May 1974; "Mexico's Population Booming," *San Antonio Express*, 3 November 1975; "Mexico Aware of High Birth Rate," *El Paso Times*, 7 February 1976; Ramon Villalobos, "Population Exploding in Mexico," *El Paso Times*, 8 February 1976; "Mushrooming Population Starts to Haunt Mexico," *Arizona Journal*, 8 August 1976; George W. Grayson, ". . . But Overpopulation Threatens Mexico," *Los Angeles Times*, 25 April 1977; James Reston, "Mexico's One Hundred Million," *Denver Post*, 31 August 1975; COMEXAZ Clippings.

31. Letter from Edmund H. Kellogg to Tanton, 2 December 1976, Box 4, Folder: Letters, 1974–1979, Tanton Papers.

32. Letter from Thomas E. Dustin to Paul Ahrens, 27 April 1978, Box 4, Folder: Letters, 1974–1979, Tanton Papers.

33. Letter from Douglas V. Bergalind to Tanton, 4 June 1975, Box 4, Folder: Letters 1971–1975, Tanton Papers.

34. Ibid. This comment is underlined in Bergalind's letter.

35. Letter from Douglas V. Bergalind to Mike McCloskey, 12 June 1974, Box 106, Folder 47, Sierra Club Papers.

36. Letter from Douglas V. Bergalind to ZPG, 9 June 1974, Box 4, Folder: Letters 1971–1975, Tanton Papers.

37. Letter from Douglas Bergalind to Sierra Club Board of Directors, 12 April 1978, Sierra Club Papers.

38. "Population and Immigration," *zPG-California Newsletter* vol. 7, no. 2 (November 1978): 3, Box 3, Folder: Immigration, 1976–1978, ZPG Records.

39. "Ten Years of Advocacy," *National Reporter* vol. 10, no. 9 (November 1978): 2.

40. Tanton, "International Migration as an Obstacle to Achieving World Stability," 221.

41. Ibid., 227.

42. Letter from Mark Horling to Tanton, Tanton Papers.

43. Letter from Adam McLane to Tanton, 10 July 1973, Box 1, Folder: Tax Law Changes, Tanton Papers.

44. Letter from Jerry Busch to Judy Kunofsky, 27 August 1980, Box 252, Folder 16, Sierra Club Papers.

45. A 1977 newspaper article also cites the recent decline in U.S. birthrates as one reason for ZPG's new emphasis on immigration (Susan Jacoby, "Anti-Immigration Campaign Begun," *Washington Post*, 8 May 1977, sec. A, p. 2).

46. Letter from Russell Mills to Tanton, 19 October 1971, Box 4, Folder: Letters 1971–1975, Tanton Papers.

47. See, for example, Letter from Frank Boseaious to Judy Senderowitz, 9 October 1974, Box 4, Folder: Letters 1971–1975, Tanton Papers.

48. Letter from Olga Thornley to Tanton, n.d., Box 4, Folder: Miscellaneous Correspondence, Tanton Papers.

49. "Ten Years of Advocacy," 2.

50. Minutes, Fifth Annual Board Meeting of the Board of Directors of Zero Population Growth, Inc., Boston, Massachusetts, 13–15 April 1974, 9, Box 4, Folder: Minutes, Board (ZPG Inc.), Tanton Papers.

51. "Resolution on Immigration," in ibid., 18.

52. Ibid., 15–16.

53. Bradley Graham, "ZPG Seeks 90 Percent Slash in Immigration," *Denver Post*, 5 July 1974, COMEXAZ Clippings.

54. Susan Jacoby, "ZPG Begins Drive to Cut Immigration," *Denver Post*, 18 May 1977, COMEXAZ Clippings.

While attributed to a largely student-based initial membership and a public perception that the population crisis was over, reasons for the drop in ZPG membership have not been decisively determined.

55. "A Funding Proposal for a Program of Applied Research, Public Education, and Policy Development on United States Immigration Policy," submitted by ZPG Inc., 20 June 1977, Box 4, Folder: Immigration Project Proposal, Tanton Papers.

56. Huss and Wirken, "Illegal Immigration."

57. "Zero Population Growth, Inc.: Annual Report, 1977," 2, Box 5, Folder: Population Policy, Tanton Papers; and "Proposal for an Immigration Reform Program," ZPG Foundation, n.d., Box 4, Folder: Immigration Project Proposal, Tanton Papers.

58. See mailing with "Bob Packwood" letterhead in Box 197, Folder 37, Sierra Club Papers.

59. Direct mail to "Dear Friend," 1977, Box 4, Folder: Direct Mail, Tanton Papers.

60. Mott Enterprises Inc. was hired to compile and send the direct mailing. In a letter regarding the first draft of the mailing, a representative of Mott commented that "The letter . . . stresses the problems of illegal immigration that it serves to alarm . . . and well it should." Letter from Daphne W. Dwyer II to Ms. Jane Bristol, 1 February 1977, Box 4, Folder: Outlet Mail, Tanton Papers.

61. "Dear Friend" direct mail, 3.

62. See, for example, letter from Tanton to Senator Bob Packwood, 28 March 1977, Box 4, Folder: Letters 1975–1979, Tanton Papers.

63. "Dear Friend" direct mail, 2.

64. For example, in a letter to Leon Bouvier at the Population Reference Bureau, Tanton questioned Bouvier's assertion that the levels of native born and immigrants are the same in a report entitled *U.S. Population in 2000—Zero Growth or Not?* by referencing Davis's September 1974 article in *Scientific American*. Letter from Tanton to Leon Bouvier, 16 October 1975, Box 4, Folder: Letters, 1971–1975, Tanton Papers.

65. Davis, "The Migration of Human Populations," 103.

66. Letter from Tanton to Judy Kunofsky, 28 July 1975, Box 2, Folder: Sierra Club Population Committee Correspondence, 1975, Tanton Papers.

67. Although Tanton makes this point in several documents, the most developed I could determine is in "The Immigration Component of Population Policy," 26 July 1975, First Draft Population Policy, September 1975, Box 5, Folder: Population Policy, Tanton Papers.

68. Letter from Vincent P. Barbara, Director, Bureau of the Census, to Honorable Patricia Schroeder, 14 August 1975, Box 4, Folder: Goals Statement Letters, 1971–1975, Tanton Papers.

69. Letter from Judy Kunofsky to Tanton, 28 August 1975, Tanton Papers.

70. Letter from Tanton to Charles Westhoff, 7 July 1975, Box 4, Folder: Letters, 1971–1975, Tanton Papers. Attached to this letter is a marginal note reading: "Same letter also sent to Kinglsey Davis."

71. Ibid.

72. Letter from Tanton to Melanie Wirken, 15 September 1975, Box 4, Folder: Goals Statement Letters, 1971–1975, Tanton Papers.

73. Letter from Tanton to Gene Matalene, n.d., Box 1, Folder: Tax Law Changes, Tanton Papers.

74. Also see "Dear Abby," 9 April 1974, *Los Angeles Times,* COMEXAZ Clippings. In this column a mother of seventeen children who fears that her husband does not love her anymore asked Abby: "Could it be because he was born and raised in Mexico and I was born and raised in Texas?" Abby's complete response is: "Maybe. Most Mexican-born men have the Old World Spanish attitude about women—they should be seen and not heard, should always have a baby in their arms and another on the way, stay at home and never complain."

75. Elaine Stansfield, director of ZPG-LA, "Testimony at Senate Commission on Immigration and Refugee Policy Hearings," Box 3, Folder: Immigration, 1979–1980, ZPG Records.

76. Ibid.

77. For example, her marginal notes upon reading an article on the issues which she is weighing in her formulation of ZPG's approach to illegal immigration read: "Inadequate. No mention of pregnant culture." See Phyllis Eisen, "Observations from a Total-Immersion Course of Illegal Immigration" (with marginal notes by Elaine Stansfield), *National Reporter* vol. 10, no. 6 (August 1978): 1, 6; ZPG Records.

78. Letter from Elaine Stansfield, director of ZPG-LA, to Phyllis Eisen, 20 October 1978, Box 3, Folder: Immigration 1976–1978, ZPG Records.

79. Ibid.

80. Elaine Stansfield, director of ZPG-LA, "Testimony at White House Hearings on Families, Los Angeles, December 13, 1979," Box 3, Folder: Immigration 1979–1980, ZPG Records.

81. For example, Douglas Bergalind, in his correspondence with Tanton (discussed earlier), asked Tanton, "please don't publish any of this as I would be

deported." In letter·from Bergalind to ZPG, 9 June 1974, Box 4, Folder: Letters 1971–1975, Tanton Papers.

82. Damman, "Dr. No."

83. Letter from Roy Morgan to Tanton, 30 August 1978, Box 4, Folder: Immigration Project Proposal; ZPG Foundation Inc. Board of Directors Meeting Minutes, 6–8 October 1978, 2, Box 4, Folder: Minutes and Agendas; Tanton Papers.

Although Tanton left ZPG in 1978 to begin his work with the Federation of American Immigration Reform (FAIR), ZPG continued its own work on the immigration front. An immigration specialist, Phyllis Eisen, was hired to represent the group at these hearings and formulate a ZPG stance on immigration.

84. "Perhaps the most encouraging development in 1979 on immigration was the establishment of the Federation for American Immigration Reform (FAIR). FAIR has already begun to make an impact on immigration legislation, and we are favorably impressed. A FAIR leaflet is enclosed. We encourage everyone interested in an effective solution to illegal immigration to join FAIR" (ZPG-Livermore, "Immigration Newsletter," no. 3 (December 1979), Box 3, Folder: Immigration: 1979–1980, ZPG Records.

85. Damman, "Doctor No."

86. *Federation of American Immigration Reform (FAIR) et al. v. Philip M. Klutznick, Secretary of Commerce, et al.* (486 F. Supp. 564) (Civ. A. No. 79-3269) (26 February 1980).

87. Damman, "Dr. No." The request for a temporary injunction was denied, and FAIR appealed to the Court of Appeals and asked the Supreme Court to take immediate jurisdiction; the appeal was denied multiple times.

88. For an overview, see Jane Kay, "Sierra Club Debates Migrant Issue," *San Francisco Examiner*, 20 October 1997, sec. A, p. 3; Bhatia, "Green or Brown? White Nativist Environmental Movements"; and J. P. Bone, "The Battle for the Soul of the Sierra Club," *Mindfield Magazine* (e-magazine), 4 March 1998; Nancy Cleeland, "Sierra Club to Take on Immigration Question," *Los Angeles Times*, 29 September 1997, sec. 1, pp. 1, 23; Florangela Davila, "Immigration Dispute Spawns Factions, Anger in Sierra Club," *Seattle Times* (online ed.) 18 February 2004; Glen Martin, "Board Election Divides Sierra Club: Environmentalists Renew Bitter Fight over Controlling U.S. Immigration," *San Francisco Chronicle* (online ed.) 11 February 2004; Glen Martin and Ramon G. McLeod, "Sierra Club Divided by Vote on Immigration," *San Francisco Chronicle*, 23 February 1998, sec. A, p. 7.

CHAPTER SIX

1. Yolanda M. Nava, "The Chicana and Employment: Needs Analysis and Recommendations for Legislation," testimony presented before the California Commission on the Status of Women on behalf of Comisión Femenil Mexicana, Los Angeles, 10 February 1973, CFMN Archives.

2. Ibid., 2.

3. Gómez, "La Feminista."

4. Collins, *Black Feminist Thought.*

5. Gutiérrez, "The Racial Politics of Reproduction."

6. MALDEF, RG 5, Box 910, Folder 1, MALDEF Papers.

7. Gutiérrez, "Policing 'Pregnant Pilgrims.'"

8. Espino, "Woman Sterilized as Gives Birth."

9. Lucio interview.

10. See Mike Goodman, "Sterilization at County Hospitals to Be Probed," *Los Angeles Times,* 22 November 1974, sec. D, p. 1; Robert Kistler, "Women 'Pushed' Into Sterilization, Doctor Charges", *Los Angeles Times,* 2 December 1974, sec. A, pp. 1, 3, 26–28; Robert Kistler, "Many U.S. Rules on Sterilization Abuses Ignored Here," *Los Angeles Times,* 3 December 1974, sec. A, pp. 3, 24–26. It was also largely through the independent efforts of Bernard Rosenfeld that different people became aware of the sterilization abuses occurring.

11. Flyer, "Birth Control Is Used as a Weapon Against Our Third World Sisters!" in possession of the author; Kathy Proppe, "Socialist Feminism in Practice," *L.A. Women's Union Newsletter* vol. 1, no. 5 (December 1974): 12–13.

12. "LA County General Is Sterilizing Women Against Their Wills," poster, Rosenfeld Papers.

13. Ibid.

14. Proppe, "Socialist Feminism in Practice," 2.

15. From pictures accompanying the article "Stop Forced Sterilization Now!" (an excerpt of the pamphlet by the same name) *La Raza Magazine* vol. 2, no. 4 (January 1975): 12–16.

16. Committee to End Forced Sterilization, Petition, Box 5, File 2, Rosenfeld Papers.

17. See documents pertaining to NCASA Inc. fundraiser, esp. NCASA to Francisca Flores, n.d., Box 27, Folder 15, CFMN Archives.

18. Vélez interview.

19. Hernández interview.

20. Hernández interview.

21. Molina interview.

22. Olivia Rodríguez interview.

23. Espino, "Woman Sterilized as Gives Birth."

24. Martínez interview.

25. "President's Message," CFMN 1978 Annual Report, Box 2, Folder 24, CFMN Archives.

26. Robert Rawitch, "State Enjoined in Sterilization Suit Filed by Women," *Los Angeles Times,* 7 October 1975, sec. A, pp. 1, 6.

27. Georgina Torres-Rizk, Los Angeles Center for Law and Justice, "Sterilization Abuses Against Chicanas in Los Angeles," 2 December 1976, RG 9, Box 95, Folder 4, MALDEF Papers. As part of the Madrigal case, lawyers introduced a draft

of suggested guidelines. At the same time, the Coalition for the Medical Rights of Women was also drafting a set of suggested guidelines, and when they found out about each other, they began collaborating. The resulting "Petition for Regulations to Prevent Coerced Sterilizations in All Licensed Health Care Facilities," submitted to the California Department of Health, can be found in RG 5, Box 10, Folder 6, MALDEF Papers.

28. CA CMRW; *Patient Education Research Project; Hastings Law School Women's Union; SFNLAF Women's Litigation Unit; MALDEF; SF Women's Health Center; Health Policy Advisory Council and Feminist Health Project of the American Friends Service Committee of Northern California v. California Department of Health,* "Petition for Regulations to Prevent Coerced Sterilizations in All Licensed Health Care Facilities," 18 April 1975, RG 5, Box 10, Folder 6, MALDEF Papers.

29. Ibid., 1.

30. Talavera, "Sterilization Is Not an Alternative in Family Planning."

31. Sandra A. Salazar, "Fight to Stop Sterilization Abuse!" 3, n.d., RG 5, Box 54, Folder 1, MALDEF Papers.

32. Chicana Rights Project, "MALDEF's Efforts in the Fight Against the Involuntary Sterilization of Third World Women," 26 August 1975, RG 5, Box 55, Folder 1, MALDEF Papers.

33. Martínez interview.

34. Molina interview.

35. Testimony of Elisa Sanchez, Sterilization Regulations hearing, n.d., RG 5, Box 54, Folder 2, MALDEF Papers.

36. "Public Hearings, State Department of Health: Sterilization Regulations," Los Angeles, San Francisco, and Sacramento, California, RG 5, Box 54, Folder 9, MALDEF Papers.

37. Martínez interview.

38. Testimony of Concha Saucedo, Department of Health Public Hearing: Sterilization Regulations, San Francisco, 1977, RG 5, Box 54, Folder 9, MALDEF Papers.

39. Testimony of Gloria Molina, Department of Health Public Hearing: Sterilization Regulations, San Francisco, 1977, 114, RG 5, Box 54, Folder 9, MALDEF Papers.

40. For the legal aspects of the debate over the regulations, see *Relf et al. v. Weinberger et al.* and *National Welfare Rights Organization v. Weinberger, et al.,* Civ. A. Nos. 73-1557, 74-243, 372 F. Supp. 1196, 15 March 1974; *Relf et al. v. Mathews et al.* and *National Welfare Rights Organization v. Mathews et al.* Civ. A. Nos 1557-3, 74-243, 403 F. Supp. 1235, 22 October 1975; and *Relf et al. v. Weinberger et al.* and *National Welfare Rights Organization v. Weinberger et al.,* 13 September 1977. For an excellent and thorough analysis of the debate as it was shaped in the public arena, see Petchesky, "Reproduction, Ethics, and Public Policy."

41. Despite the promulgation of these guidelines by HEW, however, a 1975 study found "gross noncompliance" with the regulations (Krauss, *Hospital Survey on Sterilization Policies*).

42. MALDEF, "Sterilization Abuse Challenged" (press release), 19 October 1979, Box 43, Folder 7, MALDEF Papers.

43. Brief of Amici Curiae, Comisión Femenil Mexicana and Women for Equal Health Care in Support of Plaintiffs—Appellants in the case of *Madrigal v. Quilligan* 78-3178, 19 October 1979.

44. Torres-Rizk, "Abuses Against Chicanas," 13.

CHAPTER SEVEN

The epigraph is taken from a memorandum by Tanton, "Commentary on the WITAN IV," 28 December 1988, and "Packet Attachments," n.d., Box 1, Folder: Tanton Miscellaneous Letters, Tanton Papers.

1. U.S. English is an organization that has successfully helped to dismantle bilingual education across the country. For a detailed history, see Crawford, "Hispanophobia."

2. Tanton, "Commentary on the WITAN IV."

3. Crawford, "Hispanophobia," 151. See Gordon, *Women's Body, Women's Right*; Kelves, *In the Name of Eugenics*; and Chase, *The Legacy of Malthus*, for overviews of eugenic concerns as expressed at the turn of the century in the United States.

4. Tanton, "Commentary on the WITAN IV."

5. Inda, "Foreign Bodies." For excellent theoretical and empirical examinations of the "new" nativism in historical context, see Perea, *Immigrants Out!*; and Calavita, "The New Politics of Immigration."

6. Tony Bizjak, "31.3 Million and Counting—State Grew By 654,000 in 1992," *Sacramento Bee*, 17 February 1993, sec. A, p. 3; also see Dan Walters, "State Aching for a Break," *Sacramento Bee*, 19 February 1993, sec. A, p. 3.

7. David Nyhan, "The Golden State Has Lost Its Luster," *Boston Globe*, 18 February 1993, Op-Ed section, p. 17.

8. Tony Quinn, "What is Really Driving California's Budget Woes? Demographics," *Los Angeles Times*, 22 December 1991, sec. M, p. 6.

9. As Quinn most bluntly stated, "The fiscal crisis that California has suffered in the last three years is driven by demographic change" (ibid.); see also Bizjak, "383 Million Americans By 2050?" *Sacramento Bee*, 4 December 1992, sec. A, p. 1.

10. Harold Gilliam, "Bursting at the Seams: A Torrent of New Immigrants Is Pushing California to the Limit," *San Francisco Chronicle*, 21 February 1993, sec. 1, p. 7; Dan Walters, "Our State's Population is Killing Us," *San Diego Union-Tribune*, 20 February 1993, sec. B, p. 12.

11. Debate about the financial impact of undocumented immigrants on state social resources continues. Some analysts argue that undocumented immigrants "cost" the nation billions of dollars annually; for example, Donald Huddle (*The National Cost of Immigration in 1993*) estimated that the net national cost of "illegal aliens" during 1994 was between 16 and 21.6 billion dollars, but others argue that

immigrants continue to contribute more financial resources than they utilize (e.g., Fix and Passel, "Setting the Record Straight"). However, the deficient methodology and questionable validity of many of these studies is often raised; for analysis of each of these studies as well as others, see Hinojosa and Schey, "The Faulty Logic of the Anti-immigration Rhetoric." For a comprehensive review of contrasting national-level studies of the fiscal impacts of immigrants, see Center for Immigration Studies, *The Costs of Immigration*.

12. Demographic Research Unit, California Department of Finance, Report 93 P5, *Birth Projections for California State and Counties* 2 (1993).

13. Chávez, "Immigration Reform and Nativism"; and Johnson, "An Essay on Immigration Politics," and "Public Benefits and Immigration." In an in-depth analysis of *Los Angeles Times* coverage of the immigration debates surrounding Proposition 187, Otto Santa Ana ("'Like An Animal I Was Treated'") demonstrates that public discourse about Mexican immigrants was heavily racist and rife with xenophobic sentiment.

14. Pete Wilson, "Drowning in a Flood of Immigrants," *Orlando Sentinel*, 29 August 1993, sec. G, p. 6. Also see Annie Nakao, "Assessing the Cost of Immigration," *San Francisco Examiner*, 1 December 1991, sec. B, pp. 1–3, for Wilson's early attempts to blame illegal immigrants for the state's budget problems.

15. Calavita, "The New Politics of Immigration." It is important to note that such discourses diverged from previous anti-immigrant organizers' focus on blaming immigrants for "taking" jobs from U.S. citizens. According to Calavita, this characterization of the problem as one of "immigrants-as-a-fiscal-burden" is a result of the balanced-budget conservatism prevalent in the late-twentieth-century political economy.

16. During 1993 twenty-one bills denying public housing, drivers' licenses, welfare, and other benefits were introduced in the state legislature (Robert Reinhold, "A Welcome for Immigrants Turns to Resentment," *New York Times*, 25 August 1993, sec. A, p. 1).

17. For a succinct but comprehensive summary of the history of public concern and policies about the immigrants' use of public benefits, see Johnson, "Public Benefits and Immigration."

18. Chávez, "Immigration Reform and Nativism"; Johnson, "Public Benefits and Immigration" and "An Essay on Immigration Politics"; Hondaganeu-Sotelo, "Women and Children First"; and Lindsley, "The Gendered Assault on Immigrants."

19. Wilson, "Anti-Immigrant Sentiment."

20. Pete Wilson, "Crack Down on Illegals," *USA Today*, 20 August 1993, sec. A, p. 12.

21. See Jonathon P. Decker, "Lawmakers Look to Revoke Automatic Citizenship Law," *Christian Science Monitor*, 27 December 1995, p. 3.

22. 138 Congressional Record E2572-01, E2573 (10 September 1992), cited in Roberts, *Killing the Black Body*.

23. Such legislative efforts were often made on behalf of constituents' urgings;

concerned citizens demanded that public officials take measures to stop the problem. During a town hall meeting convened by congressional representative Henry
Waxman, one constituent asked him why the children of women who "come across
the border and drop their babies" are granted American citizenship (Hill-Holtzman,
"Voters Mad as Hell, And Waxman's Taking It," *Los Angeles Times*, 10 June 1993,
sec. J, p. 1).

24. When these efforts failed, a bipartisan group of thirty California congressional delegates wrote a letter to President Clinton requesting full federal reimburse-
ment for local and state medical costs for providing emergency health services to
undocumented immigrants. In part they were expressing their belief that the president's health care proposal to set aside $1 billion a year to finance the emergency
treatment of undocumented immigrants was absurdly inadequate (Vlae Kershner,
"Lawmakers Press Clinton on Cost of Illegals; Health Care," *San Francisco Chronicle*, 23 October 1993, sec. A, p. 4; Sam Howe Verhovek, "Health Proposal Could
Leave Aliens in U.S. Without Care," *New York Times*, 25 October 1993, sec. A, p. 1.

25. Daniel B. Wood, "Confronting California's Immigration Issue," *Christian
Science Monitor*, 4 October 1993, p. 12.

Wilson repeatedly equated the provision of prenatal benefits to undocumented
immigrants with the inability to provide the same for California residents. When
asked if he thought his policies were cruel during an ABC *20/20* interview, Wilson
replied, "Let me ask you something—is it cruel to the California child who doesn't
get prenatal care because the immigrant mother does? I mean, that's what's happened" (cited in George Skelton, "Baby Delivery, Citizenship, and Tax Money," *Los
Angeles Times*, 13 January 1994, sec. A, p. 3).

26. It is significant to note that with this stance Wilson was in effect belying his
inaugural address promise that every woman in the state would receive prenatal
care (Lou Cannon, "Wilson Takes Office as Governor," *Los Angeles Times*, 8 January
1991, sec. A, p. 3).

27. Annie Caroline Schuler, "Letter to the Editor," *Los Angeles Times*, 28 November 1995, sec. B, p. 8.

28. Douglas P. Shuit, "Prenatal Care Urged for Illegal Immigrants," *Los Angeles
Times*, 8 January 1994, sec. A., p. 1; Jonathan Freedman, "Wilson's New Witch Hunt:
Prenatal Aliens," *Los Angeles Times*, 30 January 1994, sec. M, p. 5.

29. For the legislative battles which ensued after 1994 surrounding Wilson's attempts to remove prenatal care to undocumented women from the budget during
state assembly meetings, see Marc Lifsher and Daniel M. Weintraub, "Budget Cap-
tive in Assembly," *Orange County Register*, 31 July 1995, sec. A, p. 1; Robert B. Gunni-
son and Greg Lucas, "Late-Night Accord on State Budget Plan: Wilson, Legislators
Hammer Out Deal," *San Francisco Chronicle*, 4 July 1996, sec. A, p. 1; Mark Katches,
"$67.2 Billion Budget Signed By Wilson," *Orange County Register*, 19 August 1997,
sec. A, p. 4.

30. Skelton, "Baby Delivery."

31. Ibid.

32. See Nancy Cleeland, "Births to Illegal Immigrants on the Rise: State Paid Pre-natal Care for Undocumented Moms Depends on Residency," *San Diego Union-Tribune,* 20 February 1994, sec. A, p. 1; and "Blockade at Border Hasn't Cut Births," sec. A, p. 23. See also Rex Dalton, "Births to Illegal Immigrants on the Rise: California Taxpayers Finance Soaring Numbers of Foreigners' Babies," sec. A, p. 1.

33. Ibid.

34. Skelton, "Baby Delivery."

35. Ibid.

36. Sam Howe Verhovek, "Health Proposal Could Leave Aliens in U.S. Without Care," *New York Times,* 25 October 1993, sec. A, p. 1.

37. Paul Feldman and Amy Pyle, "Wilson Acts to Enforce Parts of Prop. 187," *Los Angeles Times,* 10 November 1994, sec. A, p. 1.

38. Patrick J. McDonnell and Julie Marquis, "Clinics See Fewer Patients After Proposition 187," *Los Angeles Times,* 29 November 1994, sec. A, p. 1.

While retaining their position of having the lowest rates of first trimester prenatal visits for any group of women, one study conducted by the Orange County Health Care agency found that the number of Latina mothers receiving early prenatal care jumped from 64 percent in 1992 to 77 percent in 1997 (Maria Elena Fernández, "Prenatal Education, Care Rising for Latinas," *Los Angeles Times,* 27 October 1999, sec. B, p. 1).

39. Although I cannot provide a detailed description and analysis of federal welfare reform here, its major centerpiece was the discontinuation of federal cash payments through Aid to Families with Dependent Children (AFDC) and the development of block grants to states through a new program called Temporary Assistance to Needy Families (TANF). In addition, recipients of TANF are required to work a minimum of twenty hours per week and are subject to a five-year limit for recipiency. For more thorough accounts of welfare reform in relation to immigration, see Espenshade et al., "Implications of the 1996 Welfare and Immigration Reform Acts"; Fix and Tumlin, "Welfare Reform and the Devolution of Immigrant Policy."

40. Fix and Tumlin, "Welfare Reform."

41. Representative Michael Bilirakis (Florida), H.R. Conf. Rep. No. 104–725 (1996); 142 *Congressional Record* H9392 (daily edition, 31 July 1996). Bilirakis was then chairman of the House Health and Environment Subcommittee.

42. Under the reformed welfare regulations, new immigrants are prohibited from receiving any public benefits until after residing in the United States for five years.

43. Borjas and Hilton, *Immigration and the Welfare State.*

44. Duleep and Regets, "The Elusive Concept of Immigrant Quality"; Fix and Passel, *Immigration and Immigrants;* Van Hook et al., "Public Assistance Receipt Among Immigrants and Natives."

45. Wilson officials later justified the singular focus on prenatal care, arguing that it is the most expensive and easily identifiable source of aid to illegal immigrants (Patrick J. McDonnell, "Wilson Sets Prenatal Care Cutoff Dec. 1," *Los Angeles Times,* 24 October 1996, sec. A, p. 26).

In 1997 Arizona also terminated prenatal care for undocumented women (Martin Van Der Werf and Pamela Manson, "State to End Prenatal Care For Illegals," *Arizona Republic*, 15 January 1997, sec. B, p. 1).

46. Dave Lesher and Patrick McDonnell, "Wilson Calls Halt to Much of Aid for Illegal Immigrants: Governor Uses Federal Welfare Reform to Implement Many Cuts Contained in Proposition 187," *Los Angeles Times*, 28 August 1996, sec. A, p. 1; Daniel Sneider, "California's Latest Weapon Against Illegal Aliens: U.S. Welfare Reform," *Christian Science Monitor*, 30 August 1996, sec. 1, p. 1.

47. Deborah Anderluh, "End of Prenatal Care for Illegal Immigrants Ordered," *Sacramento Bee*, 2 November 1996, sec. A, p. 1. The details of the implementation of the emergency regulations presented a veritable roller-coaster ride. While initially foiled by a preliminary injunction issued by Judge William Cahill (based upon reasoning that state officials failed to prove that an emergency situation existed), the state was forced to comply with the standard administrative procedures necessary for drafting and enacting new regulations, which take several months. Public hearings regarding the issuance of the new regulations were held as Wilson applied for an appeal, which eventually reversed Judge Cahill's decision, granting Wilson the ability to enact his emergency regulations in August 1997 (Maura Dolan, "Judge Blocks State Cutoff of Prenatal Care," *Los Angeles Times*, 27 November 1996, sec. A, p. 3; Claire Cooper, "State Asks OK to Cut Prenatal Care for Immigrants," *Sacramento Bee*, 30 January 1997, sec. A, p. 4; Patrick J. McDonnell and Dave Lesher, "Court Upholds State Plan to Cut Prenatal Care," *Los Angeles Times*, 26 August 1997, sec. A, p. 3).

48. Patrick McDonnell, "Wilson Edict Stirs Fears at L.A. Clinic," *Los Angeles Times*, 31 August 1996, sec. B, p. 1.

49. Tim Golden, "Pregnant Immigrants Wait Out Policy Storm," *New York Times*, 16 October 1996, sec. A, p. 1; William Claiborne, "Groups Sue to Save Prenatal Care," *Washington Post*, 16 October 1996, sec. A, p. 3; Patrick J. McDonnell and Virginia Ellis, "Wilson Acts to Bar Prenatal Care for Illegal Immigrants," *Los Angeles Times*, 2 November 1996, sec. A, p. 1; Hilary MacGregor, "Physicians Oppose Ban on Care," *Los Angeles Times*, 4 January 1998, sec. B, p. 1.

50. Patrick J. McDonnell, "Plan to End Funding for Prenatal Care is Assailed," *Los Angeles Times*, 17 October 1996, sec. A, p. 3; Greg Lucas and David Tuller, "Wilson Sets Date to End Care for Pregnant Illegals But Bay Area Counties Refuse to Halt Benefits," *San Francisco Chronicle*, 2 November 1996, sec. A, p. 13.

For an cogent medical argument against Wilson's efforts to halt state funding of prenatal care services to undocumented immigrant women, see Minkoff et al., "Welfare Reform and the Obstetrical Care of Immigrants and Their Newborns."

51. The legal battles surrounding the implementation of Wilson's ban on prenatal care was well documented by major newspapers in the state. In addition to the previously cited articles, see "Cutoff of Prenatal Care for Illegal Immigrants Allowed," *Los Angeles Times*, 13 November 1997, sec. A, p. 28; Patrick J. McDonnell, "Judge Upholds Wilson Ban on Prenatal Care," *Los Angeles Times*, 18 December

1997, sec. A, p. 3; Aurelio Rojas, "Judge Blocks Prenatal Care Ban," *San Francisco Chronicle*, 20 December 1997, sec. A, p. 15; "Illegal Immigrants' Prenatal Care Upheld," *Sacramento Bee*, 20 December 1997, sec. A, p. 3; Claire Cooper, "March 1 Cutoff for Some Prenatal Aid," *Sacramento Bee*, 30 January 1998, sec. A, p. 7; Patrick J. McDonnell, "Ban on Prenatal Care for Illegal Immigrants Halted," *Los Angeles Times*, 6 March 1998, sec. A, p. 18, and "Ruling Delays Prenatal Care Ban Decision," *Los Angeles Times*, 12 June 1998, sec. A, p. 3; Harriet Chiang, "Plan to Ban Medi-Cal Benefits to Immigrants Blocked By Court," *San Francisco Chronicle*, 13 August 1998, sec. A, p. 24.

52. Dan Morain, "Prenatal Care for Immigrants in Davis Budget," *Los Angeles Times*, 14 January 1999, sec. A, p. 1; "Davis Continues Prenatal Care for Illegal Migrants," *San Diego Union Tribune*, 27 July 1999, sec. A, p. 3; Patrick J. McDonnell, "State OKs Prenatal Aid for Immigrants," *Los Angeles Times*, 27 July 1999, sec. A, p. 3.

53. Students Against the Brown Peril, "Stop the Mexican Invasion: *Mata las Sucias Mexican Ratas!*" flyer on file with author, n.d.

54. Ibid.

55. Fix and Passel, "The Scope and Impact of Welfare Reform's Immigrant Provisions," 2.

56. Ibid., 30.

57. Chang, *Disposable Domestics*, 206.

58. Park et al., "Impact of Recent Welfare and Immigration Reforms." Also see Borjas, *The Impact of Welfare Reform*; Feld et al., *Immigrants' Access to Health Care After Welfare Reform*.

59. Park et al., "Impact of Recent Welfare and Immigration Reforms."

EPILOGUE

1. Castillo, "Did These Latinas Save Your Life?"

2. Joseph Rodriguez interview.

3. Ibid.

4. Ibid.

5. Ibid.

6. Haya El Nasser, "U.S.-born Hispanics Propel Growth," *USA Today*, 10 May 2006, sec. A, p. 1.

7. http://thomas.loc.gov/cgi-bin/bdquery/z?d109:h.r.00698.

8. Cosner, "Illegal Aliens and American Medicine."

9. Ibid.

10. *Lewis v. Thompson*, 252 F. 3d 567 (2d Cir. 2001).

11. Institute of Medicine, *Unequal Treatment*, 1.

12. Also see Gutiérrez, "'We Will No Longer Be Silent or Invisible.'"

13. Silliman et al., *Undivided Rights*.

14. Gutiérrez, "'We Will No Longer Be Silent or Invisible.'"

REFERENCES

ARCHIVAL SOURCES

California State Department of Health. Archives. Sacramento.

Coalition for the Medical Rights of Women. Selected Papers. Oakland, California.

Comisión Femenil Mexicana, Los Angeles. Archives, I and II. Chicano Studies Research Library, University of California, Los Angeles.

Comisión Femenil Mexicana Nacional (CFMN). Archives (CEMA 30). California Ethnic and Multicultural Archives, Department of Special Collections, Davidson Library, University of California, Santa Barbara.

Comité de México y Aztlán (COMEXAZ). News Clipping Service. Oakland, California.

Cruz, Ricardo/Católicos por La Raza. Papers (CEMA 28). California Ethnic and Multicultural Archives, Department of Special Collections, Davidson Library, University of California, Santa Barbara.

Mexican American Legal Defense and Education Fund (MALDEF). Papers. Stanford University Special Collections, Palo Alto, California.

Rosenfeld, Bernard. Papers. In possession of author.

Sierra Club. Papers. Bancroft Library, University of California, Berkeley.

Tanton, John H. Papers. Bentley Historical Library, University of Michigan, Ann Arbor.

Vélez-Ibáñez, Carlos. Papers. Personal collection (Vélez Papers).

———. Carlos Vélez-Ibáñez Sterilization Archives (Vélez Archives). Chicano Studies Research Library, University of California, Los Angeles.

Zero Population Growth, Los Angeles. Records. California State University, Northridge.

ORAL HISTORY INTERVIEWS

Benker, Karen, 26 June 2001, interviewed by Elena R. Gutiérrez.

Cruz, Frank, 16 May 2000, interviewed by Elena R. Gutiérrez.

Hernández, Antonia, 7 March 1996, interviewed by Elena R. Gutiérrez.

Lucio, Gloria, 17 May 2000, interviewed by Elena R. Gutiérrez.

Martínez, Evelyn, 16 February 2006, interviewed by Elena R. Gutiérrez.

Molina, Gloria, 12 June 2006, interviewed by Elena R. Gutiérrez.

Nabarette, Charles, May 2001, interviewed by Elena R. Gutiérrez and Virginia Espino.

Rodríguez, Joseph, 25 November 2005, interviewed by Elena R. Gutiérrez.

Rodríguez, Olivia, November 2005, interviewed by Elena R. Gutiérrez.

Rosenfeld, Bernard, July 2001, interviewed by Elena R. Gutiérrez and Virginia Espino.

Vélez, Maria Theresa, April 2001, interviewed by Elena R. Gutiérrez.

Vélez-Ibáñez, Carlos, December 1995, interviewed by Elena R. Gutiérrez.

OTHER SOURCES

Acuña, Rodolfo. *Occupied America: A History of Chicanos.* 3rd ed. New York: HarperCollins Publishers, 1988.

Allen, Ruth. "Mexican Peon Women in Texas." *Sociology and Social Research* 16 (1931): 131–142.

———. "Competitive Breeding." In *Race: Individual and Collective Behavior,* edited by E. T. Thompson and E. C. Hughes, 190–195. Glencoe, IL: The Free Press, 1958.

Albiston, Catherine. "The Social Meaning of the Norplant Condition: Constitutional Consideration of Race, Class, and Gender." *Berkeley Women's Law Journal* 9 (1994): 9–57.

Almaguer, Tomás. *Racial Fault Lines: The Historical Origins of White Supremacy in California.* Berkeley: University of California Press, 1994.

Alvírez, David. "The Effects of Formal Church Affiliation and Religiosity on Fertility Patterns of Mexican-American Catholics." *Demography* 10 (1973): 19–36.

Alvírez, David, and Frank D. Bean. "The Mexican American Family." In *Ethnic Families in America: Patterns and Variations,* edited by C. H. Mindel and R. W. Habenstein, 271–292. New York: Elsevier Scientific Publishing Co., 1976.

Amaro, Hortensia D. "Psychological Determinants of Abortion Attitudes Among Mexican-American Women." Ph.D. dissertation, University of California, Los Angeles, 1982.

Anagost, Ann. "A Surfeit of Bodies: Population and the Rationality of the State in Post-Mao China." In *Conceiving the New World Order: The Global Politics of Reproduction,* edited by F. D. Ginsberg and R. Rapp, 22–41. Berkeley: University of California Press, 1995.

Anderson, Richard K. "Obstacles to Population Control." *Journal of the American Medical Association* 197, no. 8 (22 August 1966): 126.

Andrade, Sally. "Family Planning Practices of Mexican Americans." In *Twice a*

Minority: Mexican American Women, edited by Margarita B. Melville, 33–51. St. Louis: Mosby Press, 1980.

———. "Social Science Stereotypes of Mexican American Women: Policy Implications for Research." *Hispanic Journal of Behavioral Sciences* 4 (1982): 223–244.

Appleman, Philip. *The Silent Explosion.* Boston: Beacon Press, 1966.

Aptheker, Herbert. "Sterilization, Experimentation, and Imperialism." *Political Affairs* 53 (1974): 37–48.

Aragon de Valdez, Theresa. "Organizing as a Political Tool for the Chicana." *Frontiers: A Journal of Women's Studies* 5 (1980): 7–13.

Arredondo, Gabriela F., Aída Hurtado, Norma Klahn, Olga Nájera Ramírez, and Patricia Zavella. *Chicana Feminisms: A Critical Reader.* Durham, NC: Duke University Press, 2003.

Aviaro, Hortensia. "Latina Attitudes Towards Abortion." *Nuestro* (1981): 43–44.

Baca Zinn, Maxine. "Political Familism: Toward Sex Role Equality in Chicano Families." *Aztlán* 6 (1975): 13–26.

———. "Chicano Family Research." *Journal of Ethnic Studies* 7 (1979): 59–71.

———. "Mexican American Women in the Social Sciences." *Signs: A Journal of Women in Culture and Society* 8 (1982): 259–272.

———. "Family, Feminism, and Race in America." *Gender and Society* 4 (1990): 68–82.

Bachrach, Peter, and Elihu Bergman. *Power and Choice: The Formulation of American Population Policy.* Lexington: Lexington Books, 1973.

Barnett, Larry. "A History of Zero Population Growth, Inc." *Mankind* 4, no. 12 (April 1975): 28–29.

———. "Zero Population Growth, Inc.: A Second Study." *Journal of Biosocial Science* 6 (1974): 1–22.

Bean, Frank D., and John P. Marcum. "Differential Fertility and the Minority Group Status Hypothesis: An Assessment and Review." In *The Demography of Racial and Ethnic Groups,* edited by F. D. Bean and P. Frisbie, 189–211. New York: Academic Press, 1978.

Bean, Frank D., and Marta Tienda. *The Hispanic Population of the United States.* New York: Russell-Sage Foundation, 1987.

Bhatia, Rajani. "Green or Brown? White Nativist Environmental Movements." In *Home Grown Hate: Gender and Organized Racism,* 205–225. New York: Routledge.

Black, Edwin. *War Against the Weak: Eugenics and America's Campaign to Create a Master Race.* New York: Thunders Mouth Press, 2003.

Blake, Judith, and Martha Giménez. "Coercive Pronatalism and American Population Policy." In *Population Studies,* edited by K. Kammeyer, 29–67. Chicago: Rand McNally, 1975.

Bogardus, Emory S. *The Mexican in the United States.* Los Angeles: University of Southern California Press, 1934.

Bogue, Donald J. "Demographic Aspects of Maternity and Infant Care in the

Year 2001." Paper presented at the Annual Meeting of American College of Obstetricians and Gynecologists, San Francisco, 6 May 1971.

Bordo, Susan. *Unbearable Weight: Feminism, Western Culture, and the Body.* Berkeley: University of California Press, 1993.

Borjas, George J. *The Impact of Welfare Reform on Immigrant Welfare Use.* Cambridge, MA: Center for Immigration Studies, 2002.

Borjas, George J., and Lynette Hilton. *Immigration and the Welfare State: Immigrant Participation in Means Tested Entitlement Programs.* Cambridge, MA: National Bureau of Economic Research, 1995.

Boswell, Thomas D. "The Growth and Proportional Distribution of the Mexican Stock Population of the United States, 1910–1970." *Mississippi Geographer* 7 (1979): 57–76.

Bouvier, Leon F., and Philip Martin. *Population Change and California's Future.* Washington, D.C.: Population Reference Bureau, 1985.

Bradshaw, Benjamin S., and Frank D. Bean. *Some Aspects of Mexican American Fertility,* edited by C. F. Westhoff and R. Parks. Washington, D.C.: U.S. Government Printing Office, 1972.

———. "Trends in the Fertility of Mexican Americans: 1950–1970." *Social Science Quarterly* 53 (1973): 689–696.

Briggs, Laura. *Reproducing Empire: Race, Sex, Science, and U.S. Imperialism in Puerto Rico.* Berkeley: University of California Press, 2002.

Browning, Harley L., and Dudley L. Poston. "Population and the American Future: A Discussion and Introduction to a Review Symposium." *Social Science Quarterly* 53 (1972): 445–451.

Buxton, C. Lee. "The Doctor's Responsibility in Population Control." *Northwest Medicine* 65 (1966): 112–116.

California Assembly Committee on Environmental Quality. *Report on the State's Role in Population Growth and Distribution, Demographic and Family Life, Education, and Family Planning.* San Francisco, 1972.

California Assembly Science and Technology Advisory Council. *California Population Problems and State Policy: Report to the Assembly General Research Committee.* Sacramento, 1971.

California Population Commission. *Annual Report, 1942.* Sacramento, 1943.

———. *California by 1950: A Special Report on the Future Growth of the State.* Sacramento, 1943.

California Population Study Commission. *Report to the Governor.* Sacramento, 1967.

California State Reconstruction and Reemployment Commission. *How Many Californians? Summary, Report, Estimates of Population Growth in California 1940–1950.* Sacramento, 1944.

———. *Estimated Range for Population Growth in California to 1960.* Sacramento, 1946.

Calavita, Kitty. "The New Politics of Immigration: 'Balanced-budget Conservatism' and the Symbolism of Proposition 187." *Social Problems* 43 (August 1996): 284–305.

Camarillo, Albert. *Chicanos in California: A History of Mexican Americans in California*. San Francisco: Boyd and Fraser Publishing Company, 1984.

Caron, Simone M. "Race, Class, and Reproduction: The Evolution of a Reproductive Policy in the United States, 1800–1989." Ph.D. dissertation, Clark University, 1989.

Castañeda, Antonia I. "The Political Economy of Nineteenth Century Stereotypes of Californianas." In *Between Borders: Essays on Mexicana/Chicana History*, edited by Adelaida R. Del Castillo, 213–236. Encino, CA: Floricanto Press, 1990.

———. "Engendering the History of Alta California, 1769–1848: Gender, Sexuality and the Family." In *California History*, (Summer and Fall 1997): 230–259.

Castillo, Fransizka. "Did These Latinas Save Your Life?" *Latina* (September 2005): 176–179.

Center for Immigration Studies. *The Costs of Immigration: Assessing a Conflicted Issue*. Washington, D.C., 1994.

Chang, Grace. "Undocumented Latinas: Welfare Burden or Beasts of Burden?" *Socialist Review* 23 (1993): 151–185.

———. *Disposable Domestics: Immigrant Women Workers in the Global Economy*. Boston: South End Press, 2000.

Chapa, Jorge, and Belinda De La Rosa. "Latino Population Growth, Socioeconomic and Demographic Characteristics, and Implications for Educational Attainment." *Education and Urban Society* 36, no. 2 (February 2004): 130–149.

Chapman, Leonard. "Illegal Aliens: Time to Call a Halt." *Readers Digest* (October 1976).

Chase, Allen. *The Legacy of Malthus: The Social Costs of the New Scientific Racism*. Urbana: University of Illinois Press, 1980.

Chávez, Ernesto. *My People First "¡Mi Raza Primero!" Nationalism, Identity, and Insurgency in the Chicano Movement in Los Angeles, 1966–1978*. Berkeley: University of California Press, 2002.

Chávez, Leo R. "Immigration Reform and Nativism: The Nationalist Response to the Transnationalist Challenge." In *Immigrants Out! The New Nativism and the Anti-Immigrant Impulse in the United States*, edited by J. P. Perea, 61–77. New York: New York University Press, 1997.

———. "A Glass Half Empty: Latina Reproduction and Public Discourse." *Human Organization* 63, no. 2 (Summer 2004): 173–188.

Chávez, Marisela Rodríguez. "¡Despierten Hermanas y Hermanos! Women, the Chicano Movement, and Chicana Feminisms in California, 1966–1981." Ph.D. dissertation, Stanford University, 2005.

Clark, Margaret. *Health in the Mexican American Culture*. Berkeley: University of California Press, 1959.

Clarke, Adele. "Subtle Sterilization Abuse: A Reproductive Rights Perspective." In *Test Tube Women: What Future for Motherhood?* edited by Rita Arditti, Renata

Duelli Klein, and Shelly Minden, 188–212. Boston: Pandora/Routledge and Kegan Paul, 1984.

———. *Disciplining Reproduction: Modernity, American Life Sciences, and the Problem of Sex.* Berkeley: University of California Press, 1998.

Colen, Shellee. "Like A Mother to Them: Stratified Reproduction and West Indian Childcare Workers and Employers in New York." In *Conceiving the New World Order: The Global Politics of Reproduction,* edited by F. D. Ginsburg and R. Rapp, 78–102. Berkeley: University of California Press, 1995.

Collins, Patricia Hill. *Black Feminist Thought: Knowledge, Consciousness, and the Politics of Empowerment.* New York: Routledge, 1991.

———. "Shifting the Center: Race, Class, and Feminist Theorizing About Motherhood." In *Mothering: Ideology, Experience, and Agency,* edited by E. N. Glenn, G. Chang, and L. R. Forcey, 45–65. New York: Routledge, 1994.

———. "Will the 'Real' Mother Please Stand Up? The Logic of Eugenics and American National Planning." In *Revisioning Women: Health and Healing: Feminist, Cultural, and Technoscience Perspectives,* edited by A. E. Clarke and V. L. Olesen, 266–282. New York: Routledge, 1999.

Commission on Population Growth and the American Future. *Interim Report.* Washington, D.C.: U.S. Government Printing Office, 1971.

———. *Population and the American Future: The Report of the Commission on Population Growth and the American Future.* Washington, D.C.: U.S. Government Printing Office, 1972.

———. *Statements at Public Hearings of the Commission on Population Growth and the American Future.* Washington, D.C.: U.S. Government Printing Office, 1974.

Córdova, Teresa. "Roots and Resistance: The Emergent Writings of Twenty Years of Chicana Feminist Struggle." In *Handbook of Hispanic Cultures in the United States: Sociology,* edited by F. Padilla, 175–202. Houston: Arte Público Press, 1993.

Corea, Genea. *The Hidden Malpractice: How American Medicine Treats Women as Patients and Professionals.* New York: Morrow, 1973.

Corwin, Arthur F., and Johnny M. McCain. "Wetbackism Since 1964: A Catalogue of Factors." In *Immigrants—and Immigrants: Perspectives on Mexican Labor Migration to the United States,* edited by Arthur. F. Corwin, 67–107. Westport, CT: Greenwood Press, 1978.

Cosner, Madeline. "Illegal Aliens and American Medicine." *Journal of American Physicians and Surgeons* (Spring 2005): 6–10.

Crawford, James. "Hispanophobia." In *Hold Your Tongue: Bilingualism and the Politics of "English Only,"* 148–175. New York: Addison-Wesley Publishing Company, 1992.

Critchlow, T. Donald. *Intended Consequences: Birth Control, Abortion, and the Federal Government in Modern America.* New York: Oxford University Press, 1999.

Davis, Angela. "Racism, Birth Control, and Reproductive Rights." In *Women, Race, and Class,* 202–221. New York: Vintage Books, 1981.

———. "Surrogates and Outcast Mothers: Racism and Reproductive Politics," in *It Just Ain't Fair: The Ethics of Health Care for African Americans,* edited by Annette Dula and Sara Goering, 21–55. Westport, CT: Greenwood Press, 1994.

Davis, Kingsley. "The World Demographic Transition." *Annals of the American Academy of Political and Social Science* 237 (1945): 1–11.

———. "The Migration of Human Populations." *Scientific American* 231 (3) (September 1974): 93–105.

Davis, Kingsley, and Fredrick Styles. *California's Twenty Million: Research Contributions to Population Policy.* Westport, CT: Greenwood Press, 1971.

Davis, Susan E. *Women Under Attack: Victories, Backlash, and the Fight for Reproductive Freedom.* Boston: South End Press, 1988.

Day, Lincoln H., and Alice Taylor Day. *Too Many Americans.* New York: Delta Press, 1965.

Del Castillo, Adelaida. "Sterilization: An Overview." In *Mexican Women in the United States: Struggles Past and Present,* edited by M. Mora and A. Del Castillo, 65–70. Los Angeles: Chicano Studies Research Center, UCLA, 1980.

Demeny, Paul. "Social Science and Population Policy." *Population and Development Review* 14 (1988): 451–479.

Demerath, Nicholas J., III. *Birth Control and Foreign Policy.* New York: Harper and Row, 1976.

Deutsch, Sara. *No Separate Refuge: Culture, Class, and Gender on the Anglo-Hispanic Frontier in the Southwest, 1880–1940.* New York: Oxford University Press, 1987.

Dillingham, Brint. "Indian Women and IHS Sterilization Practices." *American Indian Journal* 3 (1977): 27–28.

———. "Sterilization of Native Americans." *American Indian Journal* 3 (1977): 16–19.

———. "Sterilization Update." *American Indian Journal* 3 (1977): 25.

Donovan, Patricia. "Sterilizing the Poor and Incompetent." *Hastings Center Reports* 6 (1976): 7–8.

Dreifus, Claudia. "Sterilizing the Poor." In *Seizing Our Bodies,* edited by C. Dreifus, 105–120. New York: Vintage Books, 1975.

Duleep, Harriet Orcutt, and Mark Regets. "The Elusive Concept of Immigrant Quality." Discussion Paper PRIP-UI-28, Program for Research on Immigration Policy. Washington, D.C.: The Urban Institute, 1994.

Edwards, Ozzie. "The Commission's Recommendations from the Standpoint of Minorities." *Social Science Quarterly* 53 (1972): 465–469.

Ehrlich, Paul. *The Population Bomb.* New York: Ballantine Books, 1968.

———. "World Population: Is the Battle Lost?" *Readers Digest Reprint,* 1969.

Ehrlich, Paul R., Loy Bilderback, and Anne H. Ehrlich. *The Golden Door: International Migration, México, and the United States.* New York: Ballantine Books, [1979] 1981.

Esparza, Ricardo. "The Value of Children Among Lower Class Mexican, Mexican American, and Anglo Couples." Ph.D. dissertation, University of Michigan, Ann Arbor, 1977.

Espenshade, T. J., J. L. Baraka, and G. A. Huber. "Implications of the 1996 Welfare and Immigration Reform Acts for U.S. Immigration." *Population and Development Review* 23 (1997): 769–801.

Espino, Virginia. "Woman Sterilized as Gives Birth: Forced Sterilization and Chicana Resistance in the 1970s." In *Las Obreras: Chicana Politics of Work and Family,* edited by Vicki Ruiz, 65–82. Los Angeles: UCLA Chicano Studies Research Center Publications, 2000.

Espinoza, Dionne. "Pedagogies of Nationalism and Gender: Cultural Resistance in Selected Representational Practices of Chicana/o Movement Activists, 1967–1972." Ph.D. dissertation, Cornell University, 1996.

Feagin, Joe R. "Old Poison in New Bottles: The Deep Roots of Modern Nativism." In *Immigrants Out! The New Nativism and the Anti-Immigrant Impulse in the United States,* edited by J. P. Perea, 13–43. New York: New York University Press, 1997.

Feld, Peter, and Britt Power (Global Strategy Group, Inc.). *Immigrants' Access to Health Care After Welfare Reform: Findings from Focus Groups in Four Cities.* Washington, D.C.: Kaiser Commission on Medicaid and the Uninsured, 2002.

Fernández, Celestino, and Lawrence R. Pedroza. "The Border Patrol and the News Media Coverage of Undocumented Mexican Immigration During the 1970's: A Quantitative Content Analysis in the Sociology of Knowledge." *California Sociologist* 5 (1982): 1–26.

Fix, Michael, and Jeffrey S. Passel. *Immigration and Immigrants: Setting the Record Straight.* Washington, D.C.: The Urban Institute, 1994[a].

———. "Setting the Record Straight: What Are the Costs to the Public?" *Public Welfare* 52, no. 2 (Spring 1994[b]): 6–15.

Fix, Michael E., and Karen Tumlin. *Welfare Reform and the Devolution of Immigrant Policy.* Series A, no. A-15. Washington, D.C.: The Urban Institute, October 1997.

Flores, Francisca. "Comisión Femenil Mexicana." *Regeneración* 2 (1971): 6–7.

———. "Conference of Mexican Women: Un Remolino." *Regeneración* 1 (1971): 1–5.

Forste, Renata, and Marta Tienda. "What's Behind Racial and Ethnic Fertility Differentials?" In *Fertility in the United States: New Patterns, New Theories,* edited by John B. Casterline, Ronald D. Lee, and Karen Foote, 109–133. New York: Population Council, 1996.

Frisen, Carl M. *Changes in California's Population.* Sacramento: California Department of Finance, Budget Division, Financial Research Session, 1956.

Gallup Organization. *The Gallup Study of Attitudes Toward Illegal Aliens.* Princeton: The Gallup Organization, Inc., 1976.

García, Alma. *Chicana Feminist Thought: Basic Historical Writings.* New York: Routledge, 1979.

———. "The Development of Chicana Feminist Discourse, 1970–1980." *Gender and Society* 3 (1989): 217–238.

Ginsburg, Faye D., and Rayna Rapp. "The Politics of Reproduction." *Annual Review of Anthropology* 20 (1991): 311–343.

———, eds. *Conceiving the New World Order: The Global Politics of Reproduction.* Berkeley: University of California Press, 1995.

Glenn, Evelyn Nakano, Grace Chang, and Linda Rennie-Forcie, eds. *Motherhood: Ideology, Experience, and Agency.* New York: Routledge, 1994.

Goldscheider, Calvin. *Population, Modernization, and Social Structure.* Boston: Little, Brown and Company, 1971.

Goldscheider, Calvin, and Peter Uhlenberg. "Minority Group Status and Fertility." *American Journal of Sociology* 74 (1969): 361–371.

Gómez, Anna Nieto. "La Femenista." *Encuentro Femenil, The First Chicana Feminist Journal* 1 (1974): 34–47.

———. "Chicana Feminism." *Caracól* (1976): 3–5.

Gonzales-López, Gloria. *Erotic Journeys: Mexican Immigrants and Their Sex Lives.* Berkeley: University of California Press, 2005.

Gonzalez Baker, Susan. "Demographic Trends in the Chicana/o Population: Policy Implications for the Twenty-First Century." In *Chicanos at the Crossroads: Social, Economic, and Political Change,* edited by David R. Maciel and Isidro D. Ortiz, 5–24. Tucson: University of Arizona Press, 1996.

Goode, Erich, and Nachman Ben-Yehuda. "Moral Panics: Culture, Politics, and Social Construction." *Annual Review of Sociology* 20 (1994): 149–171.

Gordon, Linda. *Women's Body, Women's Right: Birth Control in America.* New York: Penguin Books, [1976] 1990.

Grebler, Leo, Joan W. Moore, and Ralph C. Guzman. "Distinctive Population Patterns." Chapter 6 in *The Mexican American People: The Nation's Second Largest Minority,* edited by L. Grebler, J. W. Moore, and R. C. Guzman, 105–141. New York: Free Press, 1970.

———. "The Family: Variations in Time and Space." Chapter 15 in *The Mexican American People: The Nation's Second Largest Minority,* edited by L. Grebler, J. W. Moore, and R. C. Guzman, 350–377. New York: Free Press, 1970.

Greenhaulgh, Susan. "The Social Construction of Science: An Intellectual, Institutional, and Political History of Twentieth-Century Demography." *Comparative Studies in Society and History* 38 (1996): 26–66.

Gurak, Douglas T. "Sources of Ethnic Fertility Differences: An Examination of Five Minority Groups." *Social Science Quarterly* 59 (1978): 295–310.

Gusfield, Joseph R. *The Culture of Public Problems: Drunk Driving and the Symbolic Order.* Chicago: University of Chicago Press, 1981.

Gutiérrez, David. *Walls and Mirrors: Mexican Americans, Mexican Immigrants, and the Politics of Ethnicity.* Los Angeles: University of California Press, 1995.

Gutiérrez, Elena R. "The Racial Politics of Reproduction: The Social Construction of Mexican Origin Women's Fertility." Ph.D. dissertation, University of Michigan, 1999.

———. "Policing 'Pregnant Pilgrims': Welfare, Health Care, and the Control of Mexican-origin Women's Fertility." In *Women, Health, and Nation: The U.S. and Canada Since 1945,* edited by Molly Ladd-Taylor, Gina Feldberg, Kathryn

McPherson, and Alison Li, 379–403. Toronto: McGill-Queens University Press, 2003.

———. "'We Will No Longer Be Silent or Invisible': Latinas Organizing for Reproductive Justice." In *Undivided Rights: Women Of Color Organize for Reproductive Justice,* edited by J. Silliman, M. G. Fried, L. Ross, and Elena R. Gutiérrez, 215–239. Cambridge, MA: South End Press, 2004.

Gutiérrez, Ramon A. "Community, Patriarchy, and Individualism: the Politics of Chicano History and the Dream of Equality." *American Quarterly* 45 (1993): 1.

Hall, Stuart. "New Ethnicities." In *"Race," Culture, and Difference,* edited by J. Donald and A. Rattansi, 252–259. Newbury Park: Sage Publications, 1992.

Haller, Mark. *Eugenics: Hereditarian Attitudes in American Thought.* New Brunswick, NJ: Rutgers University Press, 1963.

Hanson, D. Victor. *Mexifornia: A State of Becoming.* San Francisco: Encounter Books, 2003.

Hartmann, Betsey. *Reproductive Rights and Wrongs: The Global Politics of Population Control.* New York: Harper Collins, [1987] 1995.

Hauser, Paul. *The Population Dilemma.* Englewood Cliffs, NJ: Prentice-Hall, 1963.

Health Research Group. *A Health Research Group Study on Surgical Sterilization: Present Abuses and Proposed Regulations.* Public Citizens, Inc.: Washington, D.C., 1973.

Hellman, L. M. "Fertility Control at a Crossroad." *American Journal of Obstetrics and Gynecology* 123, no. 4 (15 October 1975): 331–337.

Hern, Warren M. "Family Planning and the Poor." *New Republic* 163 (14 November 1970): 17–19.

Hernández, Antonia. "Chicanas and the Issue of Involuntary Sterilization: Reforms Needed to Protect Informed Consent." *Chicano Law Review* 3 (1976): 3–37.

Hinojosa, Raul, and Peter Schey. "The Faulty Logic of the Anti-Immigration Rhetoric." *NACLA Report on the Americas* 29, no. 3 (November/December 1995): 18–23.

Hodgson, Dennis. "Demography as Social Science and Policy Science." *Population and Development Review* 9 (1983): 1–34.

———. "Orthodoxy and Revisionism in American Demography." *Population and Development Review* 14 (1988): 541–569.

Holmes, S. J. "Perils of the Mexican Invasion." *North American Review* (May 1929): 616.

Hondaganeu-Sotelo, Pierrette. *Gendered Transitions: Mexican Experiences of Immigration.* Berkeley: University of California Press, 1994.

———. "Women and Children First: New Directions in Anti-Immigrant Politics." *Socialist Review* 25 (1995): 169–190.

———. "Unpacking 187: Targeting Mexicanas." In *Immigration and Ethnic Communities: A Focus on Latinos,* edited by Refugio I. Rochin, 93–103. East Lansing, MI: Julian Samora Research Institute, 1996.

Horn, David G. *Social Bodies: Science, Reproduction, and Italian Modernity*. Princeton, NJ: Princeton University Press, 1994.

Huddle, Donald. *The National Cost of Immigration in 1993*. Washington, D.C.: Carrying Capacity Network, 1994.

Hughes, Edward C. "The Greatest Show on Earth/Presidential Address." *Obstetrics and Gynecology* 121 (1975): 739–744.

Huntington, Samuel P. *Who Are We? The Challenge to America's National Identity*. New York: Simon and Schuster, 2004.

Hurtado, Aída. "The Politics of Sexuality in the Gender Subordination of Chicanas." In *Living Chicana Theory*, edited by Carla Trujillo, 383–428. Berkeley: Third Woman Press, 1998.

———. *Voicing Chicana Feminisms: Young Women Speak Out on Sexuality and Identity*. New York: New York University Press, 2003.

Huss, John D., and Melanie J. Wirken. "Illegal Immigration: The Hidden Population Bomb." *The Futurist* (April 1977): 114–118, 121.

Immigration and Naturalization Service. "Report of the Commissioner [Leonard Chapman] of Immigration and Naturalization." *Annual Report*, p. iii. Washington, D.C.: Department of Justice, 1974.

Inda, X. Jonathan. "Foreign Bodies: Migrants, Parasites, and the Pathological Nation." *Discourse* 22, no. 3 (Fall 2000): 46–62.

———. "Bipower, Reproduction, and the Migrant Woman's Body." In *Decolonial Voices: Chicana and Chicano Cultural Studies in the 21st Century*, edited by A. J. Aldama and Naomi Quiñonez, 98–112. Bloomington: Indiana University Press, 2002.

———. *Targeting Immigrants: Government, Technology, and Ethics*. Malden, MA: Blackwell Publishing, 2006.

Institute of Medicine. *Unequal Treatment: What Health Care Providers Need to Know About Racial and Ethnic Disparities in Health Care*. Washington, D.C.: Institute of Medicine, 2002.

Irving, Katrina. *Immigrant Mothers: Narratives of Race and Maternity, 1890–1925*. Chicago: University of Illinois Press, 2000.

Jiobu, Robert, and H. Marshall. "Minority Status and Family Size: A Comparison of Explanations." *Population Studies* 31 (1977): 509–517.

Johnson, Kevin R. "An Essay on Immigration Politics, Popular Democracy, and California's Proposition 187: The Political Relevance and Legal Irrelevance of Race." *Washington Law Review* 70 (July 1995): 623–673.

———. "Public Benefits and Immigration: The Intersection of Immigration Status, Ethnicity, Gender, and Class." *UCLA Law Review* 42 (August 1995): 1509–1575.

———. "The New Nativism: Something Old, Something New, Something Borrowed, Something Blue." In *Immigrants Out! The New Nativism and the Anti-Immigrant Impulse in the United States*, edited by Juan Perea, 165–189. New York: New York University Press, 1997.

Johnson, Stanley P. *World Population and the United Nations: Challenge and Response.* Cambridge: Cambridge University Press, 1987.

Kaplan, David, and Ronald A. Chez. "The Economics of Population Growth." *Obstetrics and Gynecology* 103 (1969): 133–137.

Kazen, Phyllis M., and Harley L. Browning. *Sociological Aspects of the High Fertility of the U.S. Mexican-Descent Population: An Exploratory Study.* Austin: Population Research Center, University of Texas, 1966.

Keeley, Charles B. "Immigration Composition and Population Policy." *Science* 185 (1974): 587–593.

Kelves, Daniel J. *In the Name of Eugenics: Genetics and the Uses of Human Heredity.* Berkeley: University of California Press, 1985.

King, Miriam, and Steven Ruggles. "American Immigration, Fertility, and Race Suicide at the Turn of the Century." *Journal of Interdisciplinary History* 20 (1990): 347–369.

Krauss, Elissa. *Hospital Survey on Sterilization Policies.* American Civil Liberties Union, 1975.

Kuumba, Monica. "Perpetuating Neo-Colonialism Through Population Control." *Africa Today* 40 (1993): 79–95.

Lader, Lawrence. *Breeding Ourselves to Death.* New York: Ballantine Books, 1971.

Larson, Kamet. "And Then There Were None." *Christian Century* (26 January 1977): 61.

Lee, Anne, and Everett Lee. "The Future Fertility of the American Negro." *Social Forces* 37 (1959): 228–231.

Lincoln, Richard. "Population and the American Future: The Commission's Final Report." In *Population Studies: Selected Essays and Research,* edited by K. C. W. Kammeyer, 409–430. Chicago: Rand McNally, 1972.

Lindsley, Syd. "The Gendered Assault on Immigrants." In *Policing the National Body: Race, Gender, and Criminalization,* edited by Jael Silliman and Anannya Bhattacharjee, 175–196. Boston: South End Press, 2002.

Littlewood, Thomas. *The Politics of Population Control.* Notre Dame: University of Notre Dame Press, 1977.

López, David E., and Georges Sabagh. "Untangling Structural and Normative Aspects of the Minority Status-Fertility Hypothesis." *American Journal of Sociology* 83 (1978): 1491–1497.

López, Ian Haney. "Race on the 2010 Census: Hispanics and the Shrinking White Majority." *Daedalus* 134 (Winter 2005): 42–52.

López, Irís. "Agency and Constraint: Sterilization and Reproductive Freedom Among Puerto Rican Women in New York City." In *Situated Lives: Gender and Culture in Everyday Life,* edited by L. Lamphere, H. Ragone, and Patricia Zavella, 155–171. New York: Routledge, 1993.

———. "An Ethnography of the Medicalization of Puerto Rican Women's Reproduction." In *Pragmatic Women and Body Politics,* edited by Margaret Lock and Patricia A. Kaufert, 240–259. Cambridge: Cambridge University Press, 1998.

Lou, Richard. "The Sterilization of American Indian Women." *Playgirl* 4, no. 12 (May 1977): 43, 51, 57, 100.

Maciel, David R., and Isidro D. Ortíz, eds. *Chicanos at the Crossroads: Social, Economic, and Political Change*. Tucson: University of Arizona Press, 1996.

Madsen, William. *The Mexican American of South Texas*. New York: Holt, Rinehart and Winston, 1964.

Maharidge, Dale. *The Coming White Minority: California's Eruptions and the Nation's Future*. New York: Random House, 1996.

Marcum, John B., and Frank D. Bean. "Minority Group Status as a Factor in the Relationship between Mobility and Fertility: The Mexican American Case." *Social Forces* 55 (1976): 135–148.

Marks, Carole C. "Demography and Race." In *Race and Ethnicity in Research Methods*, edited by J. H. Stanfield II and R. M. Dennis, 159–171. Newbury Park: Sage, 1993.

Martínez, Elizabeth. "La Chicana." *Ideal* (5–20 September 1972): 1–2.

Mass, Bonnie. *Population Target: The Political Economy of Population Control in Latin America*. Brampton, Canada: Charter's Publishing Company, 1976.

May, Elaine Tyler. *Barren in the Promised Land: Childless Americans and the Pursuit of Happiness*. New York: Harper Collins, 1995.

McDaniel, Antonio. "Fertility and Racial Stratification." In *Fertility in the United States: New Patterns, New Theories*, edited by John Casterline, Ronald Lee, and Karen Foote, 134. New York: Population Council, 1996.

McKee, James B. *Sociology and the Race Problem: The Problem of a Perspective*. Chicago: University of Illinois Press, 1993.

Mexican Fact Finding Committee. "The Mexican Family: Its Size and Its Income." In *Mexicans in California: Report of Governor C. C. Young's Mexican Fact Finding Committee*, 209–214. San Francisco: California State Printing Office, 1930.

Milkman, Ruth. "Women's History and the Sears Case." *Feminist Studies* 12, no. 2 (Summer 1986): 375–400.

Miller, Michael V. "Variations in Mexican American Family Life: A Review and Synthesis." *Aztlán* 9 (1978): 209–231.

Mirandé, Alfredo. "The Chicano Family: A Re-analysis of Conflicting Views." *Journal of Marriage and Family* 39 (1977): 747–748.

Molina, Natalia. "Illustrating Cultural Authority: Medicalized Representations of Mexican Communities in Early Twentieth Century Los Angeles." *Aztlán: A Journal of Chicano Studies* 28, no. 1 (Spring 2003): 129–143.

Montejano, David. *Anglos and Mexicans in the Making of Texas, 1836–1986*. Austin: University of Texas Press, 1987.

———. "On the Future of Anglo-Mexican Relations in the United States." In *Chicano Politics and Society in the Twentieth Century*, edited by D. Montejano, 234–257. Austin: University of Texas Press, 1999.

Montiel, Miguel. "The Social Science Myth of the Chicano Family." *El Grito* 3 (1970): 56–63.

———. "The Chicano Family: A Review of Research." *Social Work* 18 (1973): 22–31.

Moore, Joan, and Alfredo Cuellar. *Mexican Americans.* Englewood Cliffs, NJ: Prentice-Hall, 1970.

Moynihan, Daniel P. *The Negro Family: The Case for National Action.* Washington, D.C.: Office of Policy Planning and Research, U.S. Department of Labor, 1965.

Mullings, Leith. "Images, Ideology, and Women of Color." In *Women of Color in U.S. Society,* edited by M. Baca Zinn and B. Thornton Dill, 265–289. Philadelphia: Temple University Press, 1994.

———. "Households Headed by Women: The Politics of Race, Class, and Gender." In *Conceiving the New World Order: The Global Politics of Reproduction,* edited by F. Ginsburg and R. Rapp, 122–130. Berkeley: University of California Press, 1995.

Murray, Mary John. "A Socio-Cultural Study of 118 Mexican Families Living in a Low-Rent Public Housing Project in San Antonio, Texas." Ph.D. dissertation, Catholic University of America, Washington, D.C., 1954.

Nathanson, Constance. *Dangerous Passage: The Social Control in Women's Adolescence.* Philadelphia: Temple University Press, 1991.

National Center for Health Statistics, U.S. Department of Health and Human Services. *Trends in Contraceptive Practice: United States.* Hyattsville, Maryland: Office of Health Research, Statistics and Technology, 1982.

———. *Births of Hispanic Origin, 1989–1995.* Vol. 46, no. 6 (12 February 1998).

National Council of La Raza (NCLR). *Beyond the Census: Hispanics and an American Agenda.* Washington, D.C.: NCLR, 2001.

Nelson, Jennifer. *Women of Color and the Reproductive Rights Movement.* New York: New York University Press, 2003.

Notestein, Frank W. "The Differential Rate of Increase Among the Social Classes of the American Population." *Social Forces* 12 (1933): 17–33.

———. "Population—The Long View." In *Food for the World,* edited by T. W. Schultz, 36–57. Chicago: University of Chicago Press, 1945.

Ochoa, Gilda L. *Becoming Neighbors in a Mexican American Community: Power, Conflict and Solidarity.* Austin: University of Texas Press, 2004.

Ogg, Elizabeth. *Population and the American Future.* New York: Public Affairs Committee, Inc., 1974.

Omi, Michael, and Howard Winant. *Racial Formation in the United States.* 2nd ed. New York: Routledge, 1994.

Ortiz, Sylvia, and Jesus Manuel Casas. "Birth Control and Low-Income Mexican American Women: The Impact of Three Values." *Hispanic Journal of Behavioral Sciences* (1990): 83–92.

Osborn, Frederick. "Characteristics and Differential Fertility of American Population Groups." *Social Forces* 12 (1933): 8–15.

Paddock, William, and Paul Paddock. *Famine—1975!* New York: Little Brown, 1967.

Park, Lisa Sun-Hee, Rhonda Sarnoff, Catherine Bender, and Carol Korenbrot. "Impact of Recent Welfare and Immigration Reforms on Use of Medicaid for

Prenatal Care by Immigrants in California." *Journal of Immigrant Health* 2, no. 1 (2000): 5–22.

Parsons, Jack. *Population Fallacies.* London: Elen/Pemberton, 1977.

———. *Human Population Competition: A Study of the Pursuit of Power Through Numbers.* 2 vols. Lewiston, England: Edwin Mellon Press, 1998.

Perea, Juan P., ed. *Immigrants Out! The New Nativism and the Anti-Immigrant Impulse in the United States.* New York: New York University Press, 1997.

Pérez, Emma. *The Decolonial Imaginary: Writing Chicanas into History.* Bloomington and Indianapolis: Indiana University Press, 1999.

Pesquera, Beatríz, and Denise Segura. "There Is No Going Back: Chicanas and Feminism." In *Chicana Critical Issues,* edited by N. Alarcón, 95–115. Berkeley: Third Woman Press, 1993.

———. "With Quill and Torch: A Chicana Perspective on the American Woman's Movement and Feminist Theories." In *Chicanas/Chicanos in Everyday Life,* edited by D. R. Maciel and I. D. Ortiz, 231–247. New York: Routledge, 1996.

———. "'It's Her Body, It's Definitely Her Right': Chicanas/Latinas and Abortion." *Voces: A Journal of Latina Studies* 2 (1998): 103–127.

Petchesky, Rosalind. "Reproduction, Ethics, and Public Policy: The Federal Sterilization Regulations." *Hastings Center Report* 9 (1979): 29–42.

———. *Abortion and Women's Choice: The State, Sexuality, and Reproductive Freedom.* Boston: Northeastern University Press, 1990.

Piotrow, Phyllis T. *World Population Crisis: The United States Response.* New York: Praeger Publishers, 1973.

Population Council. *Population: An International Dilemma; A Summary of the Proceedings of the Conference Committee on Population Problems, 1956–1957.* New York: Population Council, 1958.

Population Crisis Committee. *The Family Planning Services and Research Act of 1970.* Washington, D.C.: U.S. Government Printing Office, 1971.

Proceedings of the Conference on Population Growth and Public Policy. Berkeley, California, 1975.

Purvis, Trevor, and Alan Hunt. "Discourse, Ideology, Discourse, Ideology, Discourse, Ideology . . ." *British Journal of Sociology* 44 (1993): 473–497.

Ramírez de Arellano, Annette B., and Conrad Seipp. *Colonialism, Catholicism, and Contraception.* Chapel Hill: University of North Carolina Press, 1983.

Randall, C. L. "The Obstetrician-Gynecologist and Reproductive Health." *American Journal of Obstetrics and Gynecology* 129, no. 7 (1 December 1977): 715–722.

Reilly, Phillip R. *The Surgical Solution: A History of Involuntary Sterilization in the United States.* Baltimore: Johns Hopkins University Press, 1991.

Rindfuss, Ronald R., and James A. Sweet. *Postwar Fertility Trends and Differentials in the United States.* New York: Academic Press, 1977.

Roberts, Dorothy. *Killing the Black Body: Race, Reproduction, and the Meaning of Liberty.* New York: Vintage Books, 1997.

————. "Who May Give Birth to Citizens? Reproduction, Eugenics, and Immigration." In *Immigrants Out! The New Nativism and the Anti-Immigrant Impulse in the United States,* edited by J. P. Perea, 205–219. New York: New York University Press, 1997.

Roberts, Robert E., and Sul Eun Lee. "Minority Group Status and Fertility Revisited." *American Journal of Sociology* 80 (1974): 503–523.

Ruiz, Vicki L. "La Nueva Chicana: Women and the Movement." In *From Out of the Shadows: Mexican Women in Twentieth-Century America,* edited by V. L. Ruiz, 99–126. New York: Oxford University Press, 1998.

————, ed. *From Out of the Shadows: Mexican Women in Twentieth-Century America.* New York: Oxford University Press, 1998.

Rummonds, James S. "The Role of Government in Population Policy." *In Proceedings of the Conference on Population Growth and Public Policy* (8–9 February 1975), 24b,c. Berkeley, California.

Sabagh, Georges. "Fertility Planning Status of Chicano Couples in Los Angeles." *American Journal of Public Health* 70 (1980): 56–61.

Sánchez, George J. "'Go After the Women': Americanization and the Mexican Immigrant Woman, 1915–1929." In *Unequal Sisters: A Multicultural Reader in U.S. Women's History,* edited by E. C. Dubois and V. L. Ruiz, 250–263. New York: Routledge, 1990.

Santa Ana, Otto. "'Like An Animal I Was Treated': Anti-Immigrant Metaphor in US Public Discourse." *Discourse and Society* 10 (1999): 191–224.

————. *Brown Tide Rising: Metaphors of Latinos in Contemporary American Public Discourse.* Austin: University of Texas Press, 2002.

Schoen, Johanna. *Choice and Coercion: Birth Control, Sterilization, and Abortion in Public Health and Welfare.* Chapel Hill: University of North Carolina Press, 2005.

Segura, Denise A., and Beatriz M. Pesquera. "Beyond Indifference and Antipathy: The Chicana Movement and Chicana Feminist Discourse." *Aztlán* 19 (1992): 69–93.

————. "Chicana Feminisms: Their Political Context and Contemporary Expressions." In *Situated Lives: Gender and Culture in Everyday Life,* edited by L. Lamphere, H. Ragone, and P. Zavella, 193–203. New York: Routledge, 1997.

Shapiro, Thomas. *Population Control Politics: Women, Sterilization, and Reproductive Choice.* Philadelphia: Temple University Press, 1985.

Shepard, Jack. "Birth Control for the Poor: A Solution." *Look* 28 (7 April 1964).

————. "Welfare Birth Control." *America* 110 (1 February 1974).

Silliman, Jael, Marlene G. Fried, Loretta Ross, and Elena R. Gutiérrez. *Undivided Rights: Women Of Color Organize for Reproductive Justice.* Cambridge, MA: South End Press, 2004.

Solinger, Rickie. *Wake Up Little Susie: Single Pregnancy and Race before Roe v. Wade.* New York: Routledge, 1992.

Sosa-Riddell, Adaljiza. "The Bioethics of Reproductive Technologies: Impacts and

Implications for Latinas." In *Chicana Critical Issues,* edited by N. Alarcón, 183–196. Berkeley: Third Woman Press, 1993.

Spector, Malcom, and John I. Kitsuse. *Constructing Social Problems.* New York: Aldine De Gruyter, 1977.

Sretzer, Simon. "The Idea of Demographic Transition and the Study of Fertility: A Critical Intellectual History." *Population and Development Review* 19 (1993): 659–701.

Stephancic, Jean. "Funding the Nativist Agenda." In *Immigrants Out! The New Nativism and the Anti-Immigrant Impulse in the United States,* edited by J. Perea, 119–135. New York: New York University Press, 1997.

Stern, M. Alexandra. *Eugenic Nation: Faults and Frontiers of Better Breeding in Modern America.* Berkeley: University of California Press, 2005.

Styles, Frederick G. "Introduction." *Proceedings of the Conference on Population Growth and Public Policy,* 8–9 February 1975, Berkeley, California.

Sweet, James A. "Differentials in the Rate of Fertility Decline: 1960–1970." *Family Planning Perspectives* 6 (1974): 103–107.

Sybert, Richard. "Population, Immigration, and Growth in California." *San Diego Law Review* 31 (1994): 945–1015.

Symonds, Richard, and Michael Carder. *The United Nations and the Population Question, 1945–1970.* New York: McGraw-Hill, 1973.

Talavera, Esther. "Sterilization Is Not an Alternative in Family Planning." *Agenda* 7 (1977): 8.

Tanton, John H. "International Migration as an Obstacle to Achieving World Stability." *The Ecologist* 6, no. 6 (July 1976): 221–227.

Tatalovich, Raymond. "Official English as Nativist Backlash." In *Immigrants Out! The New Nativism and the Anti-Immigrant Impulse in the United States,* edited by J. Perea, 78–102. New York: New York University Press, 1997.

Thompson, Warren Simpson. *Growth and Changes in California's Population.* Los Angeles: Haynes Foundation, 1955.

Trujillo, Carla, ed. *Living Chicana Theory.* Berkeley: Third Woman Press, 1998.

Tuck, Ruth. *Not With the Fist: Mexican-Americans in a Southwest City.* New York: Harcourt, Brace and Company, 1946.

Uhlenberg, Peter. "Demographic Correlates of Group Achievement: Contrasting Patterns of Mexican-Americans and Japanese Americans." *Demography* 9 (1972): 119–128.

———. "Fertility Patterns Within the Mexican American Population." *Social Biology* 20 (1973): 30–39.

———. "Mexican American Women and Abortion Use: The Case of Alcala." In *Twice a Minority: Mexican American Women,* edited by M. B. Melville, 33–51. St. Louis: Mosby Press, 1980.

U.S. Office of Economic Opportunity. *Need for Subsidized Family Planning Services: United States, Each State and County.* Washington, D.C.: U.S. Government Printing Office, 1968.

Van Hook, Jennifer, Jennifer E. Glick, and Frank D. Bean. "Public Assistance Receipt Among Immigrants and Natives: How the Unit of Analysis Affects Research Findings." *Demography* 36, no. 1 (1999): 111–120.

Veatch, Robert M., and Thomas Draper. "Population Policy and the Values of Physicians." In *Population Policy and Ethics: The American Experience,* edited by R. M. Veatch, 377–408. New York: Irvington Publishers, 1977.

Vélez-Ibáñez, Carlos G. "Se Me Acabó la Canción: An Ethnography of Non-Consenting Sterilizations Among Mexican Women in Los Angeles." In *Mexican Women in the United States: Struggles Past and Present,* edited by M. Mora and A. Del Castillo, 71–91. Los Angeles: Chicano Studies Research Center, UCLA, 1980.

Vidal, Mirta. *Women: New Voice of La Raza.* New York: Pathfinder Press, 1971.

Westhoff, Charles. "United States." In *Population Policy in Developed Countries,* edited by Bernard Berelson, 731–757. New York: McGraw-Hill, 1974.

——. "The Commission on Population Growth and the American Future: Its Origins, Operations, Aftermath." In *Sociology and Public Policy,* edited by Mirra Komarovsky, 43–59. New York: Elsevier, 1975.

Williams, Brett. "Babies and Banks: The 'Reproductive Underclass' and the Raced, Gendered Masking of Debt." In *RACE,* edited by S. Gregory and R. Sanjek, 348–364. New Brunswick, NJ: Rutgers University Press, 1996.

Wilmoth, John R., and Patrick Ball. "The Population Debate in American Popular Magazines, 1946–1990." *Population and Development Review* (1992): 631–668.

——. "Arguments and Action in the Life of A Social Problem: A Case Study of Overpopulation, 1946–1990." *Social Problems* 42 (1995): 318–343.

Wilson, Tamar D. "Anti-Immigrant Sentiment and the Problem of Reproduction/Maintenance in Mexican Immigration to the United States." *Critique of Anthropology* 20, no. 2 (2000): 191–213.

Woofter, Thomas J. *Races and Ethnic Groups in American Life.* New York: McGraw-Hill, 1933.

Wulff, George L. "Presidential Address." Central Association of Obstetricians and Gynecologists, 1971.

Ybarra, Lea. "Empirical and Theoretical Developments in the Study of Chicano Families." In *The State of Chicano Research in Family, Labor, and Migration Studies: Proceedings of the First Symposium on Chicano Research and Public Policy,* edited by A. Valdez and T. Almaguer, 91–110. Stanford: Stanford Center for Chicano Research, 1983.

Zavella, Patricia. *Women's Work and Chicano Families: Cannery Workers of the Santa Clara Valley.* Ithaca: Cornell University Press, 1987.

——. "Feminist Insider Dilemmas: Constructing Identity with 'Chicana' Informants." *Frontiers: A Journal of Women's Studies* 13 (1992).

——. "Reflections on Diversity Among Chicanas." *Frontiers: A Journal of Women's Studies* 12 (1993): 73–84.

——. "'Playing with Fire': The Gendered Construction of Chicana/Mexicana Sexuality." In *The Gender/Sexuality Reader: Culture, History, Political Economy,* edited by Roger N. Lancaster and Micaela di Leonardo, 402–418. New York: Routledge, 1997.

———. "Talkin' Sex: Chicanas and Mexicanas Theorize about Silences and Sexual Pleasure." In *Chicana Feminisms: A Critical Reader,* edited by Arredondo et al., 228–253. Durham: Duke University Press, 2003.

INDEX

fertility (*continued*)
12, 44, 51–52, 120, 122, 126–127; in
underdeveloped nations, 78, 87, 88.
See also birth control; birthrates;
Madrigal v. Quilligan; sterilization
Figueroa, María, 42
Fix, Michael, 121
Fonda, Jane, 99
Fong, March K., 32
forced sterilization. *See* sterilization
Ford, Gerald, 26
Ford Foundation, 15, 26
Forste, Renata, 71
Fourteenth Amendment, 114, 115, 122,
125–126
Frey, William, 72

Gallegly, Elton, 114, 115
GAO. *See* General Accounting Office
(GAO)
General Accounting Office (GAO), 39
genocide, sterilization abuse as, 105–
106
Ginsburg, Faye, 8
Goethe, C. M., 11
Golden Door, The (Ehrlich et al.), 73–74,
137n83
Goldscheider, Calvin, 66–69, 150n52,
150–151nn55–56
Gordon, Linda, 29, 132n6, 138n96
Greenhaulgh, Susan, 66
Gurak, Douglas, 69–70
Gusfield, Joseph, 5, 6

Hanson, Victor Davis, 4–5
Hartmann, Betsey, 15
Harvard University, 5
Hayden, Tom, 99
health care. *See* medical care; medical
professionals; University of South-
ern California–Los Angeles County
Medical Center (LACMC)
Health, Education and Welfare Depart-

ment, U.S., 1, 16, 38, 39, 44, 102,
143n33, 158n41
Hermosillo, Consuelo, 43
Hernández, Antonia, 1–2, 35–36, 44–45,
99, 100, 104, 123, 129n4, 146n81
Hernández, Georgina, 44
Hernández, Melvina, 144n47
Hernández, Nancy, 37
HEW. *See* U.S. Department of Health,
Education and Welfare
Hispanics. *See* Chicanas; Puerto Rico
and Puerto Rican women; *and head-
ings beginning with Mexican*
Hodgson, Dennis, 150n44
Holmes, Samuel, 10
Horling, Mark, 83
Houchen Settlement, 11
Huddle, Donald, 159n11
Hughes, Edward C., 27
Hugh Moore Fund, 133n24
Huntington, Samuel, 5
Hurtado, Aida, 12
Hurtado, Maria, 43
hysterectomy, 37, 97. *See also*
sterilization

ideology: generalized ideology of domination, 12–13; and reproduction, 8,
51–54
IHS. *See* Indian Health Service (IHS)
illegal immigrants. *See* undocumented
immigrants
Illinois, 93
illnesses. *See* diseases of undocumented
immigrants
Immigrant Study Commission, 11
immigration: changing composition of
post-1965 immigration, 22; Commission on Population Growth and
the American Future (CPGAF) on,
87–88; and Federation of American
Immigration Reform (FAIR), 75,
92–93, 156nn83–84, 156n87; indirect

CPSIA information can be obtained
at www.ICGtesting.com
Printed in the USA
FSOW01n2041280715
9326FS